IPSWICH
IN THE
SECOND WORLD WAR

Unprepared to be Warriors

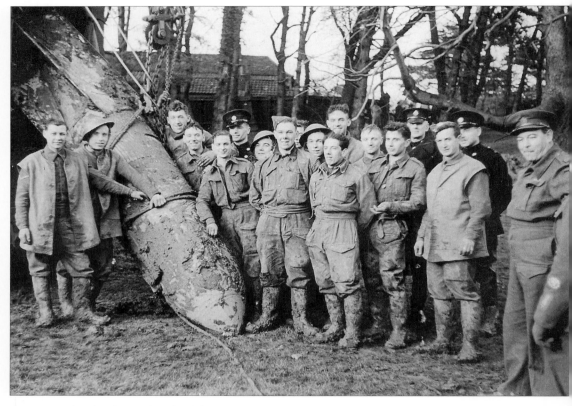

A relieved and triumphant bomb disposal team grouped around a UXB bomb recovered from Holywells Park.

IPSWICH
IN THE
SECOND WORLD WAR

Unprepared to be Warriors

David Jones

Phillimore

2005

Published by
PHILLIMORE & CO. LTD,
Shopwyke Manor Barn, Chichester, West Sussex, England

ISBN 1 86077 300 1

Printed and bound in Great Britain by
MPG BOOKS LTD
Bodmin, Cornwall

Contents

PARTING SHOTS

List of Illustrations

Acknowledgements

I would like to acknowledge the considerable help I have received from the members of the Ipswich Co-Op Oral History Group, and from their informants, from all those people who have shared their experiences with me, from David Kindred and the Ipswich Transport Museum, for help with photographs, and of course from the ever helpful and patient staff at the Suffolk Record Office in Ipswich.

I would also like to thank Paul Hyder of the Suffolk Constabulary for assistance with police records and Dave Wood for sharing some of his wealth of knowledge about local defence organisations. The project has been supported in many practical ways by the Ipswich Borough Council Museums and Galleries Service.

A Note on Sources

The Second World War produced an immense amount of official paperwork. In 1945 there was no policy concerning the preservation of local government, police and other organisations' archives. Survival was haphazard, depending on the judgement of the officer in charge in 1945 or when, later, some other plan required the use of cupboards where the documents were stored. Thus some aspects of the war in a particular locality are very well documented, while in another perhaps nothing survives.

Ipswich Museum has been fortunate in acquiring the surviving wartime papers of the Suffolk Constabulary. Essentially, these were collected by Inspector Rush of East Suffolk who was stationed at Felixstowe at the time. Rush retained large quantities of official papers, draft plans, memos, notes and so on relating to his work at Felixstowe, which police area shared a border with Ipswich. At the end of the war, Chief Constable Cresswell of Ipswich, knowing that Rush was interested, forwarded to him many of his own papers. They were handed in at amalgamation, when there was an attempt to set up a police archive and museum. There appear to be no equivalent papers for any other police area in Suffolk. The museum has still to index and assign archive numbers to these papers.

Most of the Borough of Ipswich's own records, relating to the Council's work during the war, have been deposited on loan with Suffolk Record Office. These have been fully indexed. On closer inspection, however, one discovers that the council did not save everything. What survive in fairly consistent fashion are the committee minutes for each department. The case papers or original correspondence for events mentioned in the minutes appear to be missing.

ARP in Ipswich is pretty well documented, reports made by wardens of individual incidents duly retained. Home Guard records are much weaker. So far no trace has come to light of the National Fire Service records. Museum research has led to the acquisition of other written accounts, including the work diary of the Chief Warden for the first year of the war. This was hand written for his own use and often at times when he would have been very tired. I have used this document extensively but, even with familiarity, the writing is difficult to decipher and errors may have crept in, especially over personal names.

Museum informants have sent letters, spoken with me on the telephone, or arrived unannounced and chosen to chat informally. A number were prepared to be formally interviewed and recorded, with all the necessary permission forms completed, and their tapes are retained by the museum. I have used my discretion as to when to identify sources in order to avoid embarrassing informants. When quoting from police records I have also sometimes suppressed personal names.

For anyone wishing to understand the Home Front during the Second World War there is simply no rival to Angus Calder's *The People's War: 1939-1945*. More personal in its approach is *How We Lived Then* by Norman Longmate. East Anglia as a region is well served by R. Douglas Brown's series *East Anglia 1939-1945*, with one volume for each year of the war. This relies primarily on the local newspapers and Mass Observation reports, as well as some oral history. Ipswich is well represented in the coverage. *Aviation in East Anglia* by Gordon Kinsey is, as its title suggests, more specialised but still useful. Books and pamphlets on individual aspects of the war outside Ipswich, the towns, airfields, units based in East Anglia, the development of radar and so on, are too numerous to mention

Dealing specifically with Ipswich is *Ipswich at War* by John Smith, Neil Wylie, Robert Maltster and David Kindred, an exceptionally well-researched photographic essay, and the sections on the two world wars (the book also covers other conflicts) are particularly good. The companion book *Felixstowe at War* is well worth consulting for comparisons with Ipswich. *Mr Brown's War. A Diary of the Second World War* edited by Helen D. Millgate is an invaluable source with an importance beyond Ipswich. Richard Brown was a member of both the ARP and the Home Guard in Ipswich throughout the war. He was a thoughtful man, though very much of his time, and capable of vivid description.

During the war the civil defence services occasionally published magazines. *The Warble* was the house magazine of the ARP, *The 9th Post* served the 9th Battalion Suffolk Home Guard (the 11th appears not to have had a magazine), and the Auxiliary Fire Service also published a couple of issues.

Just after the war a number of official histories relating to the civilian services and intended primarily as souvenirs were published locally in small numbers. They contain basic information that can be found here far more readily than in other sources, but of course the crisis of 1940 is seen through the triumph of 1945. Examples are the Victory Issue of *The Warble*, and *A Short Account of the Activities of the 11th Battalion Suffolk Home Guard* (Eastern Daily Times Co., 1945, the only Suffolk Home Guard unit to publish its own history).

I have also consulted R. Stanley Lewis, *Eighty Years of Enterprise 1869-1949* (W.S. Cowell Ltd), D.R. Grace and D.C. Phillips, *Ransomes. A History of the Firm and Guide to its Records* (University of Reading), R.K. McD. Morrison (ed.), *History of Engineering in Ipswich by the Ipswich Engineering Society on the Occasion of its 75th Anniversary* (Essex Telegraph Press, 1974), and *Diana Mosley* by Jan Dalley (Alfred A. Knopf, 2000)

Introduction

Towns, like people, experienced very different kinds of war. Some were more heavily bombed than Ipswich; on others hardly a bomb fell. Some were evacuated, while others received evacuees; a few had both experiences. Some were surrounded by American bases and others were far from any base; still others found whole sections of Whitehall appearing in their midst. This is an attempt to tell the story of one provincial town at war.

Ipswich in the thirties was something of a paradox in Suffolk. It was a town dominated by engineering and food processing, including malting and brewing, and the various activities associated with its Docks. A series of local family businesses, the Cobbolds, the Stokes and the Pauls amongst others, had a paternalistic attitude towards the ordinary citizen and a serious view of their social responsibilities. A particularly independent and forthright line was to be taken by both Richard and Anthony Stokes, the managers of the famous engineering firm of Ransomes & Rapier. Ipswich in the 1920s had still been a very ancient town, decrepit tenements built along the top of the mound that had been the town ramparts giving a claustrophobic, shut-in atmosphere to parts of it. In the area known as the Mount families were still living in cellars, and blood from slaughterhouses ran along the gutters. One old woman remembers being raised by her grandmother there just after the first war, and the weekly treat of looking out of the front windows to watch the grotesque antics of men staggering back from the pubs, the message being that such was the nature of husbands and how lucky she was not to have a father. My father-in-law, who was raised in George Street, used to recount how one of his father's employees, an illiterate old man, claimed to have sold his wife at a hiring fair, like the Mayor of Casterbridge. It was a town of mysterious old pubs and crumbling Tudor merchant houses which had come down in the world, with traditions of bare-knuckle fighting by gypsies, ratting, a little prostitution (but not much, there wasn't the money about), and fortune-telling in back rooms. Famously, it had a pub for every letter of the alphabet, ending with Z for Zulu.

Ipswich had the highest unemployment in East Anglia, with around 2,000 men out of work at the beginning of 1939. Conditions were bad enough to require straightforward charitable donations of free food. In February 1939, 600 loaves donated by Hovis were distributed free. The Council set up Cheap Milk Depots on its estates, open for a couple of hours each morning and selling milk at 2d. a pint to OAPs and families on relief. Some local people still remember these depots and the shame of being seen to use them, and also the rumours that local dairies were using the opportunity to off-load suspect milk onto the poor. Bitter accusations were made in Council about the free school meals system, with accusations of humiliating conditions and of suppliers selling to the Council their otherwise unsaleable produce.

This poverty was seen as inevitable, a natural disaster that it was the duty of all decent people to assist. Events like the Poor Children's Outing organised by Ipswich Motorcycle and Car Club were described as the largest in the country. They had become highly structured yearly festivals in which all levels of an intensely hierarchical society demonstrated to their own satisfaction their charity to deserving cases. On 24 June 1939 thousands watched 2,600 children leave for the country in 350 cars and lorries making the 50-mile round trip to Yoxford. There they were given tea, played games under the philanthropic gaze of the Mayor, Mayoress and Chief Constable, and had a day out that would not otherwise have been possible. The event is recorded on amateur film.

While far from being a centre of violent radicalism like the Clyde or South Wales, trades unionism, the Co-operative Society and the Labour Party were all strong in Ipswich in comparison with rural Suffolk. Such groups represented not just a political persuasion but a whole way of life, with organised clubs, recreation, education and activities for the young. There were Socialist Sunday schools and branches of the Woodcraft Folk, and an organised alternative view of society was to be found in Ipswich, one with strong links to a surviving nonconformist 19th-century radical tradition.

Ipswich was not at the forefront of events, perhaps, but at the same time it was not isolated from them. It had experienced the loss of a generation during the first war, at the end of which there had been demonstrations over food shortages. Suffragettes had taken to direct action and gone to prison in Ipswich. The town had seen strikes and mounted police during the National Strike. The Chief Constable had had to check on the behaviour of hunger marchers passing through the town and report to MI5 whether they represented any kind of threat. Fascism had affected the climate of ideas to the point where the Medical Officer of Health found it necessary to argue against compulsory sterilisation of the unfit for the good of the race in his official reports. Mrs Simpson had received her divorce in the local court amidst a hysteria of official secrecy. Mosley had spoken in the Public Hall.

At the same time, an active Council was struggling to build a better community for its people. There were lido-style open-air swimming pools at Broomhill and Pipers Vale, a new library, cinemas and skating rinks.

As Ipswich emerged from the depression the Council had already begun to build some of the biggest estates to be found in Europe. Some of the ancient neighbourhoods in the town centre had already been cleared and the communities moved out to newer estates, often as a group. So it was alleged that the people of the Mount (around St Mary Elms) had been moved to the Dickens Estate. If the Middle Ages had brought churches to the town and the Tudor period mansions, then the symbolic architecture of the thirties was the council estate. Carefully designed

1 *Neglected and unlovely traces of wartime structures lie throughout the area. These hubs of wartime activity are today quiet and forgotten. This pill box is beside Ipswich airfield.*

in gentle curving crescents, with a variety of styles and generous gardens, it was a scaled-down version of the garden suburb. Each estate was designed as a self-contained little world entered by its own trolley-bus service, with its row of small shops, its Co-op, its pub (often in one version or another of the Jacobethan style favoured by Cobbolds, the *Golden Hind*, the *Waveney*, the *Haven*, the *Margaret Catchpole* and the *Race Course*), its school, its branch library and its church.

The political idealism and involvement of the thirties was reflected in Ipswich. For the majority of people war was the supreme evil they hoped never to see again. The Peace Pledge Union was strong. People put their trust in all kinds of small-scale initiatives designed to promote international understanding. Schools actively promoted children to adopt pen-pals in Europe, including Germany. The Co-op had links with Co-op Societies on the continent. Those local people who thought about politics argued over the best methods of avoiding war, from pacifism to rearmament, but there was no dispute over the aim of avoiding war. No one argued for an aggressive military stance.

Some Ipswich businessmen had reasons to be forewarned of developments. Reavells, for example, had been involved in building submarine compressors for the Royal Navy since the 1920s. Ransomes & Rapier had helped develop ways of enabling aeroplanes to take off from naval ships. They had been experimenting with launching planes using a form of catapult, not only for the Royal Navy but also for the Russians and the Argentines. Such unpredictable and somewhat Heath Robinson experiments were to be overtaken by the development of the aircraft carrier. Smaller businesses like Saunders had purchased new machinery in Germany at the peak of the devaluation of the mark. In these and other ways, local firms were well aware of the military tensions within Europe. The official history of Ransomes & Rapier by D.R Grace and D.C Phillips claims that the firm was not as surprised by the Second World War as it had been by the First.

The RAF had had an Aeroplane and Armament Experimental Station at Martlesham for many years, and Felixstowe had been the Marine Aircraft Experimental Establishment since the first war, but other aerodromes were quickly built throughout East Anglia at Bircham Newton, Duxford, Wattisham, Stradishall, Honington and Sutton Heath.

2 *Tank traps by Heath Road.*

New civilian airports were designed with half an eye on defence. A Volunteer Reserve Flying Training School was started when Ipswich Airport was opened, to designs by Hening and Chitty, in 1938.

Important developments in connection with the municipal airport were foreshadowed by a recommendation from the Housing and Town Planning Committee that 65 acres of land adjoining the south-eastern boundary of the aerodrome be leased to the Air Ministry for ten years. A condition of the arrangement was that no objection would be raised by the Council to the use of a site on the land as a machine-gun range if required.

Already the official moral watchdogs of East Anglia were expressing concerns which were to be repeated again and again throughout the war: employment opportunities which paid better than farm labour were bringing in people from outside and were seen as a threat to village society. The organising secretary of the St Edmundsbury and Ipswich Diocesan Moral Welfare Association, in a speech at Beccles in June 1939, said that aerodromes were being built in many areas around them and very attractive young men were appearing who quite turned the heads of the village girls: 'One of the things to consider is what we can do to give these young men proper recreation and decent opportunities for meeting girls, rather than have things left to chance.'

The designs for the proposed new power station had been drawn up with war in mind, as the local newspaper made clear:

> The new station will be built with the view to providing as much protection from air attack as possible, both for the personnel and the machinery. All windows in the building are high up in the walls as a protection against blast and splinters, whilst the controls will be decentralised and duplicated and the doorways will be guarded by high concrete walls.
>
> (*EADT* 17.5.39)

3 *Entrance to Ipswich Airport.*

It was not to be built until after the war but, ironically, still with the features designed to protect it from German bombs albeit in a post–atomic age.

Both the Co-op and the local churches had been involved with aid for Spain and with help for Basque refugee children. Employees of the Ipswich Co-op had given up a part of their weekly wages to help finance aid to children taken out of Spain on potato boats. They were based at Wherstead Hall, a large property now belonging to Eastern Electricity. One local man remembers the importance given them and that they were 'holy terrors' who set fire to one house and stole his scooter. By February 1939, 600 German and Austrian Jewish refugee children had arrived as part of the Kindertransport scheme at Dovercourt (and about 200 at St Felix School in Southwold).

The charities concerned had been offered the use of a holiday camp otherwise closed down for the winter. The children were moved into wooden huts which proved bitterly cold and unsuitable for winter use. They had to be quickly removed to Barham Workhouse in Claydon, just outside Ipswich, until they could be dispersed. The house was derelict and had to be cleaned and prepared by local volunteers and furnished with second-hand furniture. By this time the original holiday camp was required for the coming summer season so the children were moved on in batches of 160. The Ipswich Quakers ran various schemes for supporting refugees.

The Council had requested its various committees and officers to look at the full range of public services it provided and think of ways of modernising them. As a county borough, this meant every aspect of public service: housing, education, the arts and sport, health, sewers, roads, slum clearance, even airports. These schemes would have transformed the public services of the town. Some had to wait thirty or forty years to be completed; others have still to come to pass or have been superseded. They were due to be presented to the Council in early 1939 and form part of the futuristic concept of a Five Year Plan, with deliberate if grandiose hints of a planned socialist community. The various plans before the Council were headed by the £2 million set aside for the power station, but the following were included: a Technical College, an Art School extension, an Art Gallery extension, a Museum extension, a new West End branch library and other branch library sites to be purchased, nine sewer schemes and extensions to the Isolation Hospital, a new maternity home, a new nurses home at the Borough Hospital, four new villas at St John's Home, and other improvements at St Clement's Mental Hospital, with a new secure female block, new male villa and new superintendent's house. Sports provision was to be increased with completion of Broomhill Baths, a sports centre, and new recreation grounds and children's playgrounds. £517,039 was to be spent on council houses, along with 11 road schemes, two bridge schemes, the completion of the airport terminal and, less glamorously but no less necessary, a public abattoir.

But when these plans were put forward in detail by the Finance Committee in early 1939 for formal approval by the Council they were clearly in conflict with the new financial demands caused by the requirements of civil defence. The opposition was happily pointing out the likelihood of mammoth increases to the rates and the Council was thrown into a quandary. It was clear that if war were to come then civil defence would have to be allocated all available finance, and these vital reforms would have to be shelved. But what if this was only another false alarm? Or what if the war were only short-lived and troops were first called up and then disbanded onto the labour market? More importantly, what was really required for civil defence? Did the town need reinforced shelters for the mass of its citizens or could it get away with a few slit trenches in school playing fields?

1938 and 1939 were years of great confusion in Ipswich, as they were for the rest of the country or indeed the rest of the world. Things were unravelling; events were simply not meant to happen like this. However, as 1939 progressed it became inescapably clear that what had been dreaded since 1918, what many had thought impossible and had struggled in various ways to prevent, was nonetheless going to happen. For the second time in a lifetime England was going to be at war. Something of the enormity of what that meant can be grasped from the local fact, tiny but evocative, that the Ipswich firm of Saunders, under contract to supply headstones for the fallen of the first war, had not fulfilled the order before the outbreak of the second.

AN AMBIGUOUS OPENING

One
Memories of the Declaration of War

There are moments in history which are remembered by nearly everyone of that generation. For the British people, Neville Chamberlain's broadcast was one such moment. There was before and there was after, and for once the wheel turned for everybody at the same time. To the historian it was little more than another inevitable step in the process, but to the people who experienced it and who recorded their experiences in diaries, in letters or recalled it in later memory this was the symbolic moment at which the fear became the reality and, however they expressed themselves, haltingly or poetically, something of this shines through all their accounts.

There is fear, bewilderment and regret at a terrible necessity, but there is no evidence of an upsurge of naive idealistic patriotism, a hunger for war, or any kind of feeling of relief that at last all the appeasement was at an end and we were about to strike a blow for democracy and make the world safe by removing a dictator.

> International situation serious. Go to bed 2.30 a.m.
>
> September 2 International situation much worse. England send ultimatum to Germany to expire on Sunday morning 11a.m. Withdraw from Poland or we fulfil our pledge to Poland.
>
> September 3 Everyone calm but anxious to know what 11a.m. will bring forth, hoping even at the last minute that war would be avoided — but determined to see things through. Sunday of all days to start a war!
>
> 11.15a.m. Premier [?] Mr Neville Chamberlain broadcasts the fatal news *that we are at war with Germany*. Awful thought! Country feels our conscience is clear — every effort for peace having been made.
>
> (Chief Warden C.J. Woods' diary)

> What were your feelings when war was declared?
>
> Very confused and very sad. I had always hoped that the horrors of the Great War would be justified by the belief that was the war to end all wars, and here we were again facing another war with horrifying weaponry for death and destruction. The howl of the air-raid sirens on the first day didn't help and it was later we realised it was only a practice exercise. I didn't have much time to worry about it for my life became very hectic as, being a Member of the National Council of the British Concrete Federation, we were called by various Ministries to work with them to organise their various requirements.
>
> (George R. Saunders 'The War Years Face to Face' typescript in Ipswich Museum)

1

At the outbreak of WW2 I was some two weeks short of my 18th birthday and, as a keen "Club Cyclist", was out on a Sunday run, and knowing that there was to be an important Radio Broadcast that morning, we stopped at the Pettistree *Three Tuns* for coffee to listen to what Neville Chamberlain had to say.

The content of that speech caused us to return straight away to Ipswich, where I went to the ARP Post at what was then known as the Borough General Hospital on Woodbridge Road East, and volunteered to become a messenger.

At home my parents were unusually subdued, but of course they had seen it all before, without the additional threat of indiscriminate bombing.

(Jack Jay letter in Ipswich Museum)

I had read all about the bombing in Spain and thought that immediately war broke out it would be the same here. Therefore the practice siren was really alarming.

(Mrs Y)

But, of all the local records of the beginning of the war, the sense of rising disquiet, the lack of certainty and the way that war cut across all other concerns is, perhaps, most clearly revealed in the letters of Basil Brown to his wife May. Basil was the talented but largely unrecognised archaeologist who had just made the greatest single find in British archaeology, the ship grave at Sutton Hoo. His letters have been preserved precisely for the light that they cast on the circumstances of the excavation and inquest that followed. They are full of details of the bitter personal feuds that the importance of the dig provoked and of Basil's own hopes and fears for what this might mean for his own career. But the war was a rising tide that slowly drowned all these normal concerns, as the letters show.

August 25 1939

If the situation gets worse we may have to make other arrangements [for the dig] but I hope war will not come, although even at present the measures are precautionary. Visitors are leaving here for their homes and it is reported that a start is being made with evacuation of children from London. Things may not be as bad as they look. We are getting the ship ready for visitors to see it September 2nd or 3rd but the situation may upset this. I shall be glad to send some of my things home in any case if you come, as I want to have as few things as possible here. You might bring my gas mask and the badges in case things worsen while I am here.

P.S. Mrs Pretty, Mr Parish and the Spiritualists do not believe there will be war.

Mrs Pretty owned the land of Sutton Hoo and had employed Basil Brown as an excavator. She was an eager Spiritualist who claimed that the spirits had revealed the site to her in a vision.

September 3 1939

Hope you are alright in all this bother of war being declared. I am today filling in the ship with bracken, etc. and hope it will remain alright. Then, if war does not last too long, it may come out alright for people to see. If not it must take its chance. I don't know where I am at present. Mrs Pretty even now thinks the war will fizzle out in a short time, but while Hitler is alive anything may happen and air raids are the danger. They are telling everyone in this village today to take gas masks with them when they go to work or anywhere. This is a worrying time. I may be home any time or perhaps stay here a few days until I know what I am going to do as everybody's plans are upset. Am sending P.O.s.

September 4 1939

I hope this war will be over soon but we may be in for a long one, but one can only make the best of a bad job. Make sure your gas mask is a good fit. I don't believe the Germans will hesitate at anything anywhere. I was called out to the ARP post this morning about 3a.m. owing to the air-raid warning going but this was bad enough. I shouldn't be surprised to be woken up again tonight. Of course Mrs Pretty thinks the war is going to be over very soon and even talks of sending me home for a fortnight. However, right or wrong, I'm preparing the boat protection to last a year.

September 6 1939

Out again this morning, German planes were flying overhead but dropped no bombs but it was not comfortable. I hear that two were brought down at Felixstowe and one at Ipswich but I don't know what did happen. [No German planes had been attacked but two British planes had been shot down in error by 'friendly fire'.] This area is rather dangerous I expect. I do hope they leave Rickinghall alone [Basil Brown's home village]. Did your hear anything? The air-raid signal has gone three times since Sunday but it was due to a mistake of the electricians. Expect the same thing will happen again tonight but hope for the best. Glad your children [evacuees] are alright. Clothes don't matter a bit. Everywhere here is full up owing to so many having to be sent. Let's hope bombs don't drop here. I expect you are safer – I trust so.

P.S. I am reporting for duty each time – ask the ARP people my position because I've no equipment and a tin hat is essential. Later, if I stop here, the ARP people are getting me equipment.

September 7 1939

I can see no signs of an early peace so we may as well prepare for a bad job. Hope your children are alright. Everywhere is packed here. We are not told all the news. I don't expect they want the Germans to know where they were the other night. Everything was quiet last night but they will try to get in again sooner or later. There were a lot of reports about but everyone must be careful of talking too much at the present time.

P.S. Look after your windows – they are very strict about a light showing.'

September 10 1939

[Following concerns about his job prospects] Had it not been for the war upsetting things, it would have come alright for me and may yet when things are quieter. I suppose you've finished with children. I see they are going to evacuate some more. If you had had any decent ones they would have been company for you while I am away but you are better off without ones like you had. We get very little war news. I heard today two German submarines were brought in [nothing is known of any such capture], if so they must be losing some and not having it all their own way sinking ships. No more air visitors but we are getting our shelter up as quickly as possible in case – I am now going to help with it so you see the people here are not feeling too secure or comfortable whatever we are told.

(Ipswich Museum Archive)

Two

The War that Wasn't

Ipswich entered the war in a whirlwind of frantic activity and with feelings of uncertainty and unreality. No fighting had taken place and the country was in a curious limbo, gearing for war yet retaining the attitudes that had prevailed during the years of peace. To make sense, now, of what happened over evacuation, ARP and other emergency services such as shelters and schooling in 1939 and early '40 it is necessary to understand that the wartime consensus to resist Hitler at all costs and press on until final victory had not yet been reached.

There were still attempts at high levels to get some kind of negotiated settlement. Lloyd-George, the last great wartime leader, was saying openly that this was inevitable. Closer to home, the local MP Richard Stokes was arguing much the same thing. Richard Stokes had become the first Labour MP for Ipswich after the botched retirement of Ganzoni in 1938. He is said to have felt uncomfortable about the family business's profitability in the first war as the East Anglian Munitions Board factory, and about Wilfred Stokes's very successful invention, the Stokes gun. He was also strongly influenced by his Catholic beliefs. In 1937 he was Chairman of the Peace Pledge Union meeting at the Public Hall. One of the other organisers was Mrs Mary Whitmore, a veteran Labour Party campaigner who after the war became the town's first mayoress. Stokes was secure enough in his position as Director of Ransomes & Rapier to take a highly independent line as the leader of the twenty or so Labour MPs in the Peace Aims Group. He had to deny frequent charges of being a pacifist and appeared to accept in public at least that Hitler's attack on France meant peace efforts had become temporarily impossible. Even as late as 25 May 1940 he was to argue in *Forward*, 'I hate Hitlerism as much as anyone, but having spent three years of the last war as a fighting soldier I remember how after a time we all longed for a negotiated peace. Such a peace obviously is not possible now but when the first great clash of arms is over an opportunity may arise and we should be ready to seize it.'

The ambiguities and uncertainties of the Chamberlain government could not fail to influence local government planning. The issue of evacuation is a vivid illustration. Ipswich planners were faced with a basic problem: the government could not decide whether or not the town should be classified as a vulnerable area. On the one hand Ipswich businesses were failing to win armaments contracts (despite Stokes offering a no-profits deal) because the government considered Ipswich too vulnerable to air attack; on the other, the government was arguing that civilian shelters were not necessary. Ipswich, bombed in the first war, was a safe place for evacuees; Norwich and Colchester, which had escaped Zeppelins, were not. Through the first year of the war the town was to go from being a centre to which children were evacuated to a town from which all non-essential people should be removed.

4   *The AFS taking delivery of sirens at Cliff Quay in 1939*

The Second World War proved to be the greatest challenge that local government in Ipswich has ever had to face. The only remotely comparable period was the crisis of the Civil War in the 1640s followed by the two Dutch Wars in the 1650s and 1660s. This time it was total war in a modern complex society, and pressures were faced throughout the entire local community.

Immediately after war broke out the Council, following central government instructions, set up an Emergency Committee of four individuals. Ostensibly this was just another Borough Committee, composed partially of councillors and reporting back to full Council. Its prime task was to deal with ARP and all matters connected with shelters and civilian defence. The rather shadowy figure of Mr Challis-King was in the chair. However, its real power and functions were much wider and were centred in a single unelected individual: the Chief Constable of Ipswich sat on the Emergency Committee, and was also the Chief Controller of the ARP. Obviously he was also *ex officio* a member of the Watch Committee, which controlled the Police, Special Constables and the Auxiliary Fire Services (as well as taxis, remand centres, petroleum licences, dog tracks, cinemas and theatres). The Home Office, the Intelligence Services, the Regional Commissioner in Cambridge and the military all communicated directly with the Chief Constable. He became by far the most powerful single man in Ipswich and much of the work of civilian wartime administration fell on him and his officers.

Local government in 1939 was faced with a number of crucial tasks. It had to organise emergency services, it had to provide shelters for its population, it had to accept its quota of evacuees and provide for them, and it had to protect its own children. Its police force had several additional security duties, and the town had to be put on a war footing ready to accept any troops billeted on it. To understand some of the decisions of the Ipswich Council during the months immediately before and after the outbreak of war requires some familiarity with the behaviour of local government. We know with hindsight that war was inevitable and that it did turn into total conflict, but at the time Ipswich Council leaders, like their colleagues in town halls across the country, had no intention of finding themselves in October 1939, with the crisis resolved by some last-minute miracle, the only council in the land to have spent every penny in its coffers on the best shelter and ARP service in England. So they prevaricated.

5 *AFS 3 engine photographed in Bolton Lane. This is still clearly the delivery van of Smiths Suitall shop which has been requisitioned and given a white visibility stripe. The headlamps do not seem to have yet been blacked out.*

6 *Private cars were transformed into fire engines by having ladders placed on their roofs and water pumps attached to trailers behind. These vehicles have been given visibility stripes and one headlamp on each provided with a blackout mask. Uncertainty over the rules for headlamp use by emergency service vehicles caused friction between ARP and other services.*

Incident after incident shows how the assumption the war would soon be over expressed itself in an obsessive concern with cutting costs and in every other detail of council decision-making, from refusing to unlock the communal shelters in the parks after the parks had closed at dusk to denying military lorries of the 32nd AA Battalion permission to use the corporation car parks without a fee (Minutes of Emergency Committee 9 July 1940, and referred to repeatedly in the minutes thereafter).

An early entry in the Minute Book records the decision not to build a special explosives store but, by an odd association of ideas, to use the cellars of the St Matthew's swimming pool instead. An unintentionally macabre entry instructed the mortuary superintendent to go ahead and order material sufficient for 500 canvas mortuary sacks from Firmins but not to have them made up in order to save on cost (Ipswich Borough Council Emergency Committee Minute Book Number 1, 14-15 September 1939).

Almost immediately, too, the Emergency Committee and Stokes crossed swords over the question of paying for the expenses of ARP wardens. At first the committee seemed sure of itself: it was not for the authorities to pay but for the employers. The committee had no problem in persuading the Transport Department of the Borough to agree with them, of course, but Stokes was a tougher nut. Emergency Committee Minute Book Number 1 never actually concedes that Stokes was correct, but it finally records that new arrangements had been drawn up, and later allowed men to be released from the Borough Surveyor's Department to attend ARP lectures, noting that their travelling time as well as their time at the lecture could be charged against the ARP account.

7 *Auxiliary Fire Service men training with a foam dispenser on wasteland near the river.*

8 *New Auxiliary Firemen pose with their trailer-pump in Derby Road. Sidney Dunlop's newsagents is proclaiming news of RAF successes*

October 28 1939

A letter from Mr A.S. Stokes referred to the handbook issued to wardens where it was stated volunteers should not be required to incur any out-of-pocket expenses in connection with their work and that they should apply for reimbursement to the local authority. It was agreed that lost time was not out-of-pocket expenses but it was decided to leave the matter in abeyance.

p.94 The Surveyor's Department enquired whether under such circumstances the men of the corporation staff would have their pay made up from civil defence funds. It was agreed this would not be allowable.

p.128 The Surveyor asked for instructions as to the men in his department attending classes during normal working hours. It was agreed that the time thus spent must be charged to the ARP account although it would not attract grant. It was further agreed that the time spent going from jobs to the lectures would be charged to the same account.

A similar drawn-out struggle was experienced in trying to get proper uniforms and protective clothing for the wardens, and is mentioned over and over in the columns of the *East Anglian Daily Times*. Nor could money be provided to supply each of the 40 wardens' posts with an electric kettle. On 19 August 1940, for example, the Emergency Committee records, 'Cook and Perry attend Committee on behalf of the Stoke wardens asking for refreshments and overalls – told of steps being taken.' In other words, no luck!

Official penny-pinching was also the experience of the emergency medical and fire services. Private cars were commandeered to be converted into ambulances. These were selected with a view to minimising compensation rather than maximising efficiency since the vans were of very poor quality. Almost immediately, Dr Pringle, head of the new medical services, was complaining and demanding money for repairs. Throughout June and July he demanded a trickle feeder to recharge the batteries. He had to agitate unsuccessfully to get steel helmets for his staff at the Orchard Street Mobile Post and beg for them to be allowed access to public shelters. Similarly, he had to agitate to get his own phone extension.

9 *Auxiliaries on the Fire Float in the Docks before the night of 9-10th April 1941 on which two were killed, one injured and one swam to safety.*

With the blackout came further adjustments and problems. It is said, for example, that on the first occasion it was tried out in Ipswich it was a great success save for one omission, the Town Hall clock! More serious was the trouble caused to the Ipswich Corporation trolley-bus service. Their poles flashed and sparked in the otherwise darkened streets in vivid fashion. They were an obvious giveaway of the town's position, and the local populace objected strongly to being harangued to 'Put that light out' and fined for lighting a match while the corporation trolley-buses were giving the equivalent of a nightly firework display.

As a partial compromise the trolley-buses stopped running at 7.30 in the evening, but the effect of this was equally disruptive. Stokes was to complain on behalf of his shift workers, who now

10 *The interior of the Norwich Road sub-station, showing a constable hard at work with a variety of phones.*

had to make long walks home after a day's exhausting work, or to the factory to start the night shift in total darkness. Trolley-bus conductors were faced with the problem of being given the wrong fares in the dark, some people apparently able to get away with wrapping copper coins in silver foil. The poor conductors had not only to stay behind to try to balance their takings but also found the employers took the losses out of their wages.

The Co-op was finding the blackout hard going, too, and published a series of posters asking for their customers' understanding and co-operation in dealing with the problems faced by baker, milk and coal delivery men. Accidents of all sorts proliferated in the darkened streets and the Emergency Committee Minutes of 7 June 1940 record how 'Two complete units of the Auxiliary Fire Service collided in Ranelagh Road from Rapier Street Station and Alfred George Smy Auxiliary Fireman killed.' They were forced to conclude on the following day, 'The method of patrolling during the emergency to be looked at as too dangerous. 10 June This is due to vehicles not having sidelights.'

The 1939 issue of the *Trumpeter*, an occasional works newsletter put out by Cranes, took care to warn its workforce against walking in the road, mentioning that three workmen had already been knocked down and injured in the blackout. On 6 March Warden Bancroft, aged 75, walked into a lamp-post in the blackout and received several cuts to his face and mouth (Chief Warden Woods' Diary). People still remember how on particularly foggy or dark nights it was possible when cycling home to find that all contact with familiar landmarks had been lost, and one had been travelling up quite the wrong street. Later on, in January 1943, the blackout led to a drowning in the Dock, and as a result the Watch Committee authorised a small searchlight in the rescue boat, two more police lamps and four large bath towels (to be used only in cases of emergency).

Ipswich Airport has the somewhat strange distinction of being the first airport from which a plane took off to bomb Germany. Five Bristol Blenheim IVs from 107 and 110 Squadrons at RAF Wattisham were moved to the airport and took part in the first RAF raid of the war. They took off at 15.55 on 4 September, one day after war was declared. The target for the Ipswich planes and ten others from Wattisham was the Kiel Dockyard and the pocket battleship *Admiral Scheer*, heavy cruiser *Prinz Eugen* and light cruiser *Emden*. It is said that Blenheim N6204 of 110 Squadron from Ipswich dropped the first bomb of the first raid on Germany. However, the raid was hardly a success. Of the 15 planes that took part, five were shot down, and of the targets only the *Emden* suffered minor damage due to its being hit by one of the downed planes. The bombs had been set with the wrong fuse and had no effect. The squadron's return was filmed and incorporated into the Korda film *The Lion Has Wings*. A few days later, on 27 September, the Commanding Officer of 110 Squadron was killed in a photographic mission over Kiel.

The full details of a second tragic event, a fight between RAF planes, were not to be made public until long after the war. Though clearly known about at the time by those, like Chief Warden Woods, in official circles, only misleading rumours reached men like Basil Brown at Woodbridge. Woods' diary reads:

> September 6 About 7 o'clock Air Raid warning sounded. Wardens arrived at posts. Cleared street. Stopped traffic into town. Foggy, could hear but not see aircraft overhead. Good practice for wardens who responded well. Doubt if German aircraft were over. *Two of our aircraft brought down by our own men in the fog.*

The full story was to emerge in the *Evening Star* of 22 September 1987. Two Hurricanes had been shot down by Spitfires. The pilot of the Hurricane that crashed at the *Ostrich* pub at Bourne Bridge, PO Frank Rose, was unharmed, but the second pilot, PO Montague Hilton-Harrap, whose plane crashed at Hintlesham, was killed by gunfire. This is how Jack Dodman of Ipswich remembered the incident:

> I was surprised to see in the *Star* about the Spitfires that shot down the Hurricanes on September the 6th 1939, as I thought no more would be heard about that now

because I was there and saw the Hurricane land in the field beside the road where I was standing at Wherstead.

What I mean is, I was the first one to speak to PO Frank Rose after he had landed. I was on my way to Brantham to pick up a load of apples. The sirens were just sounding as I was nearing the *Ostrich* pub just after seven o'clock. And at the beginning of the war they used to let vehicles out of the town but stopped them coming in till the all-clear had sounded.

It had been a bit misty that morning and as the sun was breaking there were patches of blue sky. Out of one of these I could see an aeroplane coming down low, and thinking it could be a German bomber returning after the raid and making use of the mist to shoot at anything moving before it crossed the coast, I stopped my lorry, got out and got in the ditch beside the road.

Still watching it I could see it was one of ours and it was going to land because he put his wheels down. I got out of the ditch and watched it touch down safely. I moved my lorry a few yards up the road, right opposite to where it stood, stopped the lorry, got my fire extinguisher and raced across the field because I could see smoke coming from the engine.

The pilot was just getting out of his cockpit when I got there. I asked if he had engine trouble, but he said no, but thought he had been hit by bullets. He started looking round the fuselage so I bent down and looked under the wings and I called him to tell him there were bullet holes there, two in one wing and one in the other wing.

He seemed shook up a bit and said he came from RAF North Weald, then asked me where he was and I told him. He then got his map out of his knee pocket in his flying suit, and pointed out where he was. He wanted to know where the nearest RAF station was. I told him RAF Martlesham and pointed that out to him. I said I thought the plane was on fire so I brought my fire extinguisher, but he said it was the glycol leaking on to the hot engine.

In the meantime, a young fellow came over from the farm buildings and said he worked at the farm. I told him to go back and tell his boss a fighter had landed in his field. Not long after, the village policeman arrived on his bicycle (not in a car) and wanted to know what was wrong. We told him it had been hit by machine-gun fire. I said I had seen it land. After a little while he asked for my name and address. As he was with the pilot now I went on my way to pick up my load.

On the return journey it was still there with several Air Force men checking it over to see if it could take off again. Later on that day I heard that another fighter had crashed at Hintlesham and the pilot was shot through the head.

(Jack Dodman, 76 Fitzgerald Road, Bramford, Ipswich)

Three

Spy Scares

Throughout 1939 and 1940, amongst all the other paper flooding across his desk in the newly strengthened and sandbagged Town Hall Police Station, Cresswell, the Chief Constable of Ipswich, was receiving regular circular reports and enquiries from the head of MI5, Vincent Kell, about potential German agents and likely fifth-column activities. The file survives and opens a window on to the extent of official fears about the shadowy world of subversion.

We may think of the war years as being a time of united opposition to the Nazi threat, when everyone stood by their neighbour, their community and their country. But, clearly, in 1939 and 1940 the security services thought otherwise. There was a fear not only of German spies and of foreigners of any sort but also a real concern that a section of the populace might actually help the enemy. No one can now say what grounds there were for these fears, but they were clearly taken seriously at the time.

A climate of suspicion, especially of internal subversion, went hand in hand with the fear of invasion. Of course, Cresswell was not told why he was being asked certain things, nor what further action ever took place. He was simply told what postal and telegram box office addresses to use to contact the intelligence services. Some questions were of a purely routine order, simply asking for details of people with dual nationalities who had volunteered to join the forces (about three of these), for their addresses to be checked and whether anything was known about them. Instructions to gather intelligence included:

19 September 1939

Reports regarding illicit wireless transmissions in your district – no direct action is to be taken until a full report has been furnished to this dept and advice received as to what course to adopt.

22 December 1939

A number of well-authenticated instances of illicit 'light' signalling have been reported by the Observer Corps. Such cases are in no way similar to the usual complaints. Please send reports of confirmed instances.

23 May 1940

A removal of a hedge as though to facilitate landing of aircraft has been reported, and painting farm buildings red as though for landmarks.

Another case of an individual laying in stores of red paint, clothing, shores and wire. Anything similar report.

(File marked MI5 addressed to Chief Constable Cresswell, Inspector Rush Collection, Suffolk Constabulary Archive, in care of Ipswich Museum)

As the situation worsened Cresswell received information on all the officials of the highly organised Nazi Party organisation in Britain. The Auslands Front, which also had sections for the Hitlerjugend and the Bund Deutscher Madel, existed to organise German nationals resident in England along Nazi Party lines, and Cresswell received a list of the principal officers and the places where they had set up centres throughout the country. He was also told of the 26 places in England and Scotland with branches of the equivalent Italian fascist organisations. Nowhere in Suffolk or Norfolk was among them, but the picture was still one of large, carefully organised, clandestine groups.

These were general circulars, but the Chief Constable also had had more specific allegations to deal with connected with the existence of possible real agents. On 15 February 1939 a concerned engineering assistant in Ipswich Town Hall approached the police regarding some friends of his, Mr and Mrs X [name suppressed]:

Mr X had invested as a commission agent but the business had failed and he had no apparent source of income. He had married a German girl, a Peta Valdemar. She is a good linguist and visits Berlin and Munich frequently for up to three weeks. Apparently, Mr X had said his wife worked as an espionage agent for Lever Brothers before coming to England.

Their joint current scheme is to get councils interested in purchasing surf motor boats.

They visit the Engineer frequently at his Colchester home. During the conversation on the probability of war the question of 'air defence' arose, whereupon Mrs X said, 'Are you referring to the British invention, this thing they have got at Bawdsey – the

11 *Chief Constable Cresswell at his desk in the Town Hall Police Station. There is a helmet on his duty bed, a Tilley lamp in case of power cuts, an incendiary on his desk and a diagram of another on the wall.*

Death Ray – because it is uncontrollable. If it could be controlled Herr----, he is famous Austrian professor, would be able to control it. He can't control it, and if he can't I am certain no one else can. As for it being a secret invention, what one country has, another has.' At the end of this conversation she appeared to become excited and her English deteriorated. Her husband, who was present, seemed to want to break the conversation.

I have also a friend at Bawdsey Air Station – a Corporal Bloomfield who resides at Colchester and comes every weekend. He is an electrical specialist and visits me frequently. As far as I know the Xs and Bloomfield have not met.'

Obviously rumours and speculation had blossomed about the work being undertaken at Bawdsey, and the concerns of the engineer may or may not have been misplaced.

Ipswich was covered by the Aliens Act, which meant that no foreigner could reside in the area without special permission from the Chief Constable, nor were they permitted to own cameras, binoculars or radio equipment without licence. The Chief Constable had also to prepare lists of particularly vulnerable industries in the town, about six in all, and check with their managers that they had no German, Austrian or Italian workers. (There was initially some confusion as to whether or not Czechoslovaks should be added.) On receipt of a specially coded telegram, any such workers were to be fired immediately.

A note of unconscious black comedy was provided by circular CA/110 issued by 'Box 500 Cambridge' and headed 'Secret'. It began in a suitably cloak-and-dagger fashion: 'As a result of their practical experience in dealing with German agents arriving in this country, my Head Office made a note of the following points, which would seem to merit particular attention when the identity of a suspect is in doubt.' If a policeman came across someone wandering around lost or otherwise, with lack of knowledge of the neighbourhood (point 13) but carrying large-scale maps (14) and suitcases, especially those which may contain a radio set and cameras (12), waving bundles of £5 notes about (10), wearing clothing of a foreign cut (8), with traces of strange chemicals like Pyramidon all over them (11), speaking with a foreign accent (9) and holding ration and identity cards issued to different persons (6), he should be highly suspicious! The more discerning policemen relied on subtleties like crossing the number 7 in the continental fashion or an address written in the order town, street, house number.

Other advice included, for example, suspicious Luxembourg passports, pink travellers ration cards with a CA number, or imitation crocodile-skin suitcases of light- or dark-brown colour with two catches, size about 1ft 4in. by 1ft 6in., which presumably came about from actual cases.

Four

The British Union of Fascists

It is quite rare for documents relating to the internal working of the British Union of Fascists in the first part of the war to survive. However, a file made by the police relating to the work of the BUF District Leader, Ronald Creasy of Eye, does survive in the extensive collection of wartime documents made by Inspector Rush of the Felixstowe Police. The documents stop after the banning of the party at the end of May 1940. A full run of copies of the Blackshirt paper *Action* for 1940 are also part of the file.

The police had been instructed from an early date to keep an eye on the British Union of Fascists. As far back as 8 May 1934 Schreiber had reported to the security services,

> I do not gather that it [the Fascist movement] is cutting much ice in Ipswich at the present time, but their efforts in Suffolk have so far centred on the agricultural districts and the tithe question.
>
> Sir Oswald Mosley held a meeting and spoke here on a market day about two months ago; a quiet, orderly meeting with an audience chiefly of farmers from the surrounding district: no heckling and few questions asked. They propose to hold an open-air meeting here on Thursday 5 July at the Royal Show at Ipswich, when agricultural interests will be largely centred in the town.

The Blackshirts are generally thought of as urban thugs, but the reality of the movement within Suffolk was quite different. Along the Norfolk-Suffolk border the involvement of the BUF in the tithe war had won them a following amongst farmers. Ex-officers from the first war, who had purchased farms with their severance pay and then run into considerable trouble owing to the collapse of British farming, represented a distinct category of support. It was in this way that the gentle author Henry Williamson, farming in Norfolk, became drawn into the movement.

Landowners, too, were often sympathetic. The women's District Leader for North Norfolk was Lady Downes and, as a recent biographer of Diana Mosley, Jan Dalley, has said, it is probable that it is only owing to her close friendship with the Queen Mother that she escaped internment later in the war. In other words, the BUF had contacts among the highest circles in East Anglia.

The District Leader was a man called Ronald Creasy. On 23 October 2000 Creasy described his political life, and it is best told in his own words. Even at the end of his life Creasy was a true believer, and he conjures up a moment when he at least thought that the BUF would carry all before them.

> At the age of 21 I inherited Cranley Manor, Eye, from my father (who had had interests in some eighty farms in Suffolk and Norfolk up till 1931, when the business contracted in the Depression), coupled with a certain financial contribution from a wealthy close relative of my father who died about the same time. This gave me the independence of pen and speech denied to the vast ranks unable to express themselves or in fear of what they might lose in profession or jobs.
>
> The unnecessary tragedy of the thirties provoked my whole concern for those of country and city alike, their struggle against the falsity of poverty and decay engineered by those who used them for their own ends. The current assembly of politics in the hands of Mammon appalled me, provoking a determination to take action against it. Through my writings I was approached by a member of one of the aristocratic families in England with the full literature of the BUF Movement led by Sir Oswald Mosley. After thoroughly digesting the obvious sense I arranged a personal meeting with Mosley at his headquarters in London. Our interview was brief. I explained my mission (my credentials had previously been received by him) stating I would prefer an active part and a responsible position in the Suffolk/Norfolk area of Eye, a small borough town halfway between Norwich and Ipswich. I was accepted as District Leader for the area in this already highly successful Movement in which I had already become acquainted with many leading and important figures of our country as well as European counterparts. With the help of many important County people I quickly became established. Assistant District Leaders were appointed accountable to my office at Cranley Manor, where the old Roman sign, a flash of action in a circle of unity, still acts as a weather pointer on the roof top, given to me in wrought iron and erected over sixty years ago.

Wortham, where the Blackshirts had turned up in numbers in uniform to oppose farm sales, was well within Creasy's own District. Creasy later denied any direct involvement, however, claiming to have been too important to risk getting bound over as his comrades were.

Another seam of discontent amongst the respectable was provided by the small shopkeeper. The BUF ran a front organisation, 'The British Traders Bureau', with its own newspaper, *The British Trader*. Its slogans were ''Gainst Trust and Monopoly', 'Combating the Chain Store Menace', 'British Traders First', 'Abolish Cut Prices'. What these really meant can be discerned in the circular sent by Peter Heyward, the Organiser, to Creasy and other District Leaders ahead of the election: 'With the approach of a General Election in the autumn it becomes increasingly necessary to extend our propaganda among small traders who are today suffering badly at the hands of alien and Jewish combines.'

The hatred of Jews was absolutely central to Mosley's thinking and to that of his movement. International finance, usually called the 'money power', or the 'hidden hand or plutocracy', was Jewish. This is what Creasy means by 'Mammon'. Jews cannot have the interests of a nation at their heart because they are a nation scattered throughout the world and without a homeland of their own. The Blackshirts conveniently ignored the existence of international capitalist concerns which were not Jewish, and somehow even the poorest Jew became an agent of the Hidden Hand of the Money Power. Particularly hysterical outbursts can be found in *Action* about the 'Refujews', and there are interesting premonitions of modern animosity towards refugees.

Some writers have sought to distance Mosley from anti-semitism and to link the BUF more to Mussolini and the Italian Fascists, who were indeed less obsessively racist than the Nazis. But Creasy's correspondence makes the anti-semitism obvious, as well as the other irrational ideas, if not outright fantasy and play-acting, prevalent amongst the far right.

Mosley's visit to Eye was the key moment in Creasy's career. During the leader's stay he was introduced by Creasy to the vicar, the Reverend Rea of Eye. Creasy had already briefed the British Union as follows:

> January 5 1939 His sympathies are greatly with us. He is conversant with most of the Patriotic 'secret' societies that are prevalent in England. He states that he is informed certain members of the House of Lords intend making a stand against the corruptive element of this country, such as the P.E.P. group, in the very near future and that then it will be necessary for all patriotic Movements to stand and 'fight' together.

Creasy suggested that Rea meet Mosley in Eye Vicarage. It is probably from Rea that Creasy got the several pamphlets on 'The British Mistery'. According to an article in the *Sunday Dispatch* (29 January 1939) cut out by Creasy, this secret society claimed about 20,000 members. Its principal aim was to return all political power to the King. Membership was restricted to those of Anglo-Saxon descent since 1869.

In the highly charged atmosphere of the time, Creasy was occupied in taking up the cases of members fired from their jobs for their views and in otherwise countering the opposition that he experienced. His letters are full of threats and bombast as to what would happen to their enemies when the day came. On 11 February 1939 he wrote to E.E. Green regarding his son Ronald's dismissal from A. Savill & Co. Ltd, Mellis, Eye. Creasy feels it is due to Clarke and Gill's known opposition to the British Union of Fascists. He goes on to say that,

> as a customer of theirs, and one who can influence others, I shall not hesitate to use my influence against them and to withdraw my own business. Remember those that suffer for its [British Union] cause today are those who will benefit by its greatness tomorrow, while those who have condemned in their ignorance, and live to see the birth of its renown, will do so with remorse and sorrow in their hearts.

The Ipswich Police files contain a denunciation of Creasy which, if true, shows that he and his party were prepared to consider very extreme action, little short of treason.

> 28 September 1938 to Superintendent Mr H. Potter from Detective Constable Harry Cobb.
> At 10.40a.m. today, Mrs Harris, of Brook House, Henley, called at this station with the following information.
>   She stated that her son-in-law Ronald Creasey of Cranley House, Eye, who is a Fascist, attended a meeting of this party in London on Saturday last and returned to Ipswich about 5a.m. on the Sunday morning in a Mercedes car. Creasey's wife although a member of the same organisation was not allowed to attend this meeting.

Mrs Harris is informed that at this meeting the members present agreed to assist Hitler even in the event of this Country going to war.

Mrs Harris is concerned as her son-in-law's cousin, Wilmott Creasey, is manager of the Ipswich Airport, and the former by virtue of relationship has access to the airport at all time.

From this distance, the idea of Oswald Mosley being taken seriously as the new leader of Britain, arriving at Eye to the salutes of uniformed Blackshirts, and meeting with the Rev. Rea in Eye Vicarage to discuss what Rea knew about potential coups by members of the House of Lords to replace Parliament with direct rule by the King, may sound far-fetched. So too might late-night journeys across East Anglia by a local landowner in a white Mercedes to discuss armed support for Hitler. But within the super-heated world of the British Union such events did indeed take place. There was perhaps a strong element of play-acting in all this, but the British Union wanted badly to be a serious threat, and was keen on portraying itself as such.

The government was concerned that a possible fifth column, an organised group of British far right collaborators, might spring up to aid any possible German paratroopers or raiders. It is easy to discount this as simple wartime hysteria, but given the reports Cresswell had received about Creasy, together with the accounts of unexplained signals and such like, the concern of the authorities was quite rational.

More dangerous, perhaps, than the cloak-and-dagger element of their activities was Mosley's plan to fight the election in 1940 on a peace platform. This could capitalise on the reservations of genuine pacifists, like Stokes and the Peace Pledge Union, and had the potential to mobilise wider support. In 1940 he was attempting to fight as many seats as possible, claiming that the war was a Jewish war and demanding that the people should be allowed to vote on the war aims.

Mosley's message of 1 September 1939 to all British Union members was:

The dope machine of Jewish finance deceived the people until Britain was involved in war in the interest of the Money Power which rules Britain through its press and parties. I am now concerned with only two simple facts. This war is no quarrel of the British people; this war is a quarrel of Jewish finance. So to our people I give myself for the winning of peace.

Despite a press and radio ban he was able to attract crowds around the country. Creasy's instructions were clear:

January 17 1940 to all officials from E.G. Clarke, Propaganda Administrator: Mosley has advanced in British Union the only sane and logical policy for a real BRITISH PEACE and more than that he shows the people how to get that peace. The leader has written many masterly articles and pamphlets on this subject and he has now written a great work, entitled 'THE BRITISH PEACE'. The pamphlet is written in simple language so that all can understand, and it contains over 5,000 words, for the price of ONE PENNY.

It is our duty and privilege as members of British Union to break down the press boycott and the ban of the BBC and create record sales for this new pamphlet.

Creasey was trying to organise a campaign of conscientious objection against the war, and amongst his papers is the standard information given to BUF members on appearing before tribunals.

> BUF printed advice to BUF members called up. Schedule of written statement to Tribunal.
>
> 4. The ideological grounds of conscientious objection set out as suggested in main section ('he would then express his willingness to serve his country in any ordinary war in defence of Britain or the British Empire, from whatsoever quarter attack might come. In this case, however, the government have seen fit to publish as their war aims an ideological conflict to destroy the system of a foreign country. In proof he would quote the statements on war aims of the prime minister, Mr Churchill, and other politicians to show that they intended to destroy Hitlerism and change the system of government in Germany, and confirm this interpretation from further quotations from the press. *Such war aims are contrary to the conscience of any earnest supporter of British Union.'*
>
> *The applicant should maintain throughout that the onus for the creation of his conscientious objection rests with the government which has deliberately raised the ideological issue by making one of its principal war aims the destruction of the political system of another great nation.*)

Organised opposition to enlistment through registration as conscientious objectors led to the BUF attempting to forge some strange alliances. There was even some flirting with the Peace Pledge Union, as the report of a strange meeting in the Friends' Meeting House in Ipswich makes clear:

> At the invitation of the Ipswich branch of the PPU Mr Hammond addressed a full house at the Friends House, Ipswich on Tuesday 27 February.
>
> After expressing his fear that under its original constitution, with merely a negative policy of No War, PPU could have only a very small National influence, the speaker welcomed the fact that there was now evidence of many PPU members formulating or adopting a political policy, and expressed thanks for the opportunity of presenting the case for British Union.
>
> The questions that followed proved that some of the younger members of this branch of the PPU are more deeply concerned with practical political means of preventing war than with merely salving their own individual consciences.
>
> (Action 7 March 1940)

As the year progressed Creasy and his Fascists were to encounter real and growing hostility. An increasingly desperate Creasy wrote over and over again to Donovan at the National Organisation for support and advice, and tried all he could to get police protection, but this was withheld. Donovan wrote back claiming that Creasy was the only BUF organiser facing such problems and that his sale of 20 copies of *Action* at Stowmarket was a great success; in fact *Action* published a little piece on this victory:

> On 16 March 1940 District Leader Ronald N. Creasy wrote to the Director General.
>
> On Saturday evening 16 March 1940, two active members, Arthur Hoggarth and Miss Hoggarth, and myself were selling *Action* on the street at Stowmarket [since the war a garrison town]. After a short time we were approached by thirty to forty soldiers in uniform, the ringleaders of which, one obviously a Jew, demanded that we should stop selling our papers, and that if we refused to do so they would make matters particularly unpleasant for us. We persisted in sale endeavours until surrounded by the soldiers

who were about to create an ugly scene when two officers arrived. They dispersed the soldiers who only returned a few minutes later. On four occasions I had to appeal to officers to intervene on the threatening attitude of their men, pointing out that although they were shouting about fighting for freedom against Hitlerism, which they said we represented, their whole attitude was a direct contradiction of freedom.

In the end a very disturbed Creasy was forced to abandon paper sales:

> 11 May 1940. It is with considerable regret that I must state, after careful consideration of the whole circumstances which have arisen in my district during the last week, that I have no alternative but to stop street sales of *Action* and outward public activity, until such time when it will be wise to continue. The opposition is entirely out of all control while even members of my own household are stoned while going through Eye – it would be suicide to face the crowd, every step I take outside my farm faces a possible consequence against which I am powerless to compete. I have interviewed the Chief Constable of the Norfolk Constabulary from whom I received some consideration. I have also interviewed the Chief Constable of Suffolk whose only attitude was one of discourtesy and impudent suggestions. I wish so much I could talk with you for any forced suppression of the spirit of British Union within me is as a flame consuming flesh.

Life had in fact become intolerable for the would-be plotter and scourge of the old parties. He had been beaten on the streets. Creasy was a true believer, though, and was still looking for final victory.

On 20 May 1940 he wrote to the Director General:

> On Friday morning roads leading to my house were marked with the wording 'SHOOT CREASY' possibly to intimidate a few members who regularly call on Friday evenings for a members meeting, and also to convey the desire of a certain opposition. On Sunday afternoon I left the house for 2½ hours; on my return I found a window had been forced open and a general investigation had been made in all bottom-floor rooms. Wireless wires had been severed inside and out and aerials pulled down. Young flowering trees had been snapped in two, a sundial pedestal shattered, while gates and doors had been wrenched from their hinges and thrown into the drive. All available possessions belonging to my son (aged 5½ years) had been thrown into a pond, some of which have been recovered by the police. We will march with the Leader knowing that the day of victory is ahead for now the opposition has created within us the intolerance which knows no defeat and tolerates only victory.

On 23 May Sir Oswald Mosley was arrested in his home. On the 30th his British Union of Fascists was dissolved and its publications were banned. Virtually all the Fascists who remained from Mosley's cohorts of the thirties were rounded up and imprisoned. Creasy shared their fate.

Five

Conscientious Objectors

The Peace Pledge Union had been very strong in Ipswich. Both Richard Stokes, the local MP, and other Labour Party activists had supported it, arranged public meetings and spoken from its platform, notably on 24 November 1937. But while Major S.W. Humphreys, Mayor of Lowestoft could thunder fiercely, 'I loathe a CO. I say that such a thing does not exist,' such reminders of the First World War were clearly not going to go unchallenged in Ipswich. A strong attack was made on pacifists by a group of Tory councillors, including C.G. Roper, R.W. Fison and others. They were keen that the Council should fire all the conscientious objectors that worked for it, having established that there were seven such individuals. The hawks wanted to include any teachers as well.

The Council had not properly worked out its policy towards those employees who had been called up. Their jobs would be held for them, but it was not decided whether they should receive war bonuses to bring their wages back up to their current levels. It was therefore easy to point out that if COs continued in their posts they would be eligible for any increases in council pay, war bonuses and annual increments, while employees who were called up would in all probability be taking a colossal drop in income as a private. In fact, council workers had already received an increase in April 1940 and this had not been passed on to those already called up.

Fison did not use the word dismissal but preferred to speak of giving leave of absence without pay for the duration of the war to all persons on the Council's staff who were registered as conscientious objectors. 'The question of their reinstatement should be considered by the Council after the end of the war,' he suggested. C.G. Roper said Parliament had not told any Council that they should continue to employ their COs (*EADT*, 23.7.40). This provoked a stormy session in which members of the Labour group, headed by Mr A. Victor Smith, an ex-mayor of Ipswich, walked out of the Council Chamber.

The Establishment Committee of Ipswich Borough Council (which dealt with staffing issues) had proposed a carefully worded compromise: those COs who had been registered for non-combatant duties in the forces, people who had agreed to be stretcher-bearers, for example, should be placed on the same footing as other employees serving with the forces and receive the Council's war service allowance; those objectors who were registered unconditionally and would do nothing of any kind, including first aid or munitions work, to further a war, should be given leave of absence without pay for the duration of the war, such period of absence not to count towards increments of pay.

The Labour group managed successfully to remove all distinctions between the two kinds of objector. Mr A.J. Cook said 'that this was a war of freedom. They had no right to overrule the Tribunals. If they did, then they were nothing more or less, in their humble way, than dictators – the very thing of which they were trying to clear the world.' He demanded that the Council add to its resolution these words: 'Agreeing that it is fundamental to our national cause that intellectual freedom should be preserved, this Council accepts the finding of the CO Tribunal as established by Parliament and agrees that those objectors registered unconditionally should be retained in their present conditions of service under the Council.' This resounding statement of principle brought cheering from the onlookers, much to the mayor's irritation.

Cook was supported by Alderman Jackson: 'Do nothing that will start the disintegration of our nation. The nation today is united. We shall not win this war if we start penalising liberty of conscience. We shall only win it by maintaining national unity and those things which are sacred to the liberties of Englishmen.' Here, amongst the stilted committee language, was one of the defining moments of the war. It is still worth the local community remembering and respecting these words, which sum up the motivation that enabled so many people to endure the conflict.

However, it was not to be plain sailing for COs. Inevitable feelings of hostility had been fanned locally by men like Roper, and COs who had volunteered for the civil defence services often found themselves forced out by the antagonism of their fellow-workers. It is clear that this antagonism was shared if not actively fostered by some of those in authority.

The details of these drives to clear COs out of the volunteer services are contained in Committee Minutes and in Chief Warden Woods' diary. Running alongside other debates in the Council Chamber, the events were not taken up by the press.

Emergency Committee 29 April 1940:

A letter dated 29th instant was submitted from the Fire Brigade Superintendent suggesting that Auxiliary Fireman Hawes should be asked to terminate his employment as he had registered as a Conscientious Objector and the other men at the same post were likely to resign. It was agreed that Mr Sweet should discuss the position with Hawes and report further. Hawes resigned.

C.J. Woods' Diary 6 May 1940:

Receive report from Hd Warden M & K groups of resignations of wardens from their groups if Warden Stone of M3 is allowed to remain as a warden. He has obtained exemption from military service as Conscientious Objector. Report to Chief Controller for advice. Don't want the man.

Emergency Committee 7 May 1940:

The Chief Warden called attention to James Stone of 83 Ascot Drive, a conscientious objector exempt from military service whilst he remained in the ARP service. It was agreed that the Chief Warden should interview Stone.

C.J. Woods' Diary 9 May 1940:

Receive A.M. memo from Town Clerk asking me to interview Warden Stone C.O. Will get him to retire, failing which I shall put him on reserve.

13 May 1940

Interview Warden Stone (C.O.) at Argyle Street. Inform him the Emergency Committee suggests he resigns from ARP. Exemption claimed on religious grounds. Tell him 20 wardens threaten to resign and I cannot afford to lose them. Ask him to write me his decision, then I would take further steps.

17 May

Four weeks notice to Warden Stone C.O. I advised the Head Wardens of K group.

The attempts by the Fascists to use the Tribunals and Conscientious Objector system and to co-opt the Peace Pledge Union cannot have made the position of genuine pacifists any easier and certainly not any clearer to the public. Opposition grew to such a pitch that the PPU offered to forego their hiring of the Friends' Meeting House for fear that the hostility would spread to the Quakers. The Friends met these principles with their own and allowed the meetings to continue.

Six

The ARP:
Managing the Awkward Squad

The government first appointed ARP officers in 1935, allowing four years of peace and ten months of the Phoney War in which to prepare for conflict, but recruiting in Ipswich initially ran into difficulties. While in East Suffolk volunteers had greatly exceeded the required number of wardens, 11,222 volunteers for an establishment of 3,999, with a reserve of 1,072, the reverse was true in Ipswich. By April 1939 only 481 volunteers had come forward when 1,122 wardens were needed. The town was short of 420 wardens, 125 rescue workers, 103 auxiliary firemen, 145 special constables and 99 medical volunteers. A special procession was held to drum up volunteers and mock air raids were held on 15 and 16 April.

12 *H Group Wardens outside the Town Hall. The year must be 1941 as the wardens have received their first uniforms, the blue overalls. The Head Warden and his two deputies have white-painted helmets. Two police inspectors were appointed to the warden service. H Group covered the Docks and the town centre.*

The internal struggle to create some kind of efficient force from the ever-changing group of men that made up the different categories of full-time, part-time and volunteer ARP is documented in considerable and fascinating detail by the private diary kept by Chief Warden C.J. Woods covering the years 1939-40. In his frankly terrible handwriting Woods poured out his considerable frustration with his men and the Emergency Committee. This diary makes it clear that the problem was greatest on the new estates and in the working-class parts of the town.

C.J. Woods had been appointed Chief Warden of Ipswich in August by the Emergency Committee and answered to the Chief Constable and sometimes to the Town Clerk. Two Police Inspectors, Simpson and, at various times, Church, Hammond or Charleston, were appointed as full-time liaison between the ARP and the rest of the police. The wardens in each of the 13 areas into which Ipswich had been divided were allowed to meet and elect their own area Head Wardens and Deputy Head Wardens. Woods could not appoint his own men, and at first he was not even sure if he would be allowed to dismiss them. The chain of command was weak and unclear and was to cause considerable difficulties, especially as Woods was not the best of diplomats.

At first he was relatively optimistic about the men. He was positive about the Head Wardens of A Group ('very good'), M Group ('a good chap'), F Group ('very good') and E Group ('useful'). He found a number of sectors not up to strength, and other causes for concern: M Group wardens were not such good quality but very keen – a little inclined to want to know what was to be got out of ARP personally! – and 60 per cent short of requirements in a key industrial populated district; G Group badly wanted reinforcing; F Group wanted wardens badly on new estate roads. Woods himself, as someone who had started as an unpaid volunteer well before the war began, had his own private feelings about those he saw as late-comers:

13 *An end-of-war portrait of an unknown wardens group. They are in the new blue battledress uniforms with CD badges. Although the idea had led to threats of resignation at the beginning of the war, women had finally been allowed to join. Four of the 120-odd men who managed to combine ARP and Home Guard duties can be seen.*

'September 4 Not the class of men we want: £3 a week for Full-Time service is bait no doubt. Some men could not volunteer when the duties were honorary!'

Perhaps some of the staff problems he faced were partly due to his inability to understand those unable, for whatever reason, to be as totally committed as himself. Reading between the lines of his accounts of continual friction between wardens one can see something of the underlying problem: the service was composed of two categories of men, the full-timers and the voluntary part-timers. The wages of the full-time men were such that the job was only appealing to out-of-work working-class men, a quite different group to the unpaid volunteers. The part-timers and volunteers were a potential and sometimes a real threat to the full-time wardens' jobs as the Home Office would periodically seek to replace one by the other.

The most immediate problem was the issuing of gas-mask respirators to the public. Thousands of these were being assembled at County Police Headquarters, 1,000 dispatched to Shotley as work continued on the 20,000 masks still outstanding. The public had become truly alarmed and there was particularly high demand for the baby bag respirators, which at times was close to panic: 'September 7 Spent nearly all day at Argyle St. Crowds of people for respirators. Public show up badly so far as ever having read national service booklet sent out by government. Short of respirators – hope stock is on the way!'

However, it was not until 30 October that work began on supplying the special small respirators, which finished in December. These dates reveal the bizarre attitudes

14 *Inside the D wardens post at William Cowell's printing works. Everyone is in their own clothes and the rattle is to warn of gas. Some are treating the whole thing as a joke, others are quite clearly worried.*

of officialdom. The official line had always been that the outbreak of war would be followed immediately by a devastating gas attack. Carrying gas masks was encouraged in every official medium, yet babies and children were not offered protection in Ipswich until four months had gone by. Surveying the gas-mask requirements of their areas was a never-ending job, the population being inconstant owing to evacuation. Each warden was supposed to survey his beat and produce charts showing where people slept, where potentially inflammable objects were kept, and where water mains and gas pipes were.

Just as they thought they were getting into a routine the ARP received instructions from the government to recall every single gas mask in the country to the main warden posts in each area, so the whole lot could be fitted with an improved additional respirator called Contex. Both the scale of the task and the speed with which it was accomplished were quite impressive. Without warning the wardens were told that 102,000 gas masks would have to be refitted with Contex, but the task was achieved between 22 May and 4 June 1940.

In addition, they had to police the blackout, not a popular job at all with the public for whom 'Mind that light' or 'Put that light out' became one of the principal memories of the war. Friction over lights even found its way into the pulpit:

> October 22 Sunday church parade at All Saints Church with G Group 3p.m. About 30 wardens present, beautiful service. Warden Rev. Mitton preached appropriate sermon on value of voluntary labour. After 'notices for the week' welcomed the wardens and asked people to appreciate the efforts of wardens on their behalf and not to judge them only by the fact that they sometimes had to ask them to attend to their lights! This might be copied by other groups.

This unpopularity was the least of Woods' worries. Far more difficult was the diplomatic problem wardens faced trying to get the police or military to control their lights, neither force taking too well to being ordered about by civilians. The council refuse incinerator was once fined three pounds, and not even wardens were above reproach, as Woods records: 'August 17 Find light in a warden's house in Park Road which is empty. Had to get him in from Volunteers.'

The difficulties Woods experienced in claiming for loss of earnings caused his men by their duties has already been mentioned. He was to face the same hurdles in securing a petrol ration for Head Wardens, and in getting them tea and sugar. The struggle to obtain for his men an issue of poor quality blue boilersuits with an ARP badge, as some kind of protection for their own clothes against the wet and dirty tasks they had to perform, was to turn into a lengthy cliff-hanger lasting more than a year. Everyone had to be measured in a hurry on 28 May, and on 1 June Woods sent in the last bit of paperwork, but 'July 9 Receive information that no Uniform will be provided for Wardens! All other services get theirs. There will be a fine How de do!' They still had not arrived when his diary ended late in 1940.

Meanwhile Woods had to find suitable wardens' posts for his men. This was no easy task. Many posts had problems with damp, and in some the wardens were forced to come to an understanding with neighbours so that they could use their toilets.

Initially, at least, some posts had no telephones and wardens were therefore dependent on their neighbours. One group of wardens were offered an air-raid slit trench.

The men themselves hardly helped Woods in his struggle. No sooner had he got one post set up in Dr Bartlett's garage than someone began removing the doctor's timber for use in various little jobs. In another post one warden was stealing from the others. There was fiddling of phone-call charges. Part-time men with day jobs were not turning up for their share of day duties, or were sleeping their evening duties away, sometimes even getting caught. Mr Brown, in his diary, records how group pressure obliged him to go along with missing out patrols:

Dec 26
Am just a little perturbed about the way some chaps are treating the patrol duty. Some don't do it and the last time I was on we all three stayed in and played shove ha'penny. Hope I'm not a prig but it doesn't seem the right thing to do, but I can't push against the stream on my own.
(Helen D. Millgate (ed.), *Mr Brown's War. A Diary of the Second World War*)

Nor was this unnoticed by authority. In January Woods recorded complaints against and his own defence of his men:

January 16 1940
Group comes under criticism from member of Emergency Committee re Full-Time wardens working during day and sleeping at Post at night! Enquiring into this.

January 17
Report re F5 Post recorded under 16 – much exaggerated – warden in [unclear word] does both day and night duty as required.

There were fights between wardens and continual rows leading to resignations, dismissals, petitions by loyal colleagues to reinstate wardens felt to have been hardly treated, and even protests arranged by householders on the beats covered by affected wardens. Woods noted that one warden was 85 and 'really too old'. Another was doing a good job at 65. There was public unease about the age of some men. Others Woods felt were mentally unstable, often with good reason.

September 9
Called out to 44 Westerfield Road about 9 o'clock. Mental breakdown – he is over 80. Dr Callis (?) and morphia given. Got home about 10.30. Unpleasant experience. Hardly ARP duty!

April 11
Warden X going off deep end. Not a bad chap but neurotic. Is seeing doctor, may have to get rid of him if he cannot control himself.

April 20
Busy morning, Hd Warden B Group gives me his resignation. Try to persuade him to withdraw and expect different reply Monday. Nice old chap but rather eccentric, trains his group anyway – even if he is crazy.

No sooner had he got one set of full-time men distributed around the posts and trained and organised than the government drastically cut the number of

15 *Police specials and ARP undergo training with stirrup pumps and for the removal of people overcome by smoke.*

full-time wardens. In December he had to send out 40 dismissal notices. In some cases this caused real hardship, and Woods was besieged by men begging for help, whom he tried to find part-time places. This caused a great deal of bad feeling. On 20 December he had to face the possibility of something approaching industrial action by the men of M Group, when part-timers threatened to resign in support of full-timers. In January he had to convince a warden from F Group that dismissals had been fair:

> January 1 1940
> Letter from Warden Button re his notice sent on to me by Inspector Charleston. Thinks he is badly treated. Interviewed Warden Ellwood. Satisfied him that warden being dismissed has been handled fairly.

> January 3
> Letter for son of Warden Branch I Group re his being put on Part-Time – Hard Case – but cannot alter decision. Hd Warden of F reports interview with Warden Ellwood whose attitude toward dismissal of wardens in his group has altered for the better.

Men did not go without a struggle, some complaining not only to the Regional Commissioner in Cambridge but all the way up to Sir John Anderson, the head of the Home Office. They combined complaints about their own treatment with bitter attacks on their colleagues and Head Wardens. Nevertheless, when Woods worked out how much he had paid in wages he was able to say that he had created a reduction of £190 in the total bill. By April, though, he had heard rumours of a further round of cuts, and by the 25th realised he was looking at a further reduction of 40 to 50 men.

16 *Police training slide showing a cluster bomb opened to reveal the incendiaries inside. This one had obviously failed to work.*

Having dismissed the men Woods then found he had to call some of them back to fill vacancies left by other men resigning or being called up. The number of rows and of ensuing resignations also began to mount. Woods is often unsure whether a resignation over sickness was really due to some grievance or another. He finds himself trying to talk men out of their resignations and speaks of days when there is nothing to do but deal with an epidemic of resignations.

Two months later, in June, just before the bombing campaign started, Woods found himself ordered to run a fruitless drive for more volunteers:

> June 17 Evening go off to a Loudspeaker 'whip up' for wardens in G Group – 17 enrolled.
>
> June 18 Go off at 7p.m. to G Group for further 'whip ups' – got 10 more wardens and arrived home 11 o/c.
>
> July 2 Public lecture at Springfield school – quite a good attendance who appear to enjoy Inspector's remarks. My appeal for wardens produced no response am afraid, volunteers are a past number, still we must go on trying or conscription will follow.

17 *Policemen train in how to deal with gas on waste ground near Bond Street fire station. The stick is probably being used to test for residues of mustard gas after neutralisation with bleach.*

Woods did what he could to try and improve morale: he started Sunday church parades with uplifting sermons; he attended social evenings and dances; a magazine, *The Warble*, was produced; he paid for prizes for darts competitions between posts, and sausage suppers were held, sausages being off ration.

Exercises to improve the efficiency of the men were held. Funny though some of the incidents were, they pointed up the shortcomings of the service. Things began with a series of very low-key port exercises on 15, 18 and 23 January. Woods barely mentions them. In April combined exercises with the fire and first-aid services were held. Discussions and planning started on the 6th but trouble loomed when one group threatened to resign because they refused to accept one of the umpires. In another section, wardens were claiming no knowledge of the arrangements, while their Head Warden was claiming that he had properly posted them. The actual exercise was held on 21 April and was described by Woods as follows:

> April 21 Go to Tannery, Bramford Road for opening exercise. One or two 'slip-ups' by wardens and fire service. Stay 15 minutes then to Broomhill baths, arrive same time as rescue party and mobile

MINISTRY OF HOME SECURITY

BLISTER GAS ANTIDOTE

THE PAILS CONTAIN BLEACH CREAM WHICH PREVENTS SKIN BURNS FROM BLISTER GAS

If you suspect that LIQUID blister gas has fallen upon your bare skin (for example, upon your face, neck, hands or forearm), or has soaked through thin clothing, such as stockings, to the skin beneath, you can prevent or greatly reduce blistering by the IMMEDIATE application of Bleach Cream to the skin.

Instructions for the use of Bleach Cream

Put some of the cream into the palm of one hand and rub it well into the contaminated skin for one minute. Allow the cream to remain on the skin for one more minute and then wipe it off.

If the face is contaminated take care not to get any of the cream into the eyes. Close the eyes whilst applying the cream.

If the skin is contaminated with a large drop of blister gas, or has been splashed with liquid blister gas, mop up the liquid immediately with a rag or handkerchief before applying the cream. If no cloth is available do not waste time by looking for one, but apply the bleach cream at once. The used rag or cloth will be dangerous and should be thrown into the receptacle provided.

THIS BLEACH CREAM IS PROVIDED FREE FOR YOUR USE HERE AND MUST NOT BE TAKEN AWAY.

18 *Blister gas poster.*

unit. Incident Officer has things well in hand. Go on to mustard gas incident at Ivry St. Am allowed to walk into gas without any warning! Had my respirator on as I knew what was happening. Wonder if umpire spotted the slip. Incident just closing, call in at Ellesmere Avenue at 11.15, just in time to see rescue party arrive! Something had gone wrong, ambulance had been waiting ¾ hour. Incident had not finished when 'white' went at 11.20. First aid stopped on and finished the job and took away casualties. One 'dead' still to be collected when I left, not a bad morning's work on my feet.

April 22 Umpires drop in to give general outline of incident of Sunday's exercise. Some very amusing slips made by all services.

It is hard not to wonder whether Woods was taking the exercises seriously if he was collecting tales of amusing errors. The next was held on 10 May. The result was no better but Woods was beginning to take the failings more to heart.

The 19 May exercise is mentioned is Mr Brown's diary, which gives a good idea of the type of incident arranged for the wardens and first-aid parties to deal with:

About twenty-five to thirty casualties were laid out on the waste ground and then a smoke flare went up. We approached the umpire and learnt two small HE bombs had fallen and caused forty casualties and two dead and damage to overhead cables. Wake

19 *Rescue workers search the rubble in York Road. Most of their work, often very upsetting, was done at night.*

and I tackled the casualties and found each one with a ticket ranging from sprained ankles to gunshot wounds in abdomen and broken limbs. I had a brainwave before going out and wrote out three tourniquet notices which I was able to pin on the three tourniquet cases we had – the mortuary squad took away the sandbags (dead casualties) and not a smile was anywhere as they solemnly tramped away with one bag at a time on the stretcher. We are taking these exercises much more seriously now.

Brown may have been taking the exercises more seriously, but the service was still not taking them seriously enough. The exercise turned into another series of disasters, and a total embarrassment for Woods, Simpson and the whole wardens service.

> May 19 Got off from Town Hall 10 o'clock – to Norbury Road. Most disappointed with show – bad slip up by wardens and all parties. Then to Coddenham Road. Not much better – everything going wrong that could do. Bad luck for Inspector who was very disgusted. Finished at Report Centre, discussed with Inspector Church shortcoming of my service. Town Clerk, Chief Constable and Chairman of Emergency Committee very critical! – too critical. Got back home 1.30.

> May 20 Hd Warden acting on their own bring in Report of Exercises. Minor shows went well – but many glaring mistakes. Hear that a warden put tourniquet on to a casualty with Broken Jaw! This man does not attend lectures!!

On one occasion at least it seems that gas was actually released in a training exercise in Ipswich. What is far from clear is whether it was one of the actual war gases or some less harmful substance. (On a personal note, while sorting the police collection at Martlesham I came across a glass box containing test tubes marked up with the names of the war gases, an old ARP sight sample. There were also smell sample boxes containing tubes that could be used as a guide in identifying gases; they were in fact less harmful gases treated to look and smell like the real thing. The box had to be taken away and destroyed just to be safe.)

Official records are understandably very cautious about mentioning friction between the police and the wardens over their respective duties at raids. Woods, though, gives enough detail to amplify the traces found in the more formal records:

> June 10 Letter for Chief for Special Constables giving detail of orders issued re lights on car during Raid periods. Lights to be used when moving.

> June 29 G Group wardens report police sergeants for unco-operative behaviour towards them over lights.

> August 10 Send letter to Chief Constable re the wardens' suggestions as to the police lights. Ask Inspector Simpson. I get well ticked off!

> September 19 Interview Chief Constable re treatment of wardens at incidents. Wants co-operation from police, will try and get it put into force. Head Wardens meeting 7.10. Inspector Church addresses us re police and wardens and explains position of both. Certainly did good and in his sound way put wardens in good humour.

Other indications of rivalry can be read between the lines of the reports that emerge once bombing has actually started. Head Wardens were expected to comment on the relationship with other services, especially the police, and at first do so in fulsome terms that, to the more perceptive reader, suggests concern that the two might not co-operate very well and relief whenever they did. The raid of 14 September

1940 was in fact the first for which the wardens' reports survive, and the Head Warden noted,

> *Police.* I can report in full earnestness, that the co-operation between Police and Wardens was admirable in the fullest degree. They worked together and no untoward incident was reported. I heard of outside Wardens being stopped, this is as it should be, and as per arrangements. I would therefore like to show my appreciation of this harmony.

In his accounts of the raids Cresswell appears initially to have wished to emphasise how little use had been made of the emergency services:

> The turn-out of services for incidents was sufficient. It will be appreciated that, particularly in daytime in a central area, the police immediately tackle the situation. Information from this source was very helpful. Wardens' reports were satisfactory and certainly afforded information upon which to work. As anticipated in a minor localised raid of this type, no difficulty was experienced in obtaining services quickly. Turn-out was adequate. Other services and public utility services operated efficiently.

The report of the incident by the Head Warden reveals something more of the confusion of the first minutes after the explosion. The role of the wardens is far clearer in this eye-witness account. It is worth comparing the two documents to see just what had been left out of the former:

> Mr Japhet, 'H' Group Warden residing in Bolton Lane, was one of those already out, and although only a newcomer to the service immediately sent off a message to Control, from Military H.Q. Garrett Hall, this was at 15.05. The time of the bomb was 15.02. The message was to the effect a H.E. had fallen in St Margaret's Plain, wardens on scene at once and took charge of this.
> Mr Paterson, D.H. [Deputy Head] Warden, then arrived with several other wardens at the same time, and issued further instructions to send message, at 15.08, to the effect Water Mains were damaged seriously, also Gas Mains.
> All services were speedily on the spot, and in the meantime the wardens did their best to control the people who congregated around, until police in strength arrived, and visited every house, to find any further casualties. Mr Paterson also reports that every effort was made to stop smoking by the people. Mr Wilson of 'H' 2 post went to the assistance of a Rev. Gentleman who had a casualty to deal with, suffering from a leg injury which was bleeding, the warden used his Field Am kit to cover the wound, and it was understood by me that an army official complained that he was wasting time and that he should be sent to Hospital without dressing.

Cresswell, it appears, was stressing the role of the police while playing down that of the wardens.

Even once the blitz was under way, the bombs and alert duties at times seem like interruptions in the bitter round of internal struggles. However, if one uses the diaries to construct a timetable of Woods' normal hours of service, combined with the additional hours of alerts and bombs, a truer picture appears: they were, all of them, men at the end of their tethers.

Seven

Shelters

There was no consensus whatever over policy on shelters. While the German strategy was based on communal shelters, including purpose-built reinforced cellars in blocks of flats and free-standing shelters and towers, the British government completely rejected the idea. Their line was that communal shelters would breed something called 'deep-shelter mentality'. The public, it was felt, would retreat into such shelters and refuse to come out. It is hard not to see this theory as simply a Whitehall fig-leaf designed to block what would have been the expense of building efficient shelters for the threatened people.

Some in Ipswich, Richard Stokes among them, had been planning communal shelters: one in Tower Ramparts for 800 people, a tunnel shelter in Alexandra Park for 800, and another for 600 in Wherstead Road. The government refused to sanction the local council plans for communal shelters. From September 1939 to June 1940 there was no overall council policy which allocated different levels of shelter provision to different areas of town based on the population and the perceived risks, but piecemeal and opportunistic planning offering differing amounts of protection in some areas and none at all in others.

The Emergency Committee minutes from January to June 1940 reveal how the committee experienced considerable difficulty in adjusting speedily to the realities of all-out war. Rather than taking a blanket decision that all school shelters could be used in emergency, it dealt one-by-one with demands from local residents that they might use the school trenches in the event of a raid outside school hours, referring the matter back to the Education Committee. Objections were made in each case about the difficulty of finding a keyholder. Similar pressure was faced over the use of trenches in the parks outside normal opening hours, the Council continuing to lock the parks at dusk so that public shelters remained inaccessible throughout the night. It was not until 6 July 1940 that locks and notices forbidding them to be used outside hours were removed from the public shelters, as it was proving impossible to get them all opened on a yellow warning. The true, but never clearly acknowledged, difficulty in each case was the fact that the Council would have been obliged to pay school caretakers and park keepers overtime to unlock the shelters out of hours.

Local frustration with the mixed messages being sent surfaced in the *East Anglian Daily Times* in the last months before the war, while the Council was discussing its Five Year Plan and before dissent hardened. The initial assumption had been that the Germans would raid in daylight, when most people were in the town centre or at work. Because of this, adequate public shelter was not provided in the main residential areas and council estates. On 11 May 1939 the *East Anglian Daily Times* reported the Council debates.

> How vulnerable to raids is Ipswich? Council told nobody in the town knows.
>
> The position in Ipswich in regard to ARP and evacuation is still not clear it was revealed at the meeting of Ipswich Town Council yesterday. Mr A. Victor Smith said some months ago the Council had agreed upon certain measures of shelter protection, but they were told it was not necessary because they were not a vulnerable area. He inquired whether the Council was still pressing those schemes or a modification of them.
>
> Mr F. Challis-King said it was true that Ipswich was now declared a vulnerable area but no one in Ipswich knew to what degree of vulnerability, hence the reason that the evacuation census still went on, for it was thought they were to be expected to take people and children in Ipswich as well as being a vulnerable area.

Challis-King went on to describe the situation as a 'nightmare', with no one knowing what costs could be authorised.

The Council had to be seen to be offering some kind of protection to the people so Mr Challis-King was quoted in the *East Anglian Daily Times* of 28 September 1939 giving a highly positive report on its progress towards the government's target of shelter accommodation for ten per cent of the population. It is a good example of official obfuscation. Challis-King began by listing the completed shelters, then added the nearly finished shelters, then those about to be nearly finished, then the shelters ready to be started on, and then those for which sites had been identified.

> In his summary of the above figures Mr Challis-King said by the end of the week the total accommodation in trenches and basements would be 4,431 and the total for further shelters in hand or selected 4,234, giving a grand total of 8,665. The total accommodation required for the borough was for ten percent of the population or approximately 10,000.
>
> Speaking of wardens' posts, Mr Challis-King said that 33 out of the 39 approved were almost completed – 8 were already functioning.

The reality was that only four basements and five trenches were actually ready, covering 2,896 people.

In the next months the paper was regularly to cover meetings at which Challis-King reported just how well the Council was doing. The Borough was, in fact, only requisitioning existing cellar basements, which tended to be in old commercial buildings in the town centre, and digging slit trenches in some parks. The Tower Ramparts and Old Cattle Market shelters were the public conveniences now doubling up in function. In Christchurch Park the tunnels under the road between the park and the Upper Arboretum were provided with blast walls and described as shelters.

Plotting those requisitioned cellars against the street plan demonstrates very clearly how all were concentrated within a very small area, so that in parts there were many more shelter places than people. There were places for 301 people in the Buttermarket area, and for 572 in Carr St Cox Lane, areas with no private

For the Air Raid Shelter

IMPROVED BUNKS
made by
CRANE
Strong—Comfortable—Adaptable

The Crane three-tier sleeping bunk is a sound engineering job and will stand up to every demand made upon it.

- Tubes that will not sag under full load.
- No loose joints that fail through vibration.
- Strong, quickly adjustable castraies.
- Convertible into seat with backrest.
- Handgrip extension of uprights.
- End Orders for connecting additional units.
- EXTRAS AVAILABLE Floor Flanges for feet. Wire Mesh-Bed instead of canvas.

FULLER DETAILS AND PRICES ON APPLICATION

CRANE LTD, 8151 LEMAN STREET, LONDON, E.1

20 *Cranes made special bunks for communal shelters.*

residents to speak of. These were all existing cellars of old buildings. There were none on the large estates like Nacton, Gainsborough or Racecourse, where there were no convenient cellars. Despite central government's official reluctance, some public surface shelters were built. These were heavily sandbagged, windowless, brickwork boxes with an entrance provided with a blast wall.

The tension over shelters continued until at least 1941, when the irrepressible Richard Stokes proposed a deep tunnel under Alexandra Park to provide sleeping accommodation for 672 people. The Borough Engineer's Department was talked into preparing plans for a tunnel 1,000 yards long lined with sectional concrete rings with an internal seven foot diameter. But the approach gradient would have taken up 400 feet, leaving just 400 feet with overhead cover of 50 feet. The cost was estimated at £24,000 or £36 per person. Stokes pressed the Emergency Committee to forward his plan to the Regional Commissioner's office and asked questions in the Commons. The Town Clerk forwarded the plan with a private and confidential letter that rubbished it; civil servants added comments highlighting the potential expense and the requirement for skilled technical labour.

Many people preferred to sleep in public shelters even when there was no actual raid, which meant that extra provision had to be made for sanitation. By June 1940 the public shelters appear to have been provided with electric light, first-aid boxes and a water can. Shelter supervisors could find themselves facing a difficult task, some of the public being far from easy to deal with. By 13 July the shelter supervisor at the *Brickmakers' Arms* was already finding it impossible to carry out his duties all night and his normal work during the day. He was advised that he only had to be present in the shelter when it was open for a raid, and that he could leave the problem of people sleeping in the shelter throughout the night to the police. On 6 July the Medical Officer announced plans to instruct shelter supervisors on how to deal with premature births and send for medical assistance.

In Stoke one mother was leaving her six children in the public shelter each night and then 'sleeping elsewhere', leaving the distraught shelter supervisor to deal with them. People were attempting to bring in their pets, so a decision was taken on 22 August 1940 to ban them from shelters after reports of dogs running wild and of cat and dog fights, and it is not difficult to imagine the chaos caused by several frightened and excited animals in close proximity to equally frightened and excited owners.

For those without a public shelter near their homes the official answer was, of course, the Anderson shelter, purchased at a reduced price from the government and designed to be erected by the householder. If the householder were unable to do

21 *A grass-covered Anderson shelter to the rear of a burnt-out house in Shackleton Road, 2 June 1942.*

22 *This pile of rubble is all that was left of 125 Bixley Road. The steel-framed Morrison shelter served its purpose as the family sleeping in it were all rescued.*

so they could get help from the Council, who used the unemployed to dig out the necessary hole. Many people had refused to purchase the Anderson shelters allocated to Ipswich until the Phoney War ended, and the unused shelters had been reallocated elsewhere. The worsening situation brought panicked demands for shelters, which had now to be re-ordered. Householders had sometimes paid over their 5s. deposit but not received a shelter; they were offered creosoted sandbags as an alternative. Surplus shelters were tracked down on railway sidings and attempts made to seize them. Sisam, the shelter officer, was sent to Harwich to investigate rumours of surplus shelters there. The committee agreed that policemen who had earlier turned down shelters were to be given the first choice of any new shelters that could be obtained.

Some private individuals took matters into their own hands, designing their own elaborate models. After Munich, Mr X of 262 Nacton Road dug a huge pit in his garden to a design based on suggestions in official publications. He built what was in effect a concrete box completely beneath ground level on the roof of which he placed what he called a 'concrete pillow'. It was supplied with electric light and designed to be completely gas-proof and capable of withstanding anything up to a direct hit with high explosive. It was equipped with a periscope and a speaking tube. After his experiences in the Coldstream Guards in the First World War (when he had been both blown up and gassed), Mr X was not about to trust his family to the reassurances of government, nor did he expect the Germans politely to declare war when they could simply launch a devastating air raid. Why should he believe the official line, when the headmistress of Northgate School was reassuring him that German bombers could not reach Ipswich? His girls were not going to return to school until it had completed proper trenches lined with concrete. He arranged with a few friends a private air-raid watching scheme, the neighbours taking it in turns to knock each other up.

23 *Inside Stoke Hall vaults.*

Similar concerns provided opportunities for local builders like the energetic George Saunders, who was soon marketing the 'Sleep-safe' concrete shelter. This consisted of concrete sections reinforced with steel rods that could be bolted together to make a tunnel. It was designed to be set up indoors and capable of withstanding six tons of rubble from a collapsing house. Apparently, quite a number were sold locally to those more nervous members of the middle class who could afford them. There are still occasional sightings of parts of these shelters as pig arks. The Norwich firm, Wilmot's, placed

24 *Wartime shelter hidden in the bushes by Princes Street bridge.*

adverts in Ipswich for their 'Garden Fortress', a simple underground concrete structure. Some of the households which had invested in the grander sort of shelter came to sharing arrangements with friends and neighbours.

Whatever their plans for shelters for the public, the government pressed ahead in the early years of the war with the construction of an elaborate secret bunker at the bus terminal in Cobham Road. Several rooms linked by a tunnel were built, one allegedly as an operating theatre, another as a strongbox with a special safe door added, now rumoured to hold the Town Hall silver. The documentation for the shelter, now part of the Ipswich Transport Museum, has not yet come to light.

Ransomes & Rapier built underground shelters for their workforce, and other firms in the region also built shelters well in excess of the official guidelines. The Carrow Works in Norwich actually constructed their own deep shelters, five tunnels extending 100 feet joined by a transverse tunnel ventilated by nine-inch shafts. Its width varied between five feet six inches and twelve feet. Fourteen feet underground, it could hold a thousand people.

The largest public shelters were the pre-existing cellars in Stoke Hall Road, the only shelter to hold more than 500 people. The records suggest a shelter *de luxe*. Like other public shelters, it had illuminated signs which were switched on in line with the blackout and off at 10.30 or during an alert. It was heated by a Cara stove. It had its own stirrup-pump, two buckets and fire extinguishers. In addition to a first-aid box, a section was set aside for a casualty holding section provided with extra lights. The emergency exit was purposely widened to take stretchers. A small canteen was set up at which tea and biscuits could be bought. (There were others at Smiths Suitall, Smyth Brothers, Central Cinema, Smiths Albion House, Co-op Furnishing Department and the Lads Club cellars.) As the intensity of the raids diminished so, too, did the numbers using the shelters regularly. The Emergency Committee found, on 3 April 1944, '21 families, 46 persons use the shelter habitually. Nine had no domestic shelters, two Andersons with bunks, six Andersons no bunks and four Morrisons. The shelter families allowed to continue to use Stoke Hall but felt that the Morrisons would be reallocated if needed.'

By 1 March 1945 only 14 people were still using the shelter so part of it could be closed.

Eight

Evacuation I

Evacuation has become an iconic image of the war; it is also another good example of national and local confusion. No one was sure whether Ipswich was a safe rear area to which people could be evacuated, or a danger area from which the public should be removed. This uncertainty had surfaced just before the war, when Richard Stokes complained in April that his constituency had no armament contracts worthy of the name and offered to manufacture shells on a no-profit no-loss basis. His offer was rejected because Ipswich was thought to be too exposed to attack for munitions work. It was then reclassified as a vulnerable area while a census for billeting evacuees was carried out. It is no wonder that councillors were puzzled.

The three Suffolk towns of Ipswich, Felixstowe and Lowestoft were all deemed 'safe' for evacuees, while Norwich, Yarmouth and Harwich were deemed 'neutral'. As the three Suffolk towns had all been bombed or shelled or both during the first war, but none of the others, the logic of central government escaped many.

Originally four categories of people were to be evacuated:

The classes of persons to whom priority is to be given under the Government Scheme are:
1) schoolchildren in organised units in charge of their teachers;
2) children of pre-school age accompanied by their mothers or other persons responsible for looking after them;
3) expectant mothers;
4) the adult blind and crippled population so far as removal may be feasible.

Evacuation to Ipswich seems to have been efficiently organised, as it was in great part throughout the country. Given the logistical nightmare it represented, the success of the evacuation was technically a triumphant operation. East Suffolk was to receive 23,000 refugees, 15,755 in Ipswich and the rest arriving at Saxmundham to be settled in Saxmundham, Aldeburgh, Leiston and the villages. West Suffolk was to receive 12,000 at Bury and 3,000 at Brandon.

At each railway station an official reception officer established the name of the school, what sort of school it was and how many boys, girls and adults had arrived. Parties were then sent to dispersal centres in nearby schools, guided by scouts, guides, teachers and WVS. At strategic points children were paraded through specially constructed WCs and handed emergency rations for 48 hours in carrier bags: one can of beef, milk and two 4oz. bars of chocolate. Medical inspection of heads, tongues and throats was carried out.

Schoolchildren from North Kent travelled by bus and coach to Sudbury and from Ilford by train to Ipswich. They moved as school units. A total of 400 boys and 308 girls from the Ilford County High School were evacuated to Ipswich schools. But careful planning by the national organisers was immediately negated by the failings of the local authority. Shelters would have to be provided in schools for children but the Council was prevaricating over cost. The Education Committee minutes reveal that long feasibility studies on shelters were drawn up, Education Committee surveyors talked to Borough Surveyors, their reports were placed before committees who referred them back again, while other points were referred to central government for clarification. Finally the cheapest options were selected. In practice, hardly a school in the town could re-open on time in September because none had their shelters ready. No one was going to release the money until the very last minute, in actuality not until after the war had started. Even in late September the committee was told that shelters would not be ready for a further ten weeks.

The evacuated schools had arrived and found the Ipswich schools closed. They were to remain closed for many weeks because the trenches had not yet been dug. Ipswich and Ilford headmasters were asked by the Education Committee to work out a way that some kind of schooling could be provided, and children from Roman Catholic schools in Ilford shared the premises of St Mary's, Albion Hill, an Ipswich Catholic school.

Copleston School had been taken over as a maternity hospital for those pregnant women who had been evacuated, and a house was found in 330 Norwich Road for evacuated blind and their carers. Three married couples and eight single persons with one sighted person in charge were billeted there.

In the absence of the predicted mass raids children soon began to return to their families. The official figures were reported in the *East Anglian Daily Times* on 10 November 1939:

> Replying to Mrs Lewis, Mr Challis-King said that the approximate numbers of evacuees sent to the Borough was unaccompanied children 4,810, mothers and children 3,315, of whom 1,540 and 2,576 respectively had returned home. Practically all had been billeted in private houses and the approximate number now billeted in Ipswich including women and children was 4,250.

Specific problems are not easy to identify. One man recalling his own experience to me was interrupted by his wife, who said he'd left out 'the naughty bits'. He explained that he and other children living in Aldeburgh used to stone the London children. The Londoners were billeted together in one large house and the local boys used to run down to it first thing in the morning and jam the gates shut so that the Londoners would be late to school. After he moved to Ipswich he, in turn, had been evacuated to the Midlands.

David Routh's memories are less confrontational:

> I was part of the early intake to the Western School, now Westbourne. End of September we were not able to go back because the shelters had not been dug. So we arrived at the same time as the Ilford children. The Ilford school wore grey jackets and red caps.

They had their own part of the school and each school went a full day. The Western schoolboys had no standard uniform. Football was got up between the two schools, and in the spring Ilford masters played with the Western masters in a masters versus boys match. A good schoolfriend of mine was an evacuee from London who had come privately and stayed the whole war with a friend or relation. He had a school cap decorated with bands of different colours.

In March 1940 the Ilford schools left.

The shock which the condition and behaviour of children from the inner cities gave middle-class families has been widely documented. This is no doubt true, but it is far from the whole truth. Ipswich was not without slums of its own; rural poverty was hardly unknown either. The provincial middle classes would have been no less shocked if the poor of their own towns had been billeted on them. A 1922 sample survey of Ipswich school-age children revealed that slightly more than half were suffering the typical forms of ill health brought on by poverty. The children from Ilford were likely to have come from homes as good as any in Ipswich. Schoolgirls at Northgate remember the Ilford girls as being far more sophisticated.

The Ipswich Medical Officer of Health commented on the state of children. He claimed Ipswich had got rid of vermin, impetigo and ringworm among its own children 15 years before. When Ipswich children later went to the Midlands, complaints about the state of some of them were made in turn. Stories of sick and infected children became part of the struggle between authorities for additional funding.

There were problems finding school space for all the children. The most common plan for the senior and grammar schools was to operate a double-shift system, with one school going in the morning and one in the afternoon. The extra hours during which a school had therefore to be open meant that the committee might have to black it out. This forced a change in the committee's policy, which on 18 September 1939 had ordered 'that in order to avoid expenditure estimated at £600 on blackout arrangements the afternoon session at both schools terminate before sunset'.

It also meant that children would need feeding outside the normal hours. So the local WVS volunteered to make sure all children got a hot meal. Such moves were adopted first of all for the Northgate grammar schools. There was less urgency in providing for the elementary schools. In addition, twenty to thirty children, 'mostly quite young, were attending classes in the Friends' Meeting House given by teachers from the Barking Side Lower School, Ilford under Headmistress Winifred Ashe, the teachers paying the costs themselves'. They were still there in November, and the teachers were still having to pay as the Ipswich Education Committee had refused to pay the Friends. The Museum organised educational film shows for both the evacuated children and the Ipswich children whose schools had not yet re-opened.

A report to the Education Committee of 20 November 1939 shows, firstly, the gravity of the situation for local children. Sixteen schools were fully open, three partially open and only 56 per cent of Ipswich children were back in school. It goes on to document the steady drop in the number of Ilford evacuees. Subsequent figures confirm that 3,500 Ilford elementary schoolchildren arrived in September, and by 23 October 2,700 were left, then 1,900 by 16 November and 1,785 by

4 December. By 8 January 1940 61 per cent of Ilford elementary children had returned and 31 per cent of secondary. There were 1,372 elementary and 622 secondary children still in Ipswich. It was planned that three government school camps should remove about 280 elementary children.

The changing military situation meant it was soon realised that the priority was the evacuation of Ipswich elsewhere, not of London to Ipswich. The first to go were the evacuees themselves, all of whom went to Wales on Sunday 19 May 1940. Dorothy Richardson describes the continual moves that had become part of so many children's lives, and also the kindness that they often found:

> I missed the start of the war and consequently the official trip to Ipswich as I was on holiday with my family, so didn't rejoin my school, Ilford County High School for Girls, until the Summer Term in 1940. (My father, in his wisdom, thought it would be safer to stay with relatives in, first, Staines and then Richmond, Surrey, so I spent almost a year attending Richmond County High.) As it turned out I was to live in Ipswich for only three months before we were sent to Aberdare South Wales where I saw out the rest of the war until some time in 1944, when our school returned home owing to a gradual drifting of pupils away from Wales resulting in the larger percentage being home in Ilford. I was eleven years old at the start of the war, by the way, having been at Ilford for one year only, so would have been in my twelfth year when at Ipswich.
>
> I stayed with a Mr and Mrs Tibbenham at 112 (I think) Tuddenham Road. I have since learnt that they were quite well known in the town, being in the furniture trade. There was a boy of 14 and a girl, Margaret, who was younger than me. Mrs Tibbenham was quite motherly and was recovering from an operation (gall stones, I think), which was why she hadn't taken an evacuee before. They were very good to me and did their best to make me feel at home. I used to write a weekly letter home and the Tibbenhams always used to chaff me on the things I forgot to put in. I remember there was a Saturday morning ritual of going into town and having a knickerbocker glory or the equivalent in a department store. To me this was a wonderful treat. I do remember being taken to Felixstowe by Mr and Mrs Tibbenham, where there were fairly empty beaches – maybe barbed wire but am not sure. I shared a room with Margaret – it might have been a bed as well although I seem to have a vague memory of bunk beds and I also remember thinking that she was a much naughtier child than I had been! For instance, she always tried to get out of cleaning her teeth at night, whereas I did mine as a matter of course. Regarding what possessions I took with me, I remember we were prepared during the summer of 1939 back in Ilford, being given instructions as to what to get ready. A rucksack with a blanket as well as clothes comes to mind and eventually, of course, I had to pack to go to Wales. I don't remember having any personal possessions or treasures other than clothes and not many of those – no photographs even.
>
> We shared school time with Northgate. Of course, I was near enough to walk, but I'm afraid I can't remember the routine, although I certainly can for Wales, where we attended in the afternoons and they did in the mornings. We used to traipse all over the town in the mornings attending odd lessons in small halls, etc. and for one subject, Geography, we shared Ilford Boys School Geography master as they were also in the town. Looking back over my wartime education I think credit must be given to our wonderful staff who doggedly taught in outlandish conditions as if they were the norm. They also became a sort of substitute family. I personally relied on them far more than my hostesses, and all the evacuees who lasted out the full time developed lasting bonds with the staff who had been with us. I think our actual education didn't suffer that much either – we all took our School Certificate with Matriculation Exemption when we got home (most of us that is!) and I am firmly of the opinion that the standards achieved then were higher than the present day.

Nine
Protecting the Children

Ipswich was supposed to provide shelters in each school by the time the children were back from the summer holidays in September 1939 but they were not ready by the beginning of the autumn term and the declaration of war and it was November 1939 before most primary schools re-opened, some staying closed into 1940. The school hours were changed so that they were not used during the blackout. Alterations to the length of the day mean it is really quite difficult to say just how much normal schooling Ipswich children received in 1939–40. Some schools did not open until 10, then closed for a two-hour lunch break before closing earlier than usual in the afternoons. Evening classes at the adult Schools of Art and Science were cancelled initially to avoid the expense of blacking out.

The shelters finally provided were completely inadequate and well below the government's own suggested standards and the provision made for civilians. They were without doors or, initially, seats. They weren't gas-proof, and had no curtains at the entrances, let alone the basic air-lock provision set out in one government instruction leaflet after another telling the public what to do about gas. Even though small children were supposed to spend hours in trenches during alerts in winter, these were unlit, undrained and unheated. A teacher was supposed to sit out an alert in charge of fifty children with no communication between trenches. Most schools had no telephone, and no protection, not even tape, was placed over school windows to stop them shattering until 1941. There seem to have been two reasons for this neglect: the general unspoken assumption that a peace would soon be negotiated and the fact the government paid only 50 per cent of the cost of ARP for education, compared to between 60 and 85 per cent for everything else.

Throughout 1939–41 the Education Committee became increasingly embattled as pressure was brought to bear on it by parents, teachers and headmasters' associations, the Trades Council and Labour Party and trades unions from outside, and by opposition members of the committees, especially Mrs Lewis and Mr and Mrs Whitmore. The first record of a complaint in the minutes of the Education Committee is the one submitted by the Trades Council and Labour Party on the 23 October 1939. At that meeting Mrs Lewis and Mrs Whitmore raised, besides matters concerning evacuation, the following questions (with the following results):

D) Lighting trenches hurricane lamps to be provided (further consideration later).
E) Handrails and seating (handrails for infants and juniors, seating in all).

F) Allowance in scholarship exams for children in late opening schools (to be considered).

H) Helpers for trench supervision.

The head teachers had also asked for telephones. On 4 December 1939 the committee decided against electric light in trenches but the teachers were not satisfied. On 1 April 1940 the Education Committee recorded a letter from the combined head and class teachers' associations on shelters, listing their resolutions. These (and the committee's replies) were as follows:

Electric light as in public shelters (no);
Dampness – five trenches in four schools too wet to be used (to be looked into);
Entrances to be properly protected to prevent accidents in playtimes (no);
Communication between trenches by passages or speaking tubes (expensive, no);
More teachers to improve ratio of 1:50 in trench (ask for volunteers);
Blankets and hot water bottles (no).

The Education Committee Minutes from then on reveal an ongoing contest to ensure decent shelter provision. On 27 May the committee turned down the provision of telephones for a total cost of £60. The Joint Teachers Committee tried again on 1 July 1940 with letters requesting protection at shelter entrances against blast (no), splinters (no), gas (no). Further letters discussed on 15 July 1940 came not only from the teachers but also from the Trades Council and Labour Party and involved deputations to the Emergency Committee as well. The demands had now been widened to include strengthening school windows, which was turned down, only to be looked at again in September.

The Joint Committee returned to the battle for improved entrances and camouflaging in November. It was at this point, after the experience of raids in July, that the Education Committee seems finally to have changed its mind. Apart from anything else, it must have become obvious that the war was here to stay. It was ludicrous to go on solemnly recording in June meetings that the problems of flooding reported in winter had been solved. Nor could the committee agree indefinitely to postpone weatherproofing the roofs of trenches until after trials had been carried out, only to find that bad weather prevented the trials taking place. It was becoming less and less acceptable to order headmasters to hang thermometers in trenches because without them the committee didn't know that a flooded, unheated trench with no doors was too cold for primary school children to sit still in for hours in winter.

CRISIS

———

Ten

The Seeds of Change

By 1940 the half-hearted approach to preparing for war, and in particular the petty bureaucratic meanness, was shaken to the core. For a start it looked as if the British might well be militarily defeated. Events in Norway had proved a shambles. Belgium and the Netherlands had been defeated, and France had collapsed. The reality of war had come first to the Suffolk coast. U–Boat 13 had laid mines off Orford Ness and on 10 September 1939 the freighter SS *Magdapur* was the first of three ships to be sunk by them. The surviving crew were treated at Ipswich Hospital. On the 24th of the same month the SS *Phyrne* struck another of these mines and the crew were taken again to Ipswich. (The third ship, *City of Paris*, was not sunk off Suffolk.) In the following months more ships were sunk off Suffolk but it is not specifically recorded whether the men were treated at Ipswich Hospital, although this was most likely.

Even closer to home was the sinking of the destroyer HMS *Gipsy*, which hit a mine dropped by a plane on the night of 21 November 1939 and exploded amidships, causing serious loss of life. HMS *Gipsy* had been leaving Felixstowe

25 *The Ipswich station of the National Fire Service.*

with the destroyer *Boadicea* and the Polish destroyer *Burza*, which were unharmed. The crew were picked up by ORP *Burza*, the Commander John Aitken being rescued from the sea after many hours. On 22 November a second mine exploded after coming into contact with the wreckage of *Gypsy*. Between then and May the next year five decomposed bodies were washed up on Felixstowe beaches. The 10 December 1939 saw three Polish destroyers, *Blyskawica*, *Grom* and *Burza* ('Lightning', 'Thunder', 'Storm') docked at Harwich. Harwich was also the scene of the sinking of a Dutch passenger ship *en route* for the West Indies and, in a strange irony, the Japanese liner *Terukuni Maru*, although the Japanese were still neutral at this stage of the war.

Two further disasters in this period involved Hampden bombers crashing at the mouth of the Orwell after hitting barrage balloons. On 4 June 1940 a Hampden bomber crashed and sank in the Orwell at Trimley St Mary with three dead. The Sergeant Pilot was rescued. On 13 June 1940 another hit a barrage balloon in Harwich harbour and crashed on the other side of the estuary at Felixstowe, setting fire to the grain mill and four barges, the *Golden Grain*, the *Phoenician*, the *Miller* and the *Rayjohn* lying in Felixstowe Dock, and five railway trucks. The plane's crew of five perished and one mill employee died from injuries, two others being slightly injured.

It must have seemed to those in the know that they were cursed. So far, two British fighter planes had been shot down by their own side, two bombers had crashed, managing to destroy four barges, and the enemy seemed to be having it all his own way where the coastal shipping was concerned. The Felixstowe Police

26 *Exhausted firemen from the worst affected areas were sent to Ipswich and other quiet places to recuperate. These firemen had been sent to the temporary Red House Park station and were lodging with the two women in the front row.*

Diary records eight occasions in 1940 on which Felixstowe AA defences fired on English planes in error: 25 January, 22 April (two planes from Martlesham damaged), 10 May and two occasions on 11 May, 15 May, 22 May and 12 June.

If the British forces were hardly proving effective, the crews of the barges were soon to become not just heroes but to pass into legend. The British Army was trapped at Dunkirk and there was no way the Royal Navy could get them off owing to the absence of smaller boats and the shallowness of the beach. Five barges owned by Pauls of Ipswich were among the 640 small ships commandeered by the government and manned with volunteer crews pressed into makeshift service. Wooden barges were highly suitable for the purpose because they could float in three feet of water and were invisible to magnetic mines; sailing vessels were undetectable to acoustic mines. The hope was that the soldiers could get onto the barges and from the barges onto larger rescue vessels.

The *Tollesbury*, *Doris*, *Barbara Jean*, *Ena* and *Aidie* were distributed along the east coast, finishing various commercial runs, when they received orders to proceed to Dover. At Dover the situation was explained to them and the civilian crews given the option of leaving their craft, which they refused. Even at this late stage there was some thought of re-supplying the troops for a final stand, so the five barges were loaded with military supplies, explosives and petrol as well as water, and towed behind tugs over the Channel. Once off Dunkirk the barges were left by the tugs with orders to beach themselves and take their own chances.

The *Tollesbury* under skipper Lemon Webb rowed itself onto the beach. Soldiers began to embark immediately, 273 crowding aboard eager for water and the two tins of biscuits and five loaves which represented all the food aboard. Soldiers and crew tried without success to push her off the beach until the tide rose. A little way off the shore she was becalmed. Attracted by her signals, a destroyer tried to take off the soldiers, but that made them a target for the German air force, and the destroyer could only provide covering fire. Eventually a tug got a rope onto her, but the first pulled away and a second had to be fastened before she was pulled away behind the tug, protected by two destroyers. In another wave of bombing the two destroyers were sunk. The *Tollesbury*, however, made its way back into Ramsgate.

The *Aidie* and the *Barbara Jean* were also successfully beached but got caught up in the German advance and they and their stores had to be abandoned to the enemy. The *Ena* got to the shore where it fetched up next to another barge, the *HAC*, but the Germans were closing and skipper Alfred Page and the skipper of the *HAC* were rescued by a minesweeper. However, the two barges fulfilled their mission, being spotted by a retreating group of men from the Royal Artillery and the Duke of Wellington's Regiment. They swam to the barges or floated out on an improvised canoe rowed with shovels. Under Colonel Mackay, and with men who had done some yacht sailing, the two barges limped back across the Channel, surviving Stuka dive bombers and an artillery barrage, dodging mines and coming across a drifting enemy E boat with dead crew.

Initially successful, the *Doris* beached, took up its cargo of soldiers and was pulled off by a tug that was also towing two other tugs, the *Lord Rosebery* and the

Pudge. Tragically, the tug struck a magnetic mine and sank immediately. The *Lord Rosebery* turned right over and the *Doris* was sinking, but the *Pudge* managed to pick up some of the men including its skipper.

While Dunkirk was later to acquire mythical overtones, contemporary records suggest that the soldiers who lived through the fall of France and the Dunkirk evacuation were angry and embittered by the failure of their mission and of their officers. The whole debacle must have brought home the reality of the danger. War was no longer phoney. The mood was one of considerable fear, which could express itself in unpleasant ways. By October 1939 Woods had already recorded an incident concerning a showing light:

'October 8 No duty today. But all the same had to attend to a light left burning in bedroom at 42 Westerfield Road, curtain undrawn. Angry crowd gathered. Maid arrived home, afraid to go in, suspecting burglars. Inspected house, OK. Turned off light. Police arrive.'

By 8 June 1940 it was no longer just a matter of angry crowds gathering. A Head Warden driving to an incident in his car had his lights broken by civilians who obviously thought that he was infringing the blackout. In fact, the regulations allowed both wardens and police to keep rear and sidelights on. The telephonist in charge of the exchange at Ransomes & Rapier had a French mother and had not been fully nationalised so she lost her job.

The war came closer still with the sinking of a boat belonging to the corporation. This is Inspector Rush of Felixstowe's report:

27 *Firemen resting with a cup of tea after damping down fires from a V1 raid on Halton Crescent.*

28 & 29 *The Ransomes & Rapier volunteer factory fire brigade pictured in 1942 and 1944. The earlier photograph is taken in the works yard with the new shelters visible behind the men, none of whom is wearing uniforms or helmets. One is holding a dummy. In 1944 all are paraded in front of the canteen windows, their gleaming machines marshalled behind championship shields and trophies.*

East Suffolk Police Report Felixstowe Station, 5 June 1940
I beg to report that at 12.30p.m. today the sewage boat *Sweep II* belonging to Ipswich Corporation of 145 tons gross was sunk about one mile from the Felixstowe shore between Landguard Point Felixstowe and Walton on the Naze.

The disaster is believed to be due to a mine. There was an explosion and water shot high into the air. The boat sank in about three minutes. Two of the crew of four are missing, the other two were rescued and are in Dovercourt Hospital suffering from bruises, abrasions and shock.

In July the first bomb dropped on Ipswich, and a sense of real shock comes through. There are several accounts of the event, which made more impact because it killed a successful young couple who had just moved into a pleasant home some distance from any obvious target: civilians had been killed at home in their beds. By later standards it was quite a minor raid, but even in the sober police records it was recounted at much greater length than many subsequent raids were.

From now on one begins to detect an attitude of common concern and solidarity in some of the records, a belated awareness that members of the various emergency services were risking their lives voluntarily for the common good. I have taken four trivial incidents from the Emergency Committee minutes, for each of which, whether it was opening shelters to the public or paying people who had lost work because of their civil defence duties, the committee had previously taken the opposite line. In such small ways the changed mood began to reveal itself:

29 June Pauls opened their shelters to the public.

1 July It was agreed that 8s. should be paid to C. Westbrook, a messenger who had lost a day's work on Sunday last, partly due to his oversleeping after duty on Saturday night and partly due to standing by on a Yellow Warning on Sunday morning.

8 July A letter was read from the Borough Treasurer enquiring as to the rent due from L.R. Peters of 2 Whitehouse Cottages who had been injured when the *Sweep II* was mined. It was agreed that this matter should stand over.

27 August The Chief Warden reported that J.T. Seymour, the injured warden, had to attend at the East Suffolk and Ipswich Hospital every Tuesday, Thursday and Saturday for treatment at 9a.m. It was agreed to suggest to the MO that possibly a car from Heathfields could take Seymour to the hospital and a car from Orchard St. could take him home so that no car was kept waiting while he was under treatment.

Eleven
Local Defence Volunteers

The police had been mobilised to control the civilian population and to take part in a scorched earth policy in the event of invasion, to deal with aliens and to keep an eye out for subversion. It now began to look as though there would be only a defeated, poorly equipped and demoralised regular army to meet the actual threat of military invasion. Voices of all sorts were raised nationally clamouring for some sort of militia, like Charles Remnant's Citizens' Army in London or the 'Legion of Frontiersmen' in Essex, right from the outbreak of war. Later various MPs, the British Legion and Territorial Units all started to press the government and to organise on the ground. Initially the government had been far from easy with the idea, perhaps because some elements on the left, especially former members of the International Brigade, had been campaigning for some kind of People's Militia. It was inevitable, too, that the Army should view such proposals with caution. Any spare equipment, of whatever kind, should go to them and not to some unknown quantity.

Churchill finally threw his weight behind the agitation, and the government gave the green light to the formation of Local Defence Volunteers in May 1940. Individual volunteers were then selected to be parish organisers and pick recruits from among volunteers or, if necessary, seek them out. These volunteers elected their own section leaders.

The parish approach to organisation was not suited to towns and the government finally allowed the formation of factory- or works-based units in June. Cranes apparently organised the first such unit, to be followed by an Orwell Works Unit, E.R. and F. Turner Unit and a Waterside Works Unit. There was a GPO Unit as well, but it was separate from the other Ipswich units, forming a specialised company within the Battalion of the Essex Home Guard and linked to the other GPO offices in the region, especially Colchester, the regional headquarters of the GPO. This enabled their technical expertise to be concentrated. The Railway Home Guard was also mustered with other railway companies and not with the local Ipswich battalions.

The advantages of works units were considerable. Parades and duties were formed around shift patterns. Men mounted anti-sabotage patrols around their own factories, with which they were already familiar. Athletics clubs were turned into parade grounds and in some cases at least the considerable resources of the factory were put to the use of the unit. Ransomes & Rapier, for example, appears to have produced an improvised works armoured car. (Elsewhere, Beaverbrook had a private fleet of armoured cars for his aircraft factories.)

The historian for the Orwell Works Unit recounts in *Battalion Souvenir. A Short Account of the 11th Battalion, Suffolk Home Guard* (Eastern Daily Times Co., 1945) how the typing pool, sports club and the foundry itself were used:

> Owing to the entire absence of Official Training Pamphlets we compiled our own and issued them in typewritten form. A Bayonet Fighting Assault Course was constructed at Sidegate Avenue [the Sports Club] under the supervision of Sgt P. Barker. Dummy '36' Mills grenades were cast in our foundry for practice throwing and a Miniature Range was laid down at Long Street. Our M.G. [machine gun] Section under CSM Simpson and Sgt West also invented a mobile mounting for their guns which drew general interest and approval.

The Browning machine gun was mounted on a trailer with a tow bar to either side of which were fixed two bicycles so that it could be pedalled through the streets to its site on top of the Spring Road viaduct. Ransomes, Sims and Jefferies also cast the metal mountings set in the top of concrete blocks to serve as swivels for spigot mortars. Dummy drill rifles survive which were obviously made in a local factory.

The second in command of the Ipswich Home Guard, Major Boyce-Brown, had joined the Army as a Territorial in 1904 and served in France and Salonika during the First World War and as part of the British army of occupation in Istanbul up to 1920, when he had returned for another period as a Territorial before retiring. He took charge of one of the very first LDV patrols, on the Stoke railway tunnel. For men like him the Home Guard offered another chance of a cherished military career. (Boyce-Brown carefully preserved his full blue-and-silver mess kit and his patrol kit all his life, his widow presenting them to the Museum.) They were a link to the traditions of the old Army, easily depicted as Colonel Blimps but bringing a lifetime of technical experience to the new units. Much the same could be said of the Regimental Sergeant Major of the 9th Battalion, RSM Toombs. The officers of the Ipswich Home Guard were usually members of factory management who had been officers in the First World War. The parish organisers in north-east Ipswich were R.T. Barnard, T.F.H. Bishop, C. Roper, A.G. Cobb and Cubbitt, all with managerial backgrounds.

In the early days the OTC of Ipswich School played a large unofficial role in training the newly formed units. The Captain, J.E. Young, was the school's senior Classics master, and had been slowly rebuilding the status of the OTC within the school. By 1938 127 boys belonged. The school had also promoted and supported the Gainsborough Boys Club, which organised the A Company 1st Cadet Battalion the Suffolk Regiment. The LDV unit in this area of Ipswich was particularly quick to start and was well supported.

Young gave the future NCOs of the LDV some training in drill, before being transferred himself to the LDV. Nine NCOs of the OTC joined the LDV and the OTC was put to work filling sandbags and helping with the construction of strong points around the town. The members of the OTC also volunteered to sort and clean equipment for the LDV, including removing the oil and straw from the Canadian Ross and P17 rifles, laid up since 1918, with which the LDV was issued. The rifles were completely submerged in the oil so cleaning them was a major task. (There is some question as to whether Ross rifles were issued locally. They certainly were elsewhere, but in Ipswich were rapidly replaced by the P17, if issued at all.) The OTC had their own weapons, breech-loading Martini Henrys from the Boer War and long Lee Enfields which were not requisitioned by the Army until 1941.

The LDV organised joint camps and exercises with the cadets and made full use of their band to add colour to the parades. Ceremonial occasions such as drumhead services in Christchurch Park saw both Home Guard and OTC parading together.

The LDV was notoriously short of equipment. The history of the Ipswich Home Guard rather blandly recounts that, 'Shortly after formation equipment began to trickle in and, eventually, each man possessed a suit of denims, rifle and bayonet, five rounds of ammunition, steel helmet and respirator,' then reveals that there were eight rifles for the 140 volunteers at the Orwell Works who had, therefore, to queue up to perform arms drill. The section of men posted on guard duty at Pipers Vale had only one rifle between them, which was given to the man on patrol while the rest huddled in their little tent. Initially some LDV paraded in a mixture of Army and OTC uniforms (which had First World War caps and puttees). Some paraded in their civilian clothes.

The creation of the LDV caused real problems for the ARP. The former looked like the service at the forefront of the action, and all the most active and committed members of the by now demoralised ARP were keen to resign and rejoin the LDV. Woods first mentions the LDV on May 15: 'May 15 Wardens asked about formation of Anti Parachute Force. Tell them to put warden's duty first. Do not anticipate many being required for Ipswich – more likely county. Hear 500 volunteers have offered service at Ipswich.' So keen were men to join what he privately called the 'para-shooters' that the Chief Warden had to get official confirmation warning eager volunteers that their ARP commitments took precedence: '25 May Interview Chief Constable re Wardens going "Parashooter" and phone commandant to refuse wardens to which he agrees.' This led to bitter rows, including one epic telephone argument in which a frustrated ARP man accused Woods of being a fifth columnist. Incidents of this sort continued into August: 'August 7 Interview Warden Marriot who wants to join LDV. Do not consent as he has not done his training.'

These were problems for the wardens' service over and above the loss of members. The first sign of the LDV was a proliferation of checkpoints and road blocks around the town manned by very nervous men convinced that Germans and fifth columnists would be rushing about disguised as civilians or members of other services. Wardens called out to incidents at night would be stopped at these road blocks and asked to prove their identity before being allowed to proceed. Uncertainties over whether an ARP Head Warden outranked an LDV Platoon Leader on a road block led to heated arguments and, finally, to all wardens being issued with proper warrant cards. On one occasion the wardens reported an LDV for being drunk; he was dismissed. Woods' diary is the best if not the only source for this tension. He first mentions on 24 May

1940 that 'all roads have barriers erected to stop traffic'. By 1 June he recorded that wardens were feeling very disgruntled about LDV and other matters. On 15 June he first mentions the idea of issuing wardens with identity cards with photographs. Special ones were designed for Head Wardens and other seniors to give them standing with the LDV, but it was not until 5 July that most cards had been completed, franked and issued. In the meantime, on 20 June, he notes that he had consulted with the LDV organiser (LDV officers had no official ranks as yet) about wardens being stopped at barriers on their way to post: 'August 24 Report of LDV Steel's behaviour from Warden Church which I have passed on to Chief Constable.'

On 28 May 1940 Cresswell's counterpart, the Chief Constable of East Suffolk, G.S. Staunton, circulated his superintendents and section officers with notes prepared by Major-General Majendie DSO, Commander of the 55th Division. These stated:

> It is no longer a question of 'if' the Germans come but when they will come. Work must therefore be pushed ahead with all speed. We are now in the front line and must be in a state of instant readiness.
>
> Probable method of attack will commence with bombing followed by parachutists dropped round the outside or behind the objective.
>
> No garrison of any post will ever withdraw.

Preparations to repel invasion now took on a grim urgency for all those involved. Majendie was merely following the official line in stating that the Germans would invade by parachute as they had done in Holland. In fact, they never had the capability to mount an airborne invasion and it is hard to see how the authorities failed to realise there was a significant distance between German bases and Britain. Nevertheless, the unlikely scenario was proposed by the War Office up to D-Day.

The Emergency Committee ordered the removal of the name Ipswich from school notice boards, estate agents' signs, the sides of corporation buses, the head codes of buses travelling to destinations like Ipswich Station, and even, with an attention to detail apparently unknown elsewhere, from every single bus ticket. Several meetings of the committee were taken up discussing the potential threat of enemy aeroplanes or parachutists landing in the parks and other open spaces of the town, and the setting up of obstacles, apparently in the form of piles of bricks.

As had been the case with gas, the Home Guard were trained for an attack that did not come. The result was to create considerable panic leading to unpleasant accidents when jumpy Home Guard fired upon innocent individuals or on English pilots parachuting to safety. In Ipswich at least one Home Guard was shot on duty by his fellows when he did not answer a challenge quickly enough.

Majendie's orders included one that was not spelt out to the ordinary men but discussed only at the highest level. The ordinary Home Guard were not to retreat to the countryside or towns and become a guerrilla force but were to fight and die at their anti-tank road blocks.

Ipswich was identified as a defence nodal point and its perimeter surrounded by road blocks, pill boxes and Spigot mortar sites. The Felixstowe Railway with its cuttings formed an obvious defence line to the east. Outlying services were to fall back on Ipswich and contingency plans were drawn up for their accommodation. In 1940 the RAF Martlesham CO was asking for possible emergency billeting of 1,000 troops in Ipswich. Copleston School was earmarked for them, its previous use as a maternity hospital for evacuees having ceased. At the same time the Captain of the Harwich and Parkeston Flotilla of the Royal Navy was looking for billets around the Docks for a captain, 25 wardroom officers, 10 warrant officers, 95 chief and petty officers and 206 other ranks that would have to retreat to Ipswich should Harwich be overrun. They would do this in ten Eastern County buses and so billets would also be needed for 20 drivers and conductors.

Petrol installations at Cliff Quay, Landseer Road, Chancery Road and Stanley Avenue were to be demolished and set on fire (PRO WO199.2523) and a scheme (PRO WO199.162) was drawn up to immobilise the port of Ipswich. The bridge channel was to be obstructed by two lighters and all cranes immobilised, lock gates left closed, swing bridge left open, and essential parts removed. All navigation marks on the river were to be destroyed. All rolling stock was to be removed from Cliff Quay and the swing bridge immobilised and armed merchant ships were to be tied up alongside and used in defence. As a last resort they were to be scuttled.

The police were expected to be ready to immobilise all petrol pumps with the use of metal pipes filled with cement dropped down the inflow and outflow pipes. All racing pigeons were to be killed and all phones in disused houses disconnected. All cars within 20 miles of the coast were to be immobilised, the magneto and other parts removed and taken, duly labelled, to the local police station. All major roads were earmarked as military supply roads; all side roads leading to them were to be blocked. Control of traffic to ensure military priority was a police matter in towns, a military one elsewhere.

The major rule for the civilian population was to stay put and 'stand firm', the government being concerned to prevent waves of refugees blocking the roads and causing problems. It was assumed that some private cars would make it onto the roads and vehicles from Ipswich were to be intercepted and directed to Bramford Park, Shrubland Park or Copdock House, where parties of Home Guard would destroy them. It is clear too that the occupants of the car would have been held for questioning as potential fifth columnists.

Vehicles commandeered by the various services would be issued with special coded strips to put up in their windows. Such was the air of panic, and the fear of spies and parachutists in English uniforms, that the police and others had to be instructed to use their common sense and remember that there would be vehicles that had been commandeered by the security services which would not have had the time to put up the coded strips. The police were also instructed that in the event of a major enemy landing they were to hand over all their weapons to the armed services immediately as they were in danger of being shot otherwise, not being covered by the Geneva Convention.

Lists of horse-drawn vehicles that could be left in the middle of roads were drawn up and those for Felixstowe survive. The Home Guard had to practise setting up anti-tank concrete traps and road blocks quickly.

The government assumed the invasion would involve a massive aerial bombardment followed by parachute drops. So when the largest aerial armada yet to attack, 348 bombers covered by 618 fighters, was reported on the afternoon of Saturday 7 September 1940 the invasion was thought to have begun. At 9.50 Fighter Command was authorised by the Prime Minister to issue the codeword 'Cromwell' to indicate that the invasion had started. It was a false alarm, fortunately, but it revealed the gaps in the system. In Ipswich the Home Guard received orders to 'Stand To' at 10.30p.m. and the defence lines around the town were manned soon after midnight. This was a reasonable achievement but elsewhere matters were different. In rural areas only a few of the Home Guard officers were on the telephone. The 'Cromwell' signal took nearly four hours to reach troops on the coast and the RAF signal was not received at Martlesham until 5.20 the following morning and, because it was not marked 'priority', was not decoded until 10.30a.m!

The official history of the 11th Battalion remembers the night in the following way:

> On the night of Saturday 7 September 1940 at 2230 hrs came the order for all the posts to 'Stand To'. No proper organisation was in being for such an emergency [as was in force at a later period] nor was any sound signal arranged, so it devolved on the P/Os with the help of one or two NCOs to call personally each man. This was done with such expedition that by the very early hours of the following Sunday morning 90 per cent of the men were at their posts and a defence line was manned extending from Tuddenham Road to the south side of the Rushmere Golf Clubhouse. At 0130 hrs on the Sunday morning the order to 'Stand Down' came, the threatened invasion not materialising.

D Company's historian recorded that:

> The Invasion imminent was received. All volunteers were called out and positions manned. Rifles, ammunition and equipment were issued indiscriminately to the men, and it took months to get the Quartermaster's books straight again! The strength of the company at this time was in the region of 500 men, and the length of the front was approximately 2¼ miles, so it really was only a thin red line, but nevertheless 'D' Coy was ready that night.

In keeping with the confident, up-beat tone of the history, the incident appears matter-of-fact, but it doesn't take much effort to discern the desperate attempts made to contact each man separately, and to get them somehow equipped and into a kind of defensive line. The contributor for E Company was a little more forthcoming about the enormous relief and also the sense of anticlimax that the false alarm caused: 'The big thrill!! The call out early, very early, one September morning! Man the pill-boxes, JERRY'S COMING! No he isn't, it's a try out! Happy days.'

In 1942 the police were issued with instructions concerning civilians taking arms against the enemy:

> Normally a civilian is prohibited from using arms against an enemy and where an enemy is in 'Effective Occupation' of an area the civilian is quite definitely prohibited from carrying or using arms. In no case should a civilian set out to make independent

attacks on enemy military formations, which would be futile. But circumstances may arise when a civilian may legitimately use arms, e.g. when an enemy is attempting to seize a town or village. He may then protect his hearth and home by any means in his power, in the same way as in law he may kill in self-defence a man who attacks him personally – the more people who are acquainted with the use of the rifle and Mills grenade the better, as their effective use might be most valuable in defending personal property – able-bodied men should join in the defence of their own villages with what arms they can obtain, when the defence is becoming hard-pressed. A double-barrelled shotgun is no mean weapon in street fighting.

Signed Moberly Wardens Service Staff Officer.

The Special Constables were to be given a key role in the 1942 scare, as detailed in the orders headed 'Chief Constable's office 18 April 1942 re organisation of Special Constabulary'.

> Duties on the threat of early invasion. Specials will be needed for the following duties:
> Urban areas to be evacuated by train, to assist in warning, marshalling and conducting entrainees to stations;
> Two specials to accompany each train;
> Skeleton staff to remain to prevent looting of empty houses etc, rest drafted to selected place, probably Eye, to act as a reserve.
> Urban areas not officially evacuable, to prevent wild panic and evacuation, assisting military traffic, dealing with refugees, supervise vehicle and tractor immobilisation.
> Rural duties same as second.

The assumptions behind the various official invasion scares seem misplaced with the benefit of hindsight. But to those receiving official messages, and having to contemplate their becoming a terrible reality, the effect must have been awesome.

Three very important propaganda messages were driven home: there would be a scorched earth policy; the whole community was to be totally mobilised; there would be no deal with the Germans, who would be resisted exactly as Churchill had described in his famous speech. The government had so successfully mobilised the population that there was no possibility of any other group organising a maverick Spanish Republican-style People's Militia or indeed any other movement of any significance.

A German invasion would not have found the 1940 Home Guard much of a nuisance. It does not take much imagination to envisage the results of attempting to stop Panzers with a pipe barrel on a stand shooting glass bottles powered by gunpowder (the Northover Projector). The schoolboys of the OTC had trained with the Home Guard and paraded with the Home Guard; might they not in the event of invasion have fought with the Home Guard and their Martini Henrys? The results would have been as brave but as heartbreaking and inevitable as the charges of the Polish Cavalry.

Though perhaps seriously misguided in terms of military reality, the Home Guard being liable to instant execution if taken prisoner, the policy did have immense significance for morale.

Twelve
Evacuation II: Exodus

The Ipswich authorities had now to deal with the other face of evacuation, and organise for as many people as possible to *leave* the town. This third phase was based on the fear not of bombing but of invasion. It differed in many respects from the better known evacuations from London in 1939. The intention was that the whole town should be completely evacuated of all its non-essential population, including more categories of people than the national scheme. All the elderly were encouraged to go, for example, and all non-essential adults.

Central government set different rules for towns on the coast and those, like Ipswich, a little way inland. In Lowestoft and Felixstowe the schools were ordered simply to close, and the children to move in organised groups with the whole of the staff and everything else, down to supplies of paper and pencils. In Ipswich the schools were not closed, and parents decided whether or not to register their children or themselves for evacuation. Children went in organised school groups as far as the reception areas. Once there they were fitted in anywhere. The scheme had to be organised in a secretive and low-key fashion. The London bias of most general sources has obscured this side of evacuation, which applied only to coastal eastern and southern England. Because it was connected with the military plans for coping with invasion and was, moreover, in direct opposition to the official 'stand-fast' policy, it was only notified discreetly within the area, and not by means of the press or media.

> 9 September 1940 The communication from the Regional Commissioner with regard to the Evacuation of the Civilian Population was reported, the arrangements to be put into force on Wednesday the 11th instant were discussed, and on the arrival of a messenger from Cambridge the text of the posters to be issued was agreed on.

The degree to which Ipswich and other towns were expected to be evacuated fluctuated between moving only the most vulnerable to planning for the total removal of all non-essential civilian personnel; degrees of urgency were based on central government perceptions of the immediate threat. Evacuation was intended to be a voluntary process although the scheme was heavily promoted and officially endorsed, wardens delivering notifications and councillors making pleas for people to subscribe to the scheme. The lever of closing the schools was discussed but never used.

This made the whole process more complex since the numbers of people that would go or stay could not be predicted. Many people had made their own arrangements and left, without the authorities knowing where to or for how long, so no one was sure any longer how many children were attending school.

> 20 September 1940 Mr Armitage submitted figures of the deficiency in the school rolls so far as he had been able to obtain them but he pointed out that the Priory Heath schools were closed on account of the damage which had been occasioned by bombing on the evening of the 12th. In the elementary schools there appeared to be a deficiency of 4,578 or 42 per cent and at the secondary schools a decrease of 821 or 55 per cent, a total decrease of 5,399 or 43 per cent. There were a number of factors operating which rendered these figures not entirely reliable. Mr Armitage was visiting the reception towns next week.

When the schools were due to return from the summer holidays the Emergency Committee launched its appeal for parents to register with their scheme.

> 15 September 1940 The Commissioner was still pressing for further evacuation. The handbills were being distributed that day by the wardens to every house. It was agreed to send the children home from school as soon as they assembled at 9a.m. on the 16th instant and to invite the parents to attend meetings at nine schools to be addressed by the three members of the Emergency Committee and six members of the Education Committee urging parents to allow their children to be evacuated. The Town Clerk would supply every speaker with notes. It was agreed that the schools should be opened officially on the Monday but that the teachers should have discretion as to which children should return to school after taking home the invitation to the meeting in the afternoon. Registration would proceed after the meetings until 5p.m. and on the following day.

After they had registered at the Town Hall or their school individuals were given transport vouchers, either for the trains or for the bus companies, one for every child and one for each woman per family; grannies and aunts had to make their own arrangements. The Teachers Advisory Committee had then to decide how many 'escorts' (defined as individuals going on the journey with the children and then immediately returning to Ipswich) and 'helpers' (those actually staying on to help with children in the reception areas) should go. Although the government insisted that family unity was a paramount consideration it demanded that children from the same family attending different schools had to register and move with their schools.

Certain schools only, 13 in all, were designated as Assembly Points, and children from different schools using the same Assembly Point were issued with coloured tickets to distinguish them. Further organisational headaches arose out of the demand that children use the Assembly Point nearest their house, which was not always the school they actually attended. In a rare display of generosity, the Council decided to defy the Regional Controller, who saw no need for the additional expense, and supplied buses to take the children from the Assembly Points to the station.

If adults were not engaged in war work and were free to move then policy encouraged all of them to do so. The blind and otherwise disabled had to be moved as well. So too did the elderly. The bedridden and hospital patients had little option but to go, since particular problems would have faced these groups: 'Emergency Committee 13 September 1940 The town clerk had authorised Dr Langley to provide the necessary food, bedpans and attendants for the bedridden people who were being evacuated to Bedfordshire.' The elderly poor at Heathfields had been evacuated to the Swain Street Institution in Leicester. Some of the St John's Home children were in the children's evacuation centre at 234 Fosse Road North; a further 23 were distributed in 16 billets around Leicester. Leicester had to set up a special hostel for 'difficult' children in Regent Street. In July 1942 it contained another 24 St John's Home children and was keen to see them returned to Ipswich.

The only group not to be evacuated were the mentally ill: '20 September Inmates of Handford Home. Inmates of mental institutions not to be evacuated.' (Welfare Committee reports)

By 1940 constant bombing of the railways and the need for troop and munition movements to take priority meant getting the licence for a train to take an evacuee party to their destination was not an easy matter:

> 16 September 1940 The analyses of the number of persons dealt with in the preceding week were submitted and it was reported that an intimation had been received from the Ministry of Health that they would arrange for a train to Loughborough from Ipswich on Wednesday next at 12 noon. Meetings had been held at the schools that afternoon when the matter had been explained to the parents, and Mr Armitage reported that after the meetings 127 registrations had been made. It was agreed that it was desirable that the railway company should arrange two special trains on Wednesday, one to Leicester and one to Northampton.

> 17 September 1940 It was reported that the Ministry of Health would not sanction the two trains on the 18th instant but adhered to their decision that the one train should go to Loughborough.

The experience of the evacuation journey could be very disconcerting and seem chaotic to a small child, even one accompanied by most of her family, as Jean Quinton found:

> My youngest sister Mavis was born in 1940 and that was July 18 and six weeks on from that we were evacuated because of the bombs and living near the airport that was targeted a lot. I can remember the day of being evacuated. We were taken down to the station, I think it was in an open backed lorry, with our cases and there was my sister Mavis, she was six weeks old, Peggy was four and I was six. My Auntie Ethel had Colin. I think he must have been about five, and we were all taken. Queued up on the station, put on a train and taken up to Leicester. We were all unloaded off this train and put into a big theatre there, a cinema as they called it then, and that must have been before tea and I don't know what we were given to eat or drink, or where we got it from. We must have had something. And I can remember Mum taking the clothes out of the case and laying Mavis in the case and us three, Colin, Peggy and I, were put into a gangway with coats underneath, their coats and a coat covering up. Fell asleep for the night and in the morning we woke up with people trampling all over you, and they were all wanting to go to the toilet and have a wash and we realised that in a theatre there's not many places to wash and go to the toilet and Mum said to me, 'Well, Mavis has got to be changed, would you mind (I was seven then) going

across to the bungalow across the road and asking that lady if we could all go in and change Mavis.' We went into a coach, there were several coaches, and we were taken to Market Harborough where half of us had to get off at one time and knock on doors to see who would take you because there were so many people. You weren't allocated addresses before you went, you just had to knock and take whatever there was going, some families were separated. Luckily we were kept together and Auntie Ethel and Colin were sent up the road where they were and lodged up there.

Getting people there was only the start of a bigger problem: keeping them there, especially when the feared invasion did not take place. Once again people were evacuated to places that were no safer than those they had left. Ipswich was evacuated in September to Leicester, Loughborough, Market Harborough and Northampton. On 14 November Coventry was destroyed, the flames visible from all these towns, and by the end of the month Leicester had been raided too. It is no wonder people felt they might as well die at home. Moreover, billeting and education were very hit or miss. Children often felt unhappy or were neglected by some couples. Keeping track of all of them was a continual struggle. Even when a child had gone as part of a family group and seemed relatively well placed, it was still quite easy for something to go wrong. This is what happened to Jean Quinton.

About a few weeks on Mum was taken to hospital very, very ill, at the cottage hospital at Market Harborough. And she had pleurisy because, I suppose, she caught this from Mavis being born just before we went, six weeks old, and it was very, very sad. I was allowed to go and see her and she was very, very ill and everything seemed so old-fashioned in those days. There was an old cleaner there. She came up and spoke to me and she was taking Mum's sweets off the side and I told her off and I was only seven and she said, 'I have had permission because Mum doesn't want them, she is not really well enough.' And then Dad came down for the weekend and he couldn't find us because he really hadn't been before and it took him a long, long while to find us, he told me. OK on the trains from Market Harborough, from Leicester, but not finding us from there. He found us and he went to the hospital to see Mum but the baby was still with me. And I can remember with Mum being in hospital there were three of us in the same bedroom, all very young, 7, 5 and Mavis was getting on for a few months. And there was me having to put a vial on her dummy at night and putting it in her mouth to keep her quiet and then after about a couple of weeks they found it was getting too much for me. So Auntie Ethel and Colin came and stayed. That meant four children in one bedroom which meant sometimes you didn't get much sleep.

So a seven-year-old girl found herself precipitated into caring, at least in part, for a five-year-old and a small baby on her own in an unfamiliar setting.

Ipswich Council was responsible for making payments to the people on whom children were billeted. The relevant documents try and log a child's movements but also show how difficult this was. Children would enter hospital, and therefore payments would cease for a time, and they frequently came home to Ipswich for periods of holiday during which payments were supposed to stop. They would frequently move to be with or at least closer to their mothers. Some children were completely lost sight of, or payments were made to people who denied that any such child was present in the town. In 1943 the Town Clerk, Moffat, was regularly taking people to the magistrates court to recover money paid out to them for the cost of billeting.

Not being evacuated as part of a coherent unit meant that a child's education was very difficult to ensure; it was no part of the billeting payment scheme. It had been assumed officially that the helpers, those from Ipswich staying on in the reception areas as volunteers, would be drawn from the wives of Ipswich teachers. But as male teachers were called up in any case, and as most primary school teachers were in fact unmarried women, these dutiful wifely volunteers did not appear in any large numbers. In the end only about half a dozen paid Ipswich teachers volunteered to go to the reception areas, where the task they faced must have been difficult in the extreme.

The separation of families caused all sorts of problems and worries for those concerned. What was to be done about pets? They could not be evacuated and then billeted on some unsuspecting new family:

> 15 September The Evacuation Officer submitted a letter he had received from Miss James asking for assistance in dealing with cats and dogs left by persons who had temporarily removed from the town. It appeared that the police under the Dogs Act could deal with abandoned dogs and it was agreed to refer the matter to the RSPCA as to whether they could not through their organisation deal with the cats and dogs which owners desire temporarily to leave behind pending their return.

What happened if the family concerned were living in rented property? Did they continue paying their rents to the Council or a private landlord? One concerned official begged the Emergency Committee to make sure those evacuated realised they were still liable for their council house rents.

> 20 December 1940 Mr Jewhurst asked whether any steps could be taken to correct a misunderstanding by evacuated persons that rent while they were away was excused. It was agreed that it was not within the province of the committee to issue such a statement.

How did friends and family keep in touch? Matters were not made easier by the facts that Ipswich was within a semi-restricted area for travel, making home visits difficult, and wartime rail journeys were officially discouraged, unpleasant, and subject to all kinds of delay.

All sorts of unexpected consequence arose. For example, in the absence of any works canteens how were men working shifts of 12 hours or more to feed themselves? There was simply not enough time for a man to leave his work, get home, cook a meal (assuming he knew how) and get back again. With the trolley buses ceasing to run at 7.30 this would have been next to impossible for a man on night shift in the blackout. It became a factor in the wartime pressure on firms to provide canteens:

> 16 September 1940 It was agreed to ask the various works in the town what canteen arrangements they had available and the extent to which such arrangements could be extended if the families of the workmen could be persuaded to evacuate.
>
> 17 September As to Evacuation. A number of replies were received from firms in Ipswich as to their canteen arrangements from which it did not appear that any successful scheme

could be organised based on this. It appeared that the most likely method of reaching success would be by some arrangement with the Co-Operative Society. It was agreed to issue a notice asking men who would be glad to avail themselves of communal arrangements for a midday meal to register at the Town Hall.

Evacuated women and children soon began to suffer financial difficulties and even real hardship. It had, after all, been the mothers with young families, unable to go out to work, that had been evacuated. There was concern that the various allowances paid to the husband for his dependants were not being transferred to the wives living at a distance. In fact, if the men were serving in the forces in, for example, Crete or North Africa arranging for their families to receive any money would have been a problem for the most conscientious of family men. Not all men were that responsible:

> 30 December 1940 The mayor had received a letter from a number of Ipswich women in Ibstock near Leicester asking for assistance in the provision of clothes and shoes for the children. A number of the women had been identified on the register. In the case of two of them their husbands were serving and drawing children's allowances and after discussion it was agreed to enquire from the authorities at Ibstock as to whether clothes were necessary in these cases and whether they had any organisation there for dealing with the situation.

By December 1940 those who could do had returned and there was increasing pressure to arrange for an official return of all evacuees, sending them notification that this was in order and arranging the same free transport, special trains and escorts, as had been necessary to move them in the first place. However, this would have required the government to acknowledge that the immediate invasion threat was officially over, which would have affected policy for the Home Guard. So, for the next three years, the authorities responded to pressure from central government to dispatch more evacuees with considerable lack of enthusiasm and, indeed, growing discontent.

> 30 October 1940 In view of the order by the Commissioner revoking the directions referring to restrictions on movements in the coastal area during hours of darkness, it was agreed to ask whether those persons who had temporarily removed at the request of the government in September last might not be brought back.
>
> 11 November 1940 The return of persons evacuated was discussed and it was agreed to communicate to the Regional Headquarters the information as to the large numbers who were returning.

Fairly soon the practical problems facing evacuees attempting to return home in the absence of an organised scheme began to surface.

> 26 November 1940 It was reported that a party of about 100 people returning from the Midlands to Ipswich on Sunday last had missed their connection at Bedford and found themselves stranded. The Bedford Police brought up a mobile canteen and supplied them with free refreshments and then telephoned to Cambridge and secured a special train to bring them all to Ipswich. It was agreed that a letter should be sent to the Town Clerk of Bedford thanking the Bedford authorities for the great assistance given to the Ipswich people.

27 November 1940 The Evacuation Officer raised the question of evacuees returning
to Ipswich as he was receiving many applications. The Mayor undertook to discuss the
question with the Borough Member.

In effect the authorities were forced into the compromise position of facilitating the
unannounced return of those evacuees who could make the trip under their own
steam. It seems that Lord Cranbrook had let slip an overly hopeful remark which
had then to be followed up with the traditional delay and lack of decision:

4 December 1940 A letter dated the 3rd instant was read from Lord Cranbrook
intimating that although the threat of an invasion had not yet passed those persons who
are suffering great hardship by reason of being evacuated might consider themselves
free to return. It was agreed that this would make a difficult situation and it was agreed
to enquire of Lord Cranbrook whether fares would be paid, and how the question of
hardship was to be decided.

By 1941 it was clear that government policy no longer had the support of the
whole community and that increasing dissension was being expressed by significant
groups:

10 March 1941 The meeting then proceeded to discuss the circular dated 7th instant
from Whitehall regarding evacuation and Mr Stokes reported the result of his interview
with the Regional Commissioner on this subject. The engineering firms in the town
were having a meeting in the afternoon and it was understood that they would
send a representation disapproving of voluntary evacuation. After discussion it was
agreed that if orders were received from the Regional Commissioner for voluntary
evacuation to be invited the Local Authority would do whatever they could to carry
out these orders.

However, the government maintained the official line: '27 February 1941 The
possibility of the further voluntary evacuation of the town was discussed. It was
felt strongly that the compulsory evacuation of all schoolchildren was the best line
to take if it were at all possible.'

Evacuation and the possibility of invasion became major topics of conversation
in the town, a Mass Observation report on morale in Ipswich in September 1941
noting conversations on invasions, the numbers of children evacuated and rumours
that food shortages were being created to encourage evacuation:

When the first evacuation of children to the Midlands took place in the summer of
1940, only about 10 per cent of the children went. Now there seem to be very few
children about, so presumably they have all been moved, officially or not.
     There is little fear of a blitz, but the townspeople realise that if there were an
invasion, they would immediately be in the thick of it. I was constantly being asked,
'What about invasion?', 'Do you think he'll invade?' and 'What are the chances of
Hitler's invading this country?' This also seemed to be a topic of overheard conversation.
I do not think, from long experience of the habits of Ipswich people, that there is
the slightest chance of defeatism becoming a problem in this town. But if invasion
is attempted, things might be very different. People do not know what to do in that
event. They merely know they have to take orders from somebody or other, who
will tell them what to do.

After reporting queues for cigarettes, bread and sweets, the report added,

> For some time there has been a rumour in the town that, because this is an evacuation
> area, people are deliberately being kept short of food, so that there should be no over-
> crowding. But there does not seem to be any more of a shortage in Ipswich than in
> other places.

The Regional Commissioners were still trying to evacuate Ipswich in 1942. In February the Home Defence Committee of the Cabinet approved detailed plans for a complete evacuation of Ipswich, with an estimate of two to three days necessary. So the Chairman of Ipswich Emergency Committee placed the following letter in the papers:

> Your committee has had numerous instructions from the Regional Commissioner upon
> the steps to be taken in the case of the invasion and in addition conferences have taken
> place between your committee and the Deputy Regional Commissioners, regional
> officers and the military authorities.
>   The Council will remember that instructions issued by the Government to the civil
> population and distributed to every householder urged everyone to stay where they
> were in such an emergency unless or until compulsory evacuation is ordered. This is
> still the basis of the arrangements made and the plans formulated are with the object
> of conserving stocks of food and water and providing shelter and the necessities of life
> for those whose duty it will be to stand fast in the town.
>
> (*Evening Star* 11.2.42)

However, the inclusion of a phrase like 'Those who have no cogent reason for remaining here and who can obtain accommodation inland are wise to go now,' reveals the conflicting priorities.

In March the Home Defence Committee reported that it had accumulated a five-day food reserve in Ipswich and that the only two essential war work factories in East Anglia were in Ipswich. In June 1942 further plans were made for evacuating the population and more trains left with parties on board. Chocolate and biscuits were supplied to the evacuees and mobile canteens provided tea. It seems there were plans afoot to force a wider evacuation by closing bakeries but the committee account is guarded and elliptical: '13 July 1942 The special evacuation scheme on various points which had been discussed with Mr Gaster were considered. It appeared that the retention of bakers was a matter where the Civil and Military Authorities were at variance and could only be dealt with by the regional authorities.'

ROUTINES OF CHAOS

Thirteen
Bombing

Although the Council had delayed in organising its defences, the Germans had delayed just as long in launching their attack. Now Ipswich was defended by six anti-aircraft and one rocket battery manned by the Royal Artillery. The soldiers had been billeted on the west of the town, which had taken on something of the look of a dispersed barracks. An unrecorded number of searchlight units, at least three, mostly mobile and fitted on the backs of lorries, helped pick up enemy aircraft. A series of decoy sites formed a cordon between the town and the coast. Barrage balloons, replaced a little later by salaam dummy balloons, arrived in 1942. Reservists and Special Constables had reinforced the police, the Town Hall station was strengthened, and additional stations were set up along with new police telephone boxes.

The Ipswich Fire Service had been greatly increased with 205 full-time personnel and 98 part-timers stationed in seven auxiliary fire stations. A total of 17 static water tanks, each holding 5,000 gallons, were sited all round the town. The Bond Street fire station had been given a brand new telephone exchange with a female telephonist, and a store man had been employed to look after their new stores, including 35 Worthington Simpson light trailer pumps. Deben, Gipping and Samford districts asked if the Ipswich Fire Brigade could serve them too and, for a financial contribution, this was agreed.

The wardens too were ready, around 1,000 men organised from a centre at Argyle Street into 13 districts, each with a group post and subsidiary posts, and a system of decontamination stations and laundries for gas-affected clothing.

School-age teenagers were organised into a messenger corps of cyclists. Rest centres to care for those bombed out of their homes had been set up. The shelters in all their variety, public trench, cellar and surface shelters, school trench and concrete shelters, government issue Anderson and Morrison home shelters, private garden Fortress and Sleep-safe, were all waiting.

Soon Ipswich was in the front line. Each raid brought its own dangers and challenges. Each represented potential or actual horror, chaos, disruption and damage, not in some foreign battlefield but in the middle of everyday life. Combat veterans learn not to make close friends but these bombs were falling amongst family members and neighbours. The civilians of Ipswich faced the same combat experiences as the professional soldier, but with one major difference: they had no means to fight back.

In some ways Ipswich was to be relatively lucky. There was no full blitz, no Baedeker raids, no carpet bombing, no firestorm, and the total number of deaths was small not only in comparison with London but also Lowestoft or Norwich. But the people on the ground had no way of knowing how things were going to turn out. It could easily have been a different story. Parachute mines and 1,800kg. bombs that landed on the town might have exploded before the area could be evacuated or not buried themselves harmlessly. Near misses to the Brook Nursing Homes or hospitals could have been direct hits. Residents around Cliff Lane and the Rivers estate hardly knew that a total of 12 businesses between them stored 5¾ million gallons of petroleum spirit, and 16 more stored 2,000 gallons of petroleum mixture, while Fison, Packard and Prentice stored mixed explosives at Cliff Quay near the magazine holding the munitions for HMS *Bunting* Naval Base. Had they realised that the great majority of all this was in one small area on their doorstep, they would have appreciated by the war's end just how lucky they had been.

Nor should we forget that Ipswich did not stop at the town boundary. The people of the town could hear and see the bombs fall on Felixstowe, Trimley, Kesgrave, Brightwell, Foxhall and Shotley, and if the satellite villages and its river were to be included then the number of raids is greatly increased, and with it a truer appreciation of the call on Ipswich services, particularly the hospital and Fire Brigade.

The civilians killed and the houses destroyed were nearly all the results of mistakes, of attempts to hit conventional military targets. In most raids the line of dropping bombs identified the targets easily enough as the obvious ones of the gasometer, the Dock, the railway lines, the airfield and the factories. Time after time the airport was targeted, and time after time it was missed. Raids 7, 10, 11, 13, 19, 27, 35, 36, 42, 43, 48 and 50 appear to have been intended for the airport, but only raid 48, in which an amphibious Walrus aeroplane was burnt out on the runway, and raid 50, in which a flying bomb destroyed two Nissen huts, seem to have done any damage. The airfield

30 *Wardens in overalls are picking over the wreckage of 'Kenilworth', 132 Bloomfield Street, after the 4 November 1940 raid. A mother and three children were trapped in the house. They were rescued but the seven-year-old boy was found to be dead.*

31 *The shattered ends of numbers 6 and 8 Romney Road, January 1941. Each house was hit by a bomb, numbers 1 and 2 of the raid. A seven-month-old baby was killed in 6 and both its parents seriously injured. An old lady with her head blown off was found in the wreckage of 14 Fletcher Road. Chief Constable Cresswell wrote of this raid, 'Morale of the residents was not greatly disturbed, as the people are of working-class type, used to the ups and downs of life, and seem to accept misfortune equably.'*

32 *Police made a series of slides of the raid of 28 April 1941 which they used in training. This view of St Clement's Vicarage shows the effects of counter-blast, whereby air is sucked out of a building towards an explosion.*

was never seriously damaged, and nor were the dockside installations. Of the major local industries, Cranes was hit, as was Wrinch's, Cranfields, Fisons and Ransomes & Rapier. Damaged they certainly were, but none was put out of action. The railway line between Ipswich and Felixstowe was cut for part of a day. The LNER line to Norwich was frequently targeted but never actually cut. Again, stoppages were limited to a few hours while incendiaries burnt themselves out. Given the enormous effort and expense represented by the tonnage of bombs dropped on the town, the fuel consumed and the risk to their highly trained pilots, the Germans saw little return for their efforts locally.

Large numbers of bombs never exploded at all. Raids 17, 20, 24 and 26 are perhaps best seen as total errors by the navigators or explained by the wholly understandable wish to off-load bombs as quickly and as safely as possible before returning to base.

33 *Bomb splinter damage to the TGWU office in Grimwade Street near to St Clement's Vicarage.*

However, the inability of long-range bombers to hit significant targets was no comfort to those heavily populated council estates which surrounded the targets. These areas were hit again and again and suffered quite disproportionately to the rest of the town. Of the 13 ARP sectors in the town, M sector was bombed 18 times and D sector twice. Sometimes the same house was damaged again and again.

Each raid tended to be different and all the principal types of high explosive, incendiary and anti-personnel bombs, rockets and mines were dropped by the Germans and, on two occasions, the Italians. Some of these were designed to explode in the air, some on contact, and some after a delay. Nor was the danger restricted to enemy weapons. There were also British machine-gun bullets, anti-aircraft shells and various explosive devices fixed to the wires of barrage balloons, which could break away from their moorings. There were propaganda leaflets and the silver strips called Window designed to frustrate radar.

34 *A police lecture slide showing damage in Grimwade Street.*

German, British and American planes which fell from the sky included one German Dornier shot down with four crew captured (August 1940), one German Focke Wulf 190 caught in the blast of a bomb from a comrade's plane and the pilot killed (June 1943), a Messerschmidt 410 shot down on 23 August 1943 near

35 *An Italian Fiat BR20 bomber shot down by Hurricanes from Martlesham on 11 November 1940 is being closely inspected by RAF men. A large bottle of Chianti, a complete cheese and some bread was found on board.*

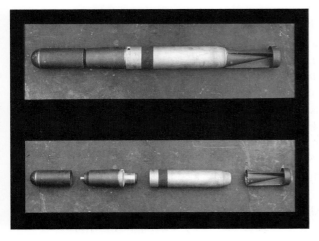

36 *Different types of incendiaries.*

Chelmondiston, two RAF Hurricanes shot down by their own side in error, one RAF Blenheim engine failure (February 1940), a Wellington bomber which crashed at Bell Lane, Foxhall (30 August 1941), a Beaufighter crashed in the Orwell (20 September 1943), a Blenheim crashed near the airport (20 October 1943), a Henley 3321 which crashed on 12 November 1943, a total of 5 Martinets (used to pull targets for AA gun training) crashed or forced to land on the airport, one American B17 Liberator returning damaged and forced to land (August 1943), a Flying Fortress 23532 which crash landed on the airport (5 November 1943) and a further three Flying Fortresses which made forced landings in 1945, and one Mustang WAF 44-14212 which overshot the runway and crashed through the fence on 3 January 1945. In August 1944 the town had a narrow escape when a plane controlling an unmanned Flying Fortress drone containing 890 gallons of napalm lost control of the drone over Ipswich. A fortunate gust of wind blew it out to sea where it exploded.

These raids produced mountains of documentation, sometimes in incredible detail, right down to which houses lost window glass in which raids. It is possible to put together overlapping but different accounts of the same incident, allowing it to be seen from multiple perspectives. Yet it can still be difficult to build up a total picture of any single major raid.

The contemporary police reports show the efforts to regularise chaos, the Chief Constable reporting how each incident had been brought under control, how morale had invariably been maintained, and how well everyone had acted. Inevitably there was concern over how the various services would co-operate, especially the sensitive relationship between the new volunteer wardens and the experienced regular police. The tone of the reports later alters to one in which co-operation is taken for granted and not remarked on, both services reporting more generously and favourably on the other. It is clear that by 27 February 1941 all the various services were responding quickly and efficiently and co-operating well.

The reports take care to record how well different kinds of shelter performed. As many people escaped unscathed from damaged houses, however, it is unclear whether or not home shelters gave much genuine protection. On two occasions, in raids 33 and 36, the reports claim that people were saved by their Andersons. Raid 36 witnessed a 250kg. bomb and the nearest Anderson was 35 feet away from the blast. But in raids 4, 9, 12, 27, 33 and 36 a total of eight Andersons were blown out of the ground by nearby bombs. None was being used, but had they been

37 *This Fiat CR42 biplane was not brought down in combat, which suggests the pilot preferred to parachute to internment than continue with a war of which he had had enough. So little damaged was the plane that it survives to this day as an exhibit in the RAF Museum in Hendon.*

matters would have been much worse. In raids 42 and 51 Andersons suffered direct hits by 500kg. of HE and a flying bomb respectively and clearly no conventional small shelter could have withstood the impact.

Morrisons are mentioned only twice, both times in connection with the Bixley Road raid. The Morrison in No.125 had been fixed to the hollow floor of the bungalow and had moved a few feet along with the floor. It was covered in fine debris but the four people inside were uninjured within a badly damaged house. The rubble from 129 and 127 had fallen onto the Morrison in No. 129 and a dead person was found inside, but the report suggests that he or she was killed not by the collapse of the house but by being trapped in the Morrison when the house caught fire.

The concrete public shelter in Silent Street, which experienced almost a direct hit in raid 38 from a 500kg. HE bomb, suffered only slight damage to the emergency exit. It was not in use at the time.

Through these dry reports a sense of the human tragedy of warfare often comes through. In one raid a man and his wife were blown out of their shelter and over their house. In another a man was thought to have gone missing on his way home

38 *Reproduced in many pamphlets and even cigarette cards, this illustration shows the different effects of blast and suction*

from work until parts of his body were found hanging from trees. Three men walking down Tuddenham Road fell to the ground to take cover; two men got up but the third, who had joined them only to help, did not, killed by a splinter from a bomb some considerable way off.

Some German pilots had perfected low level attacks, which were very difficult to detect. Bombs from these planes often travelled almost horizontally, hitting the ground and ricocheting in strange and unpredictable ways. One such buried itself in the earth, passing beneath an Anderson shelter. The vibration of its passage broke the legs of all those seated inside.

The first bomb to fall on Ipswich was probably unplanned from the German point of view and just a test for the Ipswich services. Yet its impact on the community appears to have been greater than many subsequent raids. A single German plane at high altitude dropped whistling bombs on the wealthier part of the town and

39 *Part of the same series of illustrations as number 38, this diagram seeks to show the effectiveness of taking immediate shelter*

40 *Huge crater on Ipswich golf course.*

destroyed the Andersons' house in Dale Hall Lane, a new detached house in one of the faster growing streets forming a mini garden-suburb type of development near the open-air swimming pool. A young couple lived there with their maid, the husband being a manager of one of the new stores in the town centre. They had attempted to build a strengthened refuge room but it hadn't worked. This is how the Chief Constable reported the incident:

> The Wardens knew that a man and his wife and maid were in the house, and Control Centre was notified within about three minutes. A First Aid Party and a Rescue Party were despatched and arrived on the scene in about ten minutes. The Rescue Squad set to work to remove some of the debris in an endeavour to locate the occupants of the refuge room. A second Rescue Squad was sent at 0156 hours to augment the first Squad.
>
> In a comparatively short time the body of Robert Anderson was located in a mutilated condition, the head and legs being almost missing. After about two hours the Rescue Squads were relieved by fresh parties and it was not until approximately 0700 hours that the body of Mrs Anderson [crossed out, replaced by the maid], also in a mutilated condition, was found under the wreckage.
>
> During the time that these rescue parties were working Police and First Aid Party personnel were searching the area surrounding the house and found small pieces of a third person named Miss Crawford employed by the Andersons as a domestic [crossed through, replaced by Mrs Anderson].
>
> The morale of services and public was good, but due to overkeenness and the whistling effect of the bomb, certain unconfirmed messages were reported. It was thought that bombs had fallen in many places which later did not stand investigation.

In his diary Chief Warden Woods recorded his relief that his wardens had worked well:

> 21 June 1940 11.15 Raid signal goes. Turn out and remain out till 3.30a.m. Plane very high. Searchlight unable to locate. 12.30 Bombs fall in Henley Road district. Large crater in field. Later discover house Dale Hall Lane wrecked and three killed, Anderson and maid.

> 22 June 1940 Full details of disaster available. Seven to ten unexploded bombs found. Nearly direct hit on Anderson House. Pitiful sight. 675 wardens on duty, part-timers who do work well. E & O group affected. Visit scene in afternoon and make contact with wardens most concerned. Seem to have acted with promptness and coolness. So many unexploded bombs seems surprising. Shriek of falling bomb most unpleasant.

In fact the raid had required the police, the wardens of two groups, the rescue squads of the Council, the first-aid party, the rest centre at Westbourne School and the Royal Engineers all to work successfully together. A routine had been established that covered most things, even down to harvesting the vegetables in the Andersons garden and giving them to the Heathfields Institution. At the end of the war, in the deliberately humorous accounts of the wardens of each group for the final issue of *The Warble*, the Head Warden of E Group made mention of the speed with which Woods on this occasion had taken cover at the whistle of the falling bomb. There is in the accounts an underlying feeling of profound shock, but also a sense of surprise that the system had nevertheless worked.

Other raids by single planes followed throughout the next month. Then in August took place one of the best remembered and most dramatic moments of the war. Compiling all the various records, newspaper reports and memories, we learn that on Wednesday 21 August a German Dornier 17 bomber, serial number U5, commanded by Lt. Kriensyk, had been on a mission to bomb airfields near Newmarket on a day when German activity was reported by Wattisham as particularly troublesome, and Coltishall and Horsham St Faiths airfields were bombed. A total of five Dorniers were shot down. This particular plane was engaged by Flying Officer R.E.P. Brooker of 56 Squadron from North Weald Airport and shot down, but not without damage to Brooker's plane which was forced into making a crash landing near Ipswich, at Flowton Brook, Bramford. Brooker was uninjured. The Ipswich Police had been warned of the Dornier's presence at 16.36 hours. At approximately 18.30 hours it was observed to the south-west with the

41 *Two types of incendiary bomb.*

42 *The crashed Dornier in Gippeswyk Park, 21 August 1940.*

port engine alight, flying in from the Claydon direction. It was clearly visible to many people in the town, who remember it well. One employee of Reavell's, who had kept his service pistol from his time in the Royal Flying Corps, ran home, took the pistol from his kitchen drawer and fired at the stricken plane, believing until his death at the age of 102 that he had destroyed it with a single bullet. Don Smith in a report in the *Evening Star* in 1990 remembered how,

> Alerted by the unmistakable sound of machine-gun fire, my father and I rushed into the garden and within seconds the shape of a Dornier 17Z, black crosses and swastika gleaming in the late afternoon sunlight, appeared over the rooftops.
>
> As we watched there was a further burst of gunfire from the nearest of the Hurricanes and the port engine of the bomber erupted into flames, leaving a long greasy trail of black smoke to scar the sky. At the same time its nose dipped and it commenced a dive which continued to steepen with horrible inevitability towards the crash which must follow.

Richard Brown described it in his diary:

> Saw something today which I hoped to see but never dared to expect. I saw a Dornier flying pencil come down and crash. About 6.30 I went outside just to see if I could see anything. Over Wattisham way was a plane very high up, about 12,000 to 15,000 ft. It turned towards Ipswich, then spouted smoke and two Jerries baled out. Then it turned away from the town aiming straight for me and Reavell's and two more Jerries baled out. Then as I fancied R. & Co. would cop it well and truly, it turned away, gave me a full view of its belly, the starboard engine burst into flames, and it crashed just at the back of Gippeswyk Park. It was plainly a Jerry. The crosses were visible, the thin body and the two rudders ensured that. As it came down I saw the starboard prop stationary, the port one idly turning, rather sadly; as it crashed a huge cloud of black smoke went up. Then I saw the parachutists. Two of them came down in dockland, the other two had vanished.

In the meantime Don Smith, then just a schoolboy possessed by the wartime passion for souvenirs, had jumped on his bike, pedalling in the direction of the smoke which could easily be followed. It came from the area of the railway station – and as I cycled along I realised with relief it had missed the houses and come down in the corner of Gippeswyk Park.

Few spectators had yet arrived but the fire service was fighting the fierce blaze and a solitary Home Guard complete with rifle was present to help keep others at bay. Only the rear fuselage and tail section remained and this was firmly embedded at the base of a tall tree. Wreckage was strewn around.

Other reports describe how small pieces were thrown some two hundred yards. It would appear that the plane struck a large tree, and this tree and some small bushes were set alight. Small arms ammunition was exploding, and 1kg. electron bombs burning (a few of which were unexploded).

In response to my frantic request to be allowed to take a small souvenir the kindly Home Guard agreed to turn a blind eye provided I didn't hang around. I might be in danger. I grabbed a foot long piece of crumpled metal, stuck it inside my cycle bag and was gone before more senior officialdom might arrive and disapprove.

Later when I examined my prize I discovered how fortunate I had been. It was the manufacturer's plate and it remains a treasured possession.

Don Smith was not the only boy pedalling towards the scene. Another lad, with further to go, was on his way when he discovered his route over Stoke Bridge blocked by milling crowds of people, mostly very excited women, and was unable to force his way through. The crew of four had all baled out successfully. One was picked up near Sproughton; another walked along the railway lines until captured by civilians armed with whatever came to hand. George Saunders, who owned a concrete factory near the river, wrote,

I was working late when the shift foreman came to my office, and told me what was happening, and would I come out as he expected trouble. By now they were quite low, and one seemed to be heading for our works, the other drifting some distance away. The night-shift men had stopped work and stood around, armed with their spades, one of them acting like the butcher in *Dad's Army*, and making threats about what he would do when he got at him. They really looked a murderous crowd, and I was horrified at what might happen. Fortunately he drifted just over the ridge of our workshops and into the 'Manganese Bronze Works'.

The other two had jumped just a little later and came down together. As they fell, it is said, a machine gunner on one of the patrol boats in the docks opened fire upon them. My informant thought this wrong but excused the gunner, anyway, because he had just lost his son in action. They fell onto the roofs of houses in Tyler and Puplett Streets in Stoke, one suffering minor injury. On the rooftops they were mobbed by crowds of women. Saunders described the scene:

The other one landed on the ridge of a terrace house over Stoke, his parachute ropes tangled round a chimney stack, and hung there until rescued by the police. By now a crowd of angry housewives, armed with carving knives, were shouting threats and one was heard saying she claimed 'his bits and pieces'.

Mr X, who lived next to the house onto which they had fallen, remembers the women calling out to each other that one of the men had a gun, but this turned out to be one of his gloves which he had taken off and was holding in his right hand. I have also been told that the men had worn fine watches but, by the time the police and the army had got them down and safely away, they no longer had them. They were taken away and initially detained in the church hall on St Margaret's Green before the lorries turned up to take them away. The small boy who had not been able to make his way over the bridge was rewarded by being present when the four prisoners were taken out of the hall. Fearing immediate execution, they all gave the Hitler salute, a scene which so impressed itself on his memory that he painted it 55 years later. As Saunders wrote, 'We heard after that they were very young frightened Germans and firmly believed they would be tortured and shot on landing, this propaganda being put out to prevent any pilots landing to give themselves up.'

This dramatic episode was reported only in the most guarded way by Cresswell in his official report, and setting this witness testimony alongside his version shows how important it is to read official accounts very carefully indeed. This conceals as much as it reveals:

> The other two landed on the roofs of premises quite close to each other near the river Orwell, and were taken into custody by Police and Military. All, with their equipment, were taken over by the Air Force Command at Wattisham. A certain hostile attitude was noticed amongst the public in the district where the two latter airmen were taken. Two were suffering from injuries to the thighs and received treatment. Slight damage was occasioned to the roof of two cottages by fragments thrown from the aeroplane as it crashed. There would appear to be a reluctance on the part of the public to remain in shelters when an event as outlined above occurs.

Exactly a month later the inhabitants of the Cemetery Road area of Ipswich were woken by insistent banging on their doors and shouting by wardens about an unexploded parachute mine which had fallen in the area, requiring it to be evacuated immediately. In all about 500 people were moved. The wardens were supposed to shepherd them first into the public trench shelters at Christchurch Park and the school trench shelters at the Girls High School, before the Head Wardens and police, who received a special petrol ration, conveyed them in a fleet of private cars to Northgate High School where a rest centre with beds and hot drinks had been opened.

At first the wardens were not sure what the strange object attached to the parachute was, as this was the first mine dropped on the town, but the police had been notified earlier that same day. As Cresswell put it,

> The Instructions contained in Regional Message 01.30 hrs 21st Instant, were of timely value in assisting to identify what was, to this Borough, a new form of attack. The evacuation zone therein recommended was adopted. Both Police and Wardens had been circulated with the Information from Regional, and consequently were in a position to realise the potential dangers.

In fact, a parachute mine exploding at Clacton had done spectacular damage. Another had dropped and exploded in the normal fashion on the outskirts of town but had done little damage, beyond destroying a house called 'Windy Ridge'. All went

43 *The monumental mason's yard from which the block of stone was blown into Saunders yard after the controlled explosion.*

45 *The corner of Cemetery Road and Suffolk Road after the controlled explosion of a landmine, September 1940.*

according to plan at this incident, with everyone acting promptly and efficiently. The nearest warden turned up in his pyjamas and dressing gown and put in a report 'which immediately brought the AFS' and arranged for the rescue of Mr and Mrs Woodbine from their wrecked Anderson shelter. He also took charge of their cash and valuables, and put a police guard on the damaged house.

As a mine, the powerful UXB was a naval rather than a military responsibility and so a message was sent to HMS *Vernon*, which dispatched Lieutenant Spears and a naval squad. They were joined by two Army bomb disposal officers. Even more people were evacuated, and C.J. Woods was visited by an airman and his wife who wanted a letter for the man's Commanding Officer confirming that his house had been destroyed in Cemetery Road (presumably to explain his late return from leave).

For just over a day they worked on trying to render the mine safe. The plan, apparently, was to explode the detonator cap and then remove the explosive from the main part of the mine by making a hole in the casing. The first part was successfully carried out, causing a loud explosion and puzzling Mr Brown:

There's a mystery about that one. I definitely saw an explosion and heard it but people say that only the nose cap exploded, which is ridiculous. Anyway they dared not move it so built up sandbags and detonated it. The bang was huge, shook the house and brought out many windows in Woodbridge Road, Carr Street and even Tacket Street and Elm Street.

The second part of the operation couldn't be done and it was thought too dangerous to try and move the live bomb through the streets of Ipswich and explode on waste ground. Therefore, two days after it had fallen it was deliberately set off where it had fallen at about 8 o'clock in the evening. The explosion and the resulting damage was enormous and greater than had been expected. There is a strong defensive tone in Cresswell's report:

It was difficult to foresee the actual result of destroying the mine in situ, but it is correct to say that the actual result of the explosion appeared to exceed in violence what was generally anticipated.

The mine exploded at about 2000 hrs. It cratered to about 50 feet across and 25 feet deep. In the immediate zone of the explosion there was considerable total destruction of property and from there on there were zones of destruction of decreasing severity. The most remote effect was the shattering of shop windows in the main street some ⅜ of a mile distant.

C.J. Woods' diary makes it clear that the damage was even greater than Cresswell reported:

23 September Find damage by explosion very severe. Hundreds of windows blown, some at Argyle St, also door damage. Huge crater and one house completely disappeared. About 70 houses will have to be pulled down. Damage in Main St. very bad and from Spring Road Bridge to Barrack Corner more or less.

In other words, from one end of the central shopping area to the other. One lady remembers walking past Frasers large store in Princes Street, well over a mile and a half away, when all the plate-glass windows blew out. Dorothy Gray was taking a walk along the docks when the same thing happened.

George R. Saunders, typically, reported the kind of bizarre incident that provided the opportunity for some black comedy:

Things remained peaceful for a time until a very large landmine fell in the works of Clary and Wright stonemasons in Cemetery Road and fortunately failed to explode. The site was 50 yards away from one of our Memorial Works and, as Mr Wright was informed that the ticking had stopped and the mine was harmless, I went along to have a look and saw this huge mine about eight feet long with its nose buried under a block of redstone. A group of naval mine experts arrived a few days later to extract the explosive charge; when this was considered done a small controlled explosion was arranged to enable the casing to be removed. A time was arranged and as a safety precaution the area was vacated. The mine exploded on time but went off with a shattering explosion and badly damaged over 200 houses in the Cemetery, Suffolk and Norfolk Roads to the horror of all concerned. When we were allowed back I stood looking at the huge crater with Mr Wright and he said he wondered where the block of redstone had gone. I told him it had arrived in the middle of our works 50 yards away, and he said he hoped that I would buy it from him as his works were finished, and with a brave smile he said at least you won't have to pay for delivery.

44 *Mr and Mrs Woodbine's house, 'Windy Ridge' on the Woodbridge Road, after the first of the two naval mines was exploded.*

An audience member at the Chatsworth Ladies Club told me that on returning to her house she found a huge lump of masonry had landed on the bed she shared with her sister and damaged it. Because of the shortage of furniture in wartime the bed was somehow repaired by their father but always sagged in the middle so the two girls ended up on top of each other. Mrs Goldsmith lived through the event and remembers it as follows:

> It was a landmine that was dropped not a hundred yards away from here. We'd gone to bed that night and next thing we knew, terrific noise. Wondered where we were, we were sitting up in bed, couldn't think what was happening. Air-raid wardens were going round telling us to get dressed and get OUT. My daughter was ten months old, right the early part of the war. It happened early hours of the morning, we came down stairs, the police and air-raid wardens and that came round, 'Dress and get out. Can we find somewhere to go.' I got my little dog, I got my babby and put her in the pram, took as many of her clothes as I could, took my handbag, my insurance papers. We dressed ourselves and my next-door neighbour was very good. Her mother was a housekeeper in Bixley Road so she said, 'Come with me,' and she took my husband and I and the baby and we walked from here to the Bixley Road, well over half an hour. It was a brilliant moonlit night but it was in the middle of the night, early hours of the morning and there was a lot of activity overhead. Searchlights, guns firing, you name it. Everybody was out up on the Colchester Road. We watched the planes caught in the searchlights. Quite a few of them were ours, looking for the raiders. It was a long walk and people came out and asked us, had we got somewhere to go, were we alright? And we stayed up there two or three days. We couldn't come back next day because they'd got bomb disposal squad and they got as much of the dynamite out of the landmine as they could possibly get and the rest they had to explode. And they exploded it the next day and after that we came back here to see if we could move into here and we couldn't for a day or two. We took a house down Cromer Road. Couldn't settle down there, I suppose the shock of the air raid, and we moved all our furniture out of here down to Cromer Road. I moved it all back, all the smaller stuff in the baby's pram, and the Voluntary Fire Service were marvellous. They brought all my big stuff back for me and I was laying lino and moving the furniture around and here I have been ever since.

Conventional high explosive and mine attacks were followed by another type of weapon, the anti-personnel or butterfly bomb. When first used, on 27 October 1940, these bombs were a deadly novelty, not recognised for what they were. There appears to have been something about their bizarre shape that encouraged people of all sorts, who should have known better, to fiddle with them. They were an example of a weapon devised out of pure malice rather than for any significant military purpose.

They were dropped from a group of Messerschmidts that also attacked Martlesham and went on to bomb Little Bealings, Buxhall, Foxhall, Holbrook, Kelsale, Melton, Middleton, Nacton, Playford, Ramsholt, Southwold, Sproughton and Stoke Ash. This air raid, the tenth in Ipswich, started with only a few minutes warning at about 16.40 on the Sunday evening. A small high explosive bomb, probably of about 50kg., was dropped in a field about 55 yards from the Westerfield–Felixstowe railway line at Westerfield, making a small crater a few feet in width and doing no material damage. Cresswell once again reported the official view:

> At about 18.20 hours these enemy bombers flew over the southern part of the town at a very low altitude. At first the bombs were confused with machine-gun fire. Statements made after the raid alleged that machine guns and possibly cannon were being used by the aircraft, and following one plane in particular were orange bursts in the air. The first report was of two casualties, one an auxiliary fireman on duty and one civilian, stated to have been wounded by machine-gun fire. This was later shown to be by small pieces of shrapnel or bomb case.

The wardens' reports show this to have been at the AFS fire station attached to Cobham Road bus depot, the civilian being the caretaker.

> Following reports gave damage to overhead trolley-bus wires and telephone wires, and damage to windows in a district which has suffered bombing on two previous occasions. Again it was alleged that damage was caused by machine gunning or by the explosion of cannon shells. Then came reports of High Explosive bombs being used which produced a very small crater and only damaged windows and tiles. Further reports of telephone wires and electric cables damaged in the same district were received and later messages

46 *A butterfly bomb hidden in the grass.*

spoke of many craters in close proximity, all very small. Then came reports referring to small cylinders with fans. Air Raid Message 'White' was received at 18.59 hours.

The later messages quoted High Explosive bombs but at this point they were still unknown as regards type. No reports had been received of serious structural damage. A sample of the fan-like metal objects was soon received at Control and messages asking for information were despatched to Regional Control. Information was soon at hand that some of these metal objects had a small cylinder attached and Police and Wardens were active in locating these. A party of three police and one auxiliary policeman were moving one of these latter when it exploded, and seriously injured all four, one dying shortly afterwards. The wounds were described as multiple gunshot wounds, and at this stage it was thought that the bombs contained shot. Later it was established that it was due to the fragmentation into tiny pieces of the cast-iron case of the bomb.

The warden reports this incident in tragic detail and perhaps explains why Cresswell was so tight-lipped in reporting the death of one of his own men. It appears that the police had not been very sensible:

At about 21.15 there was a loud explosion in Shackleton Road. Wardens were quickly on the spot and it was found that three policemen, later identified as Inspector Harrington, Sgt Coe and Special Constable V. Revett were badly injured, and that a PC Doylend had been killed. First aid was given by wardens and civilians to the casualties and a report was put through giving particulars of the incident. In a short while two ambulances arrived, but no first-aid party, and they took the casualties away.

It would appear from enquiries that some unknown person had placed an unexploded bomb in a bucket and that the police had taken it out and were trying to unscrew the top. This is perhaps borne out by the remark of Sgt Coe, who told the wardens while his wounds were being dressed that there was another bomb in the car and also one at the corner of Hatfield Road, and on no account to unscrew the tops.

Cresswell went on,

Reports continued to come in and showed that a distance of approximately one mile with a maximum width of a quarter of a mile was sprinkled with this new type of weapon. Each area, as it was discovered, was isolated and marked off; guards were posted throughout the night.

On the morning of the 28th at about 07.00 hours a report was received that an explosion had taken place in Messrs Ransomes & Rapiers Waterside Works, Ipswich. Investigation showed that one of these new weapons had been found in a small enclosed yard in a part of the works near the river Orwell, had been taken into a shop (the Turnery) and was being examined when it exploded, killing six men and wounding two others. It was then seen that the roof of the works, which consists mainly of corrugated sheets was filled with small holes. At the time of the raid on the previous evening the workshops were unoccupied, the night shift coming on later. No structural damage was occasioned in the works. The morale of the workers was somewhat shaken as it was not at first understood that the small bomb had been brought in from outside. It was considered expedient to close the works until a thorough search of the premises had been made, and production was suspended until 14.00 hours the same day. Part of the vanes of the exploded bomb was found in the yard, but very little else has been reported. Examination of the shores of the river close by showed many small craters in the mud and three unexploded bombs of this miniature type.

This was another incident that shook the populace and is still vividly remembered. Dorothy Gray's husband was called upon to identify the remains of a close friend who had been killed, and was only able to do so by the new shoes that he had been proudly wearing. The shoe still contained his friend's foot. Parts of the bodies had got into the machinery and were still being found weeks later. Another informant spoke of a family acquaintance who had just been successful in getting a job at Ransomes & Rapier, rather than cycle to Colchester each day for work, but was amongst the killed. The board of Ransomes met to discuss the tragedy on 1 November, listing the killed and wounded. C.F. Cripps, H.L. Judd, F. Whiting, M.A. Roberts, C.G.A. Lambton and S.W. Cornish were killed, and L.W. Dawkins and A.L. Giddons injured.

Cresswell's report then continued with the rest of the raid.

During the morning reports came in that other unexploded bombs had been found, in the same line as reported on the previous night, but extending over the works of Messrs Ransome & Rapier to the west as far as Belstead Road, the total distance covered by them being two miles. A member of the bomb disposal squad located in Ipswich had been called on the Sunday night with reference to the new weapon, and he advised that they be treated as unexploded High Explosive bombs. On the Monday a representative from the Bomb Disposal Headquarters at Cambridge, together with the local Bomb Disposal Squad of the Royal Engineers, investigated the new weapon, as a result of which Regional Control issued details at 18.15 hours on Monday 28th.

A Naval Party dealt with unexploded miniature bombs which had fallen near the railway lines of the Anglo-American Tank Farm and were hindering rail traffic. On the Tuesday morning at about 12.00 hours one of these bombs being dealt with by the Naval Party in St Clement's shipyard exploded, resulting in the immediate death of one naval officer and, later, two ratings, after removal to hospital. One other rating was slightly wounded.

At about 13.00 hours on this day two children found a small bomb in an unexploded state in some wooded land and were injured when it exploded. [They were dealt with by wardens from L Post.] Loudspeakers had covered that district during the day and all schools in the vicinity had been definitely warned during Monday morning.

From Monday 28th to Friday 1st November the local Bomb Disposal Squad and the Naval Party dealt with 54 of these new-type bombs. It is very difficult to give an estimate as to the number of bombs used in the raid, but there must have been several hundreds.

Steps have been taken to warn the public of the danger of meddling with any strange object dropped from aircraft, and schoolchildren and Civil Defence workers have been given full details of this new weapon. The affected area covered key points and finished near to the Municipal Aerodrome, both districts being possible objectives of the enemy. The residents of the affected area reacted to this new form of attack very well, and morale was maintained. A few people in the vicinity of the unexploded bombs decided not to sleep in their houses but to go to neighbouring friends. No trouble was experienced in this matter.

Elsewhere in Suffolk the raid caused further damage. Two wards at St Audrey's Hospital, the county mental hospital at Melton, was seriously damaged, and a patient and two nurses killed. Houses and a poultry farm at Martlesham were also hit and Kesgrave church damaged. In all there were one female and 18 male injuries.

The butterfly bombs had exercised their fatal attraction on the curious, killing police, naval crews, workmen and schoolchildren. But all this havoc was the result of interfering with the unexploded bombs. Once the message got through to leave the things well alone their lethal power disappeared, and the subsequent raids in which they were used produced little or no effect at all. There is an unusual postscript to this story. Mr Bacon has been kind enough to furnish me with a copy of a letter he received from Dieter Lukesch of the ex-KG76 aircrew association in 1992. The relevant section reads,

> To Ipswich. From memory I know that a crew, after the return to their base at Cormeille, reported that they had missed the target, an airport [Wattisham], and that on their way back flew over Ipswich, where they had dropped their SD2s [butterfly bombs].
>
> I know that the crew were severely punished, as attacks on civilian targets were against specific orders. There were also spirited discussions by all the crews, who condemned the bombing; that is why it has remained in my memory. The crew concerned were from the III group Staffel, but I do not know their names any more.

In 1941 German tactics changed once again and concerted attempts were made to hit two targets in the town: the Docks, on 27 February 1941, 9 and 10 April 1941, 28 April 1941, 19 October 1942 and 2 June 1943; and Cranes Factory in the Nacton Road, on 8 January 1941, 24 March 1941, 4 May 1941, 9 May 1941, 12 May 1941, 11 and 26 August 1942 and 23 August 1943. The attack on the Docks on the 9-10 April 1941 was the first concerted attempt to push home a raid with repeated bombing runs.

Despite the obvious weakness of the town's defences, no German losses being caused either by anti-aircraft fire or the RAF, these raids on obvious military targets were not very successful either, and on 2 June 1942 they attempted to set the town on fire. However, the Starfish decoys, strips laid out in fields to imitate streets, appeared to do their work and most of the incendiaries fell onto the heath side of Bixley Road. The way some areas were hit repeatedly is demonstrated by the events of 25 and 26 August 1942, when two consecutive raids hit the Nacton Road between Cranes and the airport. There are surviving Chief Constable's reports, warden reports and the memories of a woman who was a girl at the time. They give a very complete picture of the incident and the experience of being bombed. It was the second bomb of the raid that did the most damage, according to Cresswell's report.

47 Bixley Road after the raid of June 1942 involving both HE and incendiary bombs. Taken from the tower of St Augustine's church, this photograph shows the importance of the decoy sites. They had been activated that night and most of the incendiaries fell on the heath on the eastern side of the road, which was then the boundary of the town. Had they been released a few seconds later they would have caused very much more damage.

(2) Again believed a 500kg. SD, but this time fitted with a steel fin and drum. This bomb exploded on top of an Anderson shelter at the rear of 501 Nacton Road. A women and eight children in the shelter were killed. [From various informants I have learnt that they were the Nunn family, the boys went to a deaf and dumb school in Colchester, the girls had only just returned from a dance at Cranes; the father was alive, relatively unhurt, but he is said to have died of despair.] The father of the family was seriously injured and found between the entrance to the shelter and the damaged property, which was only nine feet away. A man from the adjoining house, who was near his Anderson shelter, and the two men at the next pair of houses, one of whom was partly in an Anderson shelter, were killed. The pair of houses, 501 Nacton Road and 2 Lindbergh Road, was seriously damaged.

Jean Quinton remembers:

We were down the air-raid shelter and dad was blown down the air-raid shelter by a wind that seemed like a gust of wind from something and he reckoned that was the bomb that actually flew past him across the road where I was living and it killed actually eight people down one air-raid shelter. When Dad got his breath back he was first over there and he had never seen a sight like it. They were just intermingled with all the corrugated, it was awful, and it was quite funny 'cause that evening we were only talking to those people. I think most of the family were deaf and dumb, and all from the same family and they were home on holiday for the summer and to think that they were talking to us on this very hot evening, summer evening, outside our

48 *Workmen are digging among the scattered sheets of corrugated iron from the Anderson shelter in which the Nunn family of Lindbergh Road were killed. The men in white helmets are inspecting the neighbouring shelter, the earth on the roof of which was not disturbed according to the police report.*

bungalow garden and then they were dead the next morning. And Dad went next door to my friend Peggy's and touched her father standing up in the porch way and he fell frontwards. The blast had caught him and killed him. How long he was stood there I don't know but it just shows how quick Dad was over there to help.

The very next night, the 26th, Cresswell reported,

At about 22.50 hours an aircraft approaching the town from the east released four ABB 500 incendiary bomb containers in a line from Ipswich Airport to Avondale Road, just over half a mile.

A small number of bombs entered dwelling houses, and about twelve incipient fires were dealt with by street fire parties, etc. The fourth container failed to open in the air and penetrated an Anderson shelter at the rear of 65 Avondale Road. Three people were buried under the earth from the top of the shelter, street fire parties tackled the incendiaries and it is stated they were beaten back on more than one occasion by gusts of fire and hot air. The NFS controlled the burning bombs and helped a Rescue Party in digging operations. The remains of a man and two women were found. Very slight damage was occasioned to glass at the rear of the houses.

Head Warden McLeason was pleased with his men's work:

From all reports and my own personal observations, it appears that these parties did a splendid job of work, both in the Airport area and at 65 Avondale Road. In the former case all fires were under control within a quarter of an hour and in the case of 65

Avondale Road the fire parties, together with the wardens, worked like heroes on the blazing heap of incendiary bombs which were going off all the time. I think you will agree with me that this is most encouraging. It shows that the wardens and street fire parties are working well together.

The people in the road, however, did not share his confidence:

One night Dad called us up from the air-raid shelter, which he never did, and told us just to run and we ran up Lindbergh Road. I remember my sister getting quite worried, she wasn't very old then because she lost her shoe, and, thinking of her, I ran back to get her shoe and Mum shouting, she'd got Mavis in her arms.

We had to knock on somebody's door and go in their air-raid shelter, so that was as bad as that. We were in our night clothes and the incendiary bombs were just lighting up. You'd be running and they'd be a few yards to one side and then another side and Mum was quite frightened because she'd be in front of us a little while and with us a little while and they were just all in between us you know.

Mrs Quinton's father decided to evacuate the family once more, despite their previous bad experience.

The reports for raids 10, 18, 19, 23, 25, 28, 32 and 37 specifically mention bombed-out families being taken care of by friends and neighbours. People still remember the care they were shown:

My family and I were rescued by wardens one night in April 1941 [not sure of date] when a block of four houses in Bonington Road took a direct hit. Four people were killed. At 20 Bonington Road Mrs Waters and her teenage son Billy were killed, her teenage daughter Joyce badly injured and her daughter Daphne aged five years also badly injured. At 22 Bonington Road Mr and Mrs Harry and Violet Taylor were both killed. At 24 Bonington Road Mrs Brown (my mother), sister Roma, 11 years old, and myself, six years old, were only slightly injured.

I know that Mr Marsh, a dock labourer (Christian names unknown to me), was involved in our rescue, my sister and I were taken to his house in Bonington Road after being dug from the rubble. I also know that there were several other bombs dropped in the dock area that night.

(Personal communication from Mrs Jean Pooley)

They recall how property left in empty houses was safe:

When my husband came home it was a stick of bombs that had gone down near Long Street and New Street and his mother and father had got faces like, all black, all the soot. And the windows were shattered, the doors were all off their hinges of course, they were in a state naturally but the house was left 'cause they had to find somewhere to sleep that night, 'cause you couldn't clear it up then, and they went up to his sisters to sleep and for a week that house was not shut up. There was no locks on the doors, there was no windows in, and there was good stuff in that house that was never touched, never touched.

(Dorothy Gray)

Perhaps it is because of their prosaic nature that the police reports describe more vividly than the propaganda of the time the mutual aid so readily offered. They include many instances of ordinary members of the public, not members of the voluntary services, eager to help even at some considerable risk to themselves.

Their over-eagerness sometimes proved a danger to those trapped:

> Report Raid 19
> In the Fletcher Road incident the public had commenced rescue operations prior to the arrival of the Wardens and Police, and had to be tactfully persuaded by Police to stand aside.
>
> Report Raid 25
> In one particular instance they were in time to prevent over-willing helpers from moving a large beam which may have disturbed debris with a harmful effect to trapped persons. Prompt first aid in some cases was given by qualified people on the spot in the few minutes prior to the arrival of regular services.
>
> Report Raid 30
> A man and a youth at the Anglo-American installation did extremely well. Almost everywhere there was evidence of fire prevention, i.e. of burnt incendiary bombs covered with sand, and charred timbers, etc.

Evening Star 17.11.1956:

> In one of his few off-duty periods during the blitz of 1941 war reserve policeman William Arthur Goode went to the rescue of an Ipswich couple trapped in the debris of a bombed building. By tunnelling single-handed through the tangled wreckage PC Goode reached the couple and saved their lives. Gassed by a broken main and injured in the back, he collapsed from his efforts and spent a fortnight in hospital recovering. For the rescue PC Goode received a mention in the *London Gazette*, a medal for brave conduct and a citation signed by Sir Winston Churchill.

While the official reports give the details and dwell on how quickly control was established, how well the services performed and how morale was maintained, the memories of those who experienced bombing tend to focus far more on its surreal nature, on the grotesqueness of it all, and on luck and fate, both good and bad, and the odd coincidences. In the case of one couple killed in the last bombing raid on Seymour Road, it was thought significant that they had been married in St Margaret's church during a raid earlier in the war, and had only just moved to the house in Seymour Road where they were killed. One woman left her chair to make a cup of tea but found an incendiary where the chair had been on her return. Girls who had been strictly ordered to come home on time from a dance did so, just in time to be bombed. A woman who thought her mother was dead discovered she was unharmed but covered with jam.

Vivid glimpses of this sort build into a kind of picture whose disjointed nature captures something of that feeling of disorientation and chaos that people experienced and the air of unpredictability hanging over everything. There is little evidence either in police records or in oral accounts of anything that could be taken as a serious breakdown in morale. No signs of 'deep shelter mentality' or fear affected people's efficiency or gave rise to the wish to make peace at any price and bring the raids to an end. The warden service was civilian, mostly part-time and, of necessity, not made up of the fittest and healthiest young men. Yet it seems to have operated effectively and did not break down under the strain, including the accumulated effects of sleep deprivation.

Fourteen

Home Guard Exercises

The Home Guard enlivened the streets and parks of Ipswich with regular exercises in which they took the role of gallant defenders and the regular Army that of the invading hordes, all under the inquisitive if not downright scornful eye of local children. Many men remember, as boys, watching their fathers dressed in unfamiliar uniforms and dodging about in back gardens in all seriousness, pretending to shoot at one another. In the earliest exercises, when equipment was in short supply, all sorts of 'token' devices stood in for barricades, weapons or vehicles, making them even easier to confuse with an elaborate adult version of Cowboys and Indians.

> Token road blocks, token weapons, token mines, token trenches and token reinforcements
> – all these were commonplaces in the early stages of our career. The Home Guard
> needed considerable imagination in those days, and sometimes a generous endowment
> of good humour in order to take the will for the deed.
>
> We remember an exercise in which most of the road blocks consisted of such
> devices as a tape stretched across the road, or a plank balanced precariously on a couple
> of tubs, so perhaps it was hardly surprising that enemy tanks (generally Bren carriers as
> 'tokens') heartlessly swept them aside in their attacks on our positions.
>
> *(History of the 11th Battalion Suffolk Home Guard)*

"You fool, you've brought a case of Light Tobbolds"!

49 *Cartoon of Home Guard exercise. Instead of Molotov cocktails, the recruit has brought along a case of Cobbolds Light Ale.*

91

Dorothy Gray recalls one exercise in Stoke in which bags of flour were used as bombs. David Routh, however, remembers being a lot more impressed by an exercise in which a group of three armoured, tracked vehicles drove down the Valley Road over the tops of all the roundabouts, leaving tracks still visible months later. Even the official history of the Ipswich Home Guard records very mixed feelings about the major exercises, which were entitled 'Kangaroo', 'Joker', 'Scorch', 'Exercise' (universally nicknamed 'Freeze'), 'Orwell' and 'Stalk II' in turn.

After the immediate invasion threat was over, when it was obvious to all but the government that paratroopers were unlikely to drop onto Chantry Park, exercises seem to have been looked upon as somewhere between an enjoyable rough and tumble and an uncomfortable and boring nuisance. A minor injury is recorded in the minutes of the Watch Committee:

50 *Three photographs taken at a street-fighting exercise in Ipswich.*

> 16 January 1942. It was reported that during the Scorch military exercise on the 6th ultimo Special Constable G.W. Goodman had sustained an injury to his eye owing to the discharge of a blank cartridge and he now submitted an account for medical treatment amounting to £1. It was resolved to reimburse.

Operation 'Scorch' was very well described by Richard Brown, who took an enthusiastic part in it, writing it up at length on Sunday 7 December 1941. His

51 *The crack spigot mortar (Blacker Bombard) team from Cranes factory unit (D Company). Even though one shell exploded in the mortar, this team went on to achieve a formidable rate of fire and accuracy.*

account combines the elements of make-believe, the awe that David Routh felt in seeing the Bren carriers ignore roundabouts, the general feel of an extended game that could not be allowed to interfere with tea times but held the exciting if dangerous possibility of getting out of hand, and the injury to Special Constable Goodman:

> Well, our looked-forward-to exercise has ended. The invader eventually captured the town, I fancy, but not until the Home Guard let them through, having decided to go home for a rest − the enemy distinguished by a yellow St George's cross on hats and vehicles. The town was only defended by Home Guard in our district anyway, and all we saw were yellow crosses, and no white ones which were British troops.
>
> I was the mutt at the telephone and missed a little fun. While hanging on I heard the police had nobbled a fifth-columnist officer and had arrested him. He yelled to two passing carriers, who rescued him firing blank rifle shots. The police tried to truncheon one stopped carrier and I could stand the other chaps' comments no longer. I dropped the damn phone, and my sense of duty, and had a glimpse in time to see the police attack repelled by rifle and revolver fire. One poor devil had a blank charge in the eye at about one foot range and came to our post half-blinded.
>
> I came home to tea at 17.15hrs and returned at 18.00hrs to find the post surrounded, the enemy in charge and established at the *Royal George*, sentries along Sidegate Lane and Colchester Road, with Brens in gateways and a soup kitchen in Bertie Beechener's driveway.

52 *The old army inspects the new. Using their engineering skills, the Orwell Works B Company has devised a mount for the Browning machine gun which they are proudly demonstrating to Major-General Aizlewood resplendent in First World War uniform.*

He gives an even more lively account of the fight in a later exercise in which he took part as a member of the Home Guard and not as a warden. His platoon caught up with four Bren carriers, which they turned back with clods of earth, thunder flashes, rifle fire and chalk bags (possibly the 'flour bags' which Dorothy Gray saw used in Stoke).

The sense of physical exhilaration, fitness and excitement that such exercises gave to men like Richard Brown, who worked all day in a drawing office, comes through very strongly. The more bizarre element of the Home Guard is revealed by

53 *Three photographs of combined Home Guard and Army Cadets camp at Levington.*

the glimpse we get of William Butcher's being detailed to guard all the men's pushbikes while they were on company exercises in the bushes of Piper's Vale.

Big weekend exercises were something of a trial, involving long hours, night guards and stress for the officers trying to do well, enlivened by a few periods of intense activity, which seemed to contain elements of a free-for-all and the possibility of getting injured.

The boredom and discomfort of night exercises in winter is also captured in some detail:

The notorious 'Scorch' was invented by the higher-ups to test our fighting qualities and it rained all through the night. Nor is the exercise familiarly christened 'Freeze' likely to be forgotten, for on this occasion the landscape was covered with many inches of snow, almost obliterating the tombstones in the cemetery! From the point of view of 'action', however, 'Freeze' was something of a 'frost'. On such occasions there might be a solitary Home Guard standing exposed to the wintry blast, because his weapons pit existed only in the imagination, while he himself represented a Squad in token.

The nearness of our house to a Platoon HQ and easy means of access by way of the back garden meant, on different occasions, soup making in bulk for transport at dead of night to snowbound warriors; or the sitting room handed over to a Platoon Cdr and his 2i/c (the fire came in handy for drying their rain-soaked socks).

(History of the 11th Battalion)

There is an unmistakable air of men playing with fireworks. After one exercise in 1942 some 60 windows of Cliff Lane school were blown out. The attitude must have been particularly galling for those officers trying to take the exercises seriously who adopted the ponderous terminology of high strategy:

The exercise with the Royal Engineers on 11.4.43, to test their infantry training, was an attack on our Company front only. It was carried out by two companies of REs and provided evidence of the fallacy of holding a statically defended front against a superior and better armed force. Another purely Company effort was a night exercise on Piper's Vale, employing half the Company against the other; Major Burch, at his concealed HQ, was surprised by the appearance of the CO and the Adjutant, climbing through the 'Danert Wire' brandishing a huge electric torch, which quickly became the focal point of the attacking force. This exercise proved the value of men being thoroughly familiar with all features of the ground they were holding.

(History of the 11th Battalion)

54 *The Home Guard frequently provided a new career for retired professional soldiers such as Major W. Boyce-Brown and RQMS S. Toombs.*

Perhaps more effective, and also more bizarre for the general public, were the street-fighting exercises for which one of the warrens of small streets around the Mount or behind Carr Street was selected. Platoons divided into scouts, and assault parties with blackened faces, armed with stens, crept around in carpet slippers (for silence), setting up positions for their Browning heavy machine guns and EY rifles and disturbing courting couples.

It is difficult to assess fairly the value of the Home Guard. In relieving the regular Army of the necessity of guarding docks and factories they were clearly very useful, as they were in manning checkpoints throughout the country during the period when an invasion was a real possibility. They provided useful initial training to many 17-year-olds waiting to be called up. They were a tremendous boost to civilian morale, and the frustration felt by many desperate to protect their homes was channelled in an organised manner.

But, had there been an invasion in 1940 the Home Guard would have fought and died bravely and tragically. Their equipment was so poor and the military tasks they were given, such as manning static road blocks against armour, so suicidal that their lives would have been thrown away to little purpose. As the instructions issued to the police made clear, the British government was well aware it was on tricky ground in terms of international military law with the Home Guard, who were unlikely to be treated as POWs. Moreover, the Germans had made it clear they would be considered civilians in arms and therefore subject to summary execution.

In its early days the Home Guard had the harmful effect of siphoning off many of the eager and fitter men from the other organisations like ARP and the Fire

55 *Home Guard parade on the sports ground near Bourne Park.*

56 *The management of Cranes is gathered around Major J.H. Webster as the officers of D Company 11th Battalion Ipswich Home Guard, which covered the eastern part of the town. These group photographs, one of which survives for nearly every company, were taken late in 1944 just before the final stand down.*

Services where they were desperately needed. Later on, people who had originally been part of a volunteer organisation with some control over its selection of officers found themselves stuck in what had become an extension of the regular Army, with parades, guard duties and exercises for conventional military roles carried out after working long hours at full-time jobs. Nationally, the TUC leader Lord Citrine was calling for an end to it on the grounds that compulsory pointless parades after long and exhausting shifts was simply too much.

Between 1943 and 1944 the Magistrates Calendar lists at least 25 offences of being absent from Home Guard duty. These attracted a great variety of sentences, from being discharged with a warning up to fines of £10 or one month in prison. The variety shows that magistrates were prepared to listen to individual stories of hardship; in comparison, everyone guilty of showing lights got exactly the same fine, £3. The contrast with the other services is striking. Over the same period there were just a couple of cases of people failing to do their ARP fire-watching duty and only one case of an NFS fireman refusing a lawful order.

In Ipswich at least 113 individual Home Guard were discharged before a medical board. A further 40 were discharged for hardship at the authority of the commanding officer in 1943-4. Eight people were discharged on a single day, 29 March 1943, and five on 26 June 1944. A smaller number are marked as discharged, directed in error, perhaps about half a dozen in total. Four are discharged for being under-age and one as over-age. One was discharged owing to facial injuries sustained while riding a bicycle on duty, one displaced a cartilage, one was taken ill on fire picket and one was killed in a road accident. Some were discharged to special duties, one to learn how to use the new Smith gun, three to join the secret Auxiliary Units and one to duty with the National Pigeon Service.

Fifteen

Work and More Work

Apart from children and the elderly, everyone in Ipswich, man or woman, was at work. This in itself was a very great change: no more unemployed, no more people living on their investments, no more women, married or otherwise, spending their time at home. They were in work for very long periods and surrounded by slogans saying, not incorrectly, that 'In this war everything depends on you'. The war was in great part a struggle between production systems to create the most destructive objects and the factory was a front-line target. Despite all this, the world of work is one of the hardest areas to investigate. Work is, after all, work, and as a subject has none of the glamour or heroism that other aspects of wartime seem to have had. Businesses in Ipswich had to adapt to changed conditions, and in fact the government came to rely on business to help organise parts of the war. Factories had to manage their own protection, change what they made, and adapt to the loss of one workforce and train a totally new one. The government told firms who they could employ and who they could dismiss.

Managers were expected to provide air-raid shelters for their employees, their own camouflage and blackout and their own wardens, organise fire watching and, in large factories, provide their own fire services. They had to concede that parts of their workforce could also be expected to disappear at unpredictable moments to fulfil their duties as wardens. Woods records how he had to arrange that wardens could go to their duties straight from their work bench without finding a supervisor and requesting permission.

By 14 December 1942 Ransomes & Rapier had spent a total of £34,904 6s. 0d. on ARP, of which blackout had cost £2,758 4s. 2d., shelters £8,908 2s. 9d. and camouflage painting £827 16s. 9d. (Ransomes & Rapier Minute Book 8). All engineering firms had to prepare for war by having Barcograph copies of their precious technical drawings made and safely stored.

There were also the interruptions of air raids and deciding on routines to be followed given the twin imperatives of minimising loss of production and safety. At first, all production ceased as soon as an air-raid warning was given and the workforce retreated to the shelters for the duration of the alert. Some elderly workers still remember with pleasure night shifts spent drinking tea and playing cards in shelters. Pretty soon, however, the ARP system of warnings became more sophisticated. Woods records the introduction of air-raid warning 'Purple' on 22 July 1940: 'Received siren system of warning introducing "Purple" to signify outside lights at factories and railways must be extinguished.' So production was no longer stopped whenever raiders were in the vicinity; work continued until they were actually overhead.

Large factories remained very jealous of their territory and unwilling to let wardens on to their premises. This is recorded in the report of the Head Warden of I Group, B.G. Halliday, for the raid on 9 and 10 April 1941, during which the Docks were under concerted attack and incendiaries and High Explosive were falling all around Ransomes & Rapier: 'I immediately went to Ransomes & Rapier works to get information for reporting, but was told by the Works Manager, Major Blair, that the Works could do all the reporting that was necessary. Therefore there was a delay in reporting the incident.' Woods records the somewhat schizophrenic attitude of A.S. Stokes to the wardens and to him in particular: 'June 28 Interview with Mr A.S. Stokes re ARP matters – wants to help but at same time tells us where to get off!'

Stricter controls were imposed on businesses seeking licence to store inflammable goods, and more non-productive work for managers to organise generally certainly did little to make life easier for business, to say nothing of interruptions to production, additional calls on budgets and shortages of raw materials, fuel and spare parts,

But by far the greatest change was the fact that all but the most skilled men and supervisors were called up and replaced by women. Better wages, and the kind of freedom that came with being part of a large group of people one's own age, rather than isolated and under the direct eye of employers, proved quite attractive to many young unmarried women and an alternative to domestic service or shop work. Women who had worked part-time now had the chance to work full-time, but volunteers alone did not provide enough labour. Compulsion was necessary, although only unmarried women between 20 and 30 were called up at first and offered a choice between the services or other essential war work.

All the various practices and traditions that made it hard for women to work full-time were attacked. Some of these were deeply engrained, however. The rule that demanded all women teachers resign on marriage was amended on 10 March 1941 to allow married women to continue as supply teachers, and in June 1942

57 *Women welding at Orwell Works but dressed suspiciously in skirts and wearing their hair styled.*

58 *Women filing the corners of teeth for Rolls-Royce Merlin engine timing gear. The lady in the front has since disclosed that she was working in the office but asked to pose by the vice 'because she was pretty'.*

the rule was finally scrapped in practice (although even then the Educataion Committee said it was just a wartime relaxation). In 1944 this rule was finally abolished nationally. Even then it was said to be just a wartime measure. Around three years of total war was needed to effect this simple change. On 15 July 1941 the Public Health Committee followed suit and Nurse Stribling was allowed to continue working after marriage.

The arrival of women on the factory floor had a civilising effect on factories. I have been told that Reavells brought in toilets for the non-office staff at the same time. Women on the factory floor meant that a bucket round the back of the yard was no longer feasible. Richard Brown lists the changes he had seen, in a passage that reveals a very traditional set of attitudes:

> Compared with pre-war treatment the chaps in the works are pampered today. They have the tea wagon each morning and afternoon, a works council which acts as an intermediary with the employers, concessions such as leaving off early on pay day so as to be able to draw money and be off at the usual time, are allowed to smoke all day and they somehow get away with a slightly lower standard of work.

Larger firms even increased or appointed welfare officers and nurses.

Women appeared everywhere doing all the things it had been said they were unsuitable for and proving their ability, just as they did by their work in the services and civil defence. They worked as conductors and, eventually, as drivers on the buses, and took over the factory floor.

Mr Brown vividly describes their appearance in Reavells in his diary:

> This time they wore green overalls and there are lots of them in our works, and it's pretty they look, except for one thing. The overalls are boiler-suit type with legs and they show off, or accentuate a little, the ladies' extra width across the hips. In other words, their bottoms are more prominent and made even more so by high-heeled shoes. It seems ever so peculiar to see a large stern taper down to two one-inch heels.

Contemporary photographs show lines of women at Ransomes, Sims and Jefferies wearing welding masks and dressed in flowery aprons and skirts with fashionable shoes. One rather suspects that such pictures are posed, as snapshot views taken at

59 & 60 *These outstanding photographs of women engineers at Ransomes Sims & Jefferies should be contrasted with the posed series.*

Mann Egertons show the more practical adoption of boiler suit and sensible footwear. Not even those jobs felt to be most physically demanding excluded women. They worked around kilns of maltings on the Docks for example. Not surprisingly, at this hard end of physical work it was acknowledged that more women were required to do the same task.

Propaganda then and now suggests that housewives were only awaiting the opportunity cruelly denied them for so long before rushing to become 'Rosie the Riveter' in the nearest factory. The truth is more complex. Firstly, in most cases women moved from one type of job to another rather than never having previously worked. Secondly, married women were not the principal targets for conscription into the

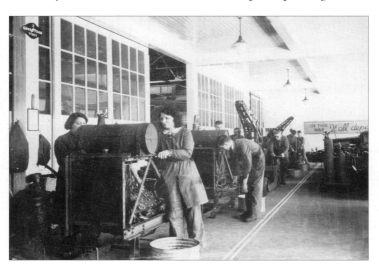

61 *An unposed snapshot of women working alongside younger lads on engines for the D-Day landing craft in Mann Egerton's garage in Princes Street. The slogan on the wall reads 'In this war it all depends on you.'*

workforce. In fact, as Mr Brown was to write in his diary (3 October 1941), 'Naturally some are unpatriotic enough to dodge it and get married for that purpose as it is reckoned that if a woman has a husband and home to look after, she can be exempt.'

Later the rules were tightened up. By 1943, unless they were looking after children under school age, or a war worker was billeted on them, few women under 40 could avoid war work and all women under 51 had to be registered. There were special provisions for the wives of servicemen, however.

As the register of cases in the Magistrates Court between February 1943 and June 1944 makes clear, the name of William Nightingale, National Service Officer, was to figure large in the nightmares of many women and some men. At practically every sitting there was a series of cases brought by him in his official capacity, detailing various aspects of wartime employment law. There were six cases of women failing to attend an interview with the National Service Officer, one of which was dismissed, the rest facing fines of up to £2. Failing to comply with direction was particularly serious. On 12 April 1943 one woman got three months in prison. On another occasion a woman was fined £5 for failing to accept work as a resident housemaid. A man also got a three month sentence.

Once directed to a job people were supposed to stay there. There were nine cases, predominantly female, of workers absent without permission from their employment, and attracting fines from 10s. to £5, and eight cases of women leaving work without permission, their sentences ranging from a £1 fine to one month in prison. Both men and women received fines for being persistently late of between 10s. and £3 and one man did 14 days. There was a single case of a man absent from essential work and three cases, one withdrawn, of youths not entering employment as coalmining trainees. In addition there was a slowly growing number, nearly all men, of those refusing to take medicals.

62 *Ipswich County Borough employed more women as conductors and drivers on buses than any other local authority, and this photograph taken at the end of the war, probably at Constantine Road, includes most of them.*

63 *Female bus driver.*

But perhaps the most serious consequence of the stereotype is that it ignores the real hardships that women conscripted into factory work had to face. At the very least, factory work was hard and involved long hours in unheated, noisy and dirty buildings. At its worst it was also exploitative and carried out in a dangerous and harmful environment. The need to preserve blackout meant that windows were often painted shut and the environment became even more stuffy and oppressive than before. Women found themselves doing things they had been assured were beyond them, but many of these things were in fact unpleasant, boring and potentially harmful. Accidents were not unusual though it has so far proved impossible to say how many people died or were injured in the workplace in Ipswich during the war. Dorothy Gray's memories of the factory include her own escape from the foundry floor. She had started work at fourteen, three years before the war started:

They wanted so many people to go out to Stowmarket, Suffolk Iron Foundry, and my name just happened to be one of them. I had done nothing in a workshop prior to that. I was sent to Suffolk Iron Foundries to make bomb trolleys, which was their bit of war effort, and when I got out there they took me through the factory to be an inspector. They sat me in front of a box of wooden handles for hand drills and I had to sit there all day sorting out wooden handles to make sure there were no flaws in them.

I nearly died of boredom but their telephonist-receptionist was having a baby so I suppose they looked down their lists and said, oh well she can do the same job for the same money, and they put me in as telephonist-receptionist there, which was quite nice really because some of the girls (it was heart-breaking) some of the country girls were put in the foundry and the foundry was no picnic for anybody, it was hell, and if you went through there it was like walking through hell. There was several of them come from Coddenham, girls who had never been in service before had to go in the foundry and make these moulds. What they were made of a lot of it was horse muck. It stained your hands and stunk to high heaven but it was one of the things from which they were made. They were very nice girls some of them.

Mrs B. Stiff worked in the jewellery and fancy goods department of a large local store, in a job she loved, until two or three months after she was married. Then she was called up and offered the choice of ATS, Army or war work and was eventually directed into Ransomes & Rapier:

64 *Two women help maintain an Eastern Counties gas-producer unit. This replaced petrol as fuel.*

I was painting patterns, patterns which they put in the cores they make the metal of; they have to have the pattern of what they make and the patterns are painted different colours for the type of metal they use, and they're a work of art and you even shellac them and rub them down, and you work at the pattern shop. I was the only girl in there with forty men. I hated it. I didn't like the back chat. I was very naïve, actually I hated it. Every time I moved they wanted to know where I was going. Oh, it wasn't nice. They hadn't had women before you see, it was a man's job, their family job. I didn't like it.

The Medical Officer of Health in Ipswich was to point to a steep rise in the rate of still births during the war, and link this directly to exhaustion and stress. In 1945 he wrote, 'It is apparent that the strain of war-time existence, the multitude of worries, the diminution and monotony of diet have undoubtedly contributed to this increase of still births and neo-natal mortality.' The pre-war rate was 26.8 per thousand live births and the 1944 rate 31.9 per thousand. The worst year was 1940.

Another report, by the Ipswich Youth Committee in October 1942 on the registration of 16- to 18-year-olds in the town, revealed much the same thing:

Many young people are working too long and too hard. There is some danger of devitalising the nation in the earlier years. The effect of strain was manifest, both with the girls and the boys, but especially in the case of the girls, who declared that they were too tired to go out at night.

65 *The sight of a woman conductor wrestling with the pole to reconnect the trolley bus was a common one.*

It was discovered that some youngsters were working 12 to 14 hours a day, doing fire-watching duties as well or travelling long journeys.

Dorothy Gray herself became exhausted and ill after her father died. Diagnosed with severe anaemia, and with the full support of her doctor, she couldn't simply cease work, though. She had to go before a board and plead her case, using contacts and advice to ensure the decision went the right way. At first the board tried simply to switch her employment from Stowmarket to the sugar beet factory in Ipswich, but she was too ill to work there:

And the doctor advised me to pack up and actually she said to me, if you've got some sense you'll go in for having a baby, otherwise you'll still have to keep going to Stowmarket. But then they tried to get me to go to the sugar beet, but there again the doctor said that it just wasn't to be possible. I was right down to just about seven stone.

Oh you had to go to work. Yes, I used to go with my aunt cause she was something to do with the Red Cross and I used to go with her as much as I could, so (um) the lady who used to be my boss at Rapiers, the first place I worked, she was on the committee that had to deal with people. I mean, they sent the police after you if they thought you were skiving and (um) we went in front of her and she agreed with the doctor's report and such-like. That was the most sensible idea, otherwise I would just fizzle out and that would be it. I mean you were just so weak.

But not all war work was unrelieved labour or drudgery. There were the moments of humour when the routine was flouted, as Dorothy described in the early years of the war while she was still at Ransomes & Rapier:

Crummy old office actually, but it had got a brick wall in front of the windows which looked out onto the river, and the other end of the office had glass windows and the top half of the windows was clear and we were right opposite the strong room which had the great big heavy safe and such-like, and also the stairs which went up to the drawing office. And (um) there was Hazel, myself, Denise and Lily, four of us in that office, and that was the time the song 'A tisket, a tasket' came out. We started having a song session, singing 'A tisket, a tasket, a brown and yellow basket', and there were all these men standing on the stairs up to the drawing office watching us and when we finished they all clapped. (Giggle.) Major Blair who was in the office next door came round to wonder what all the noise was about and we got choked off. Misbehaving at work. We were told not to do it again.

The Mass Observation social survey also recorded a detailed description of an 18-year-old girl's day in an Ipswich factory (possibly Manganese Bronze) in February

1943, which, for all its length, is worth repeating here for its vivid depiction of the way that individual personality persists in wartime despite all the drama of raids and the official encouragement of selfless devotion to the national war effort. It takes more than the background of total war to change a teenage girl.

Mother called me at 7.45. She had overslept so I did not get my usual cup of tea in bed. I cycled to work (this takes about three minutes) and arrived there at 8.15 instead of 8. I am the only one who starts at 8 in the physical testing laboratory so, as usual, I was alone for the first hour. A friend who works in the nearby machine shop came in soon after I arrived. He wanted some plywood. I went into the chemi-lab, borrowed an empty case, and broke it up for him. We chatted until 9, when George, 'the boy', came in, swept up and cleaned the machines.

I then went into the chemi-lab again and made some nitrogen iodide (when dry this explodes at a touch). I took some over to the office block and sprinkled it on the passage floor to dry out. This was a joke I had been planning for some days. About half an hour later there was a phone call from the office. A female voice said, 'Will you come and clear up whatever it was you put over here?' I feigned ignorance and rang off.

At 9.20 the chief inspector arrived and, after his usual remarks about the weather, his indigestion and his car, sat down with the *Daily Mail*.

I went over to the office block to reconnoitre. The typists had discovered that the stuff could be exploded by scraping the floor with their feet. This they were doing, screaming with delight at each little bang; they accosted me and asked me what it was – said they wanted to take some to a dance. I muttered something about 'secret formula' and hurriedly left.

Back in the test room I did some tensile tests until 10.30 when I lunched – Marmite sandwiches. Afterwards I sat for a while looking through catalogues of gramophone

66 *This image is from a series of photographs taken to illustrate Ransomes Sims & Jefferies village out-stations which were set up in all kinds of buildings to give women basic engineering tasks. The site shown is probably the first such at Playford.*

67 *Inside an engineering out-station.*

records. Then a yarn in the chemi-lab, more yarns in the machine shop, then at 12.45 home to dinner. During my dinner hour, apart from eating (potato pie, greens, sponge pudding), I glanced through father's *Daily Herald*, played Sibelius' 'Karelia Suite' on my 'gram, and read a of *Maradick at Forty* by Hugh Walpole. Back to work at 2p.m.

Until 4 I worked fairly steadily – pulling tensile tests, graphing and writing certifi-cates. At 4 the chief went off to the canteen for tea and my friend from the machine shop came in. We discussed making some ultra-modern stools from tubular bronze. I don't expect this ever to get beyond discussion. A little more browsing in a record catalogue passed the time until 5.30 p.m. I had tea in the works canteen – Welsh rarebit, bread and butter cake and tea (6d.). I left about 6.30 and went to see the film *In This Our Life*. I returned home by 11p.m. – supper and bed.

In other words, in a working day which was officially eight and a half hours long, by her own account she actually worked at her job for three hours, and it seems that neither her 'friend' in the machine shop, nor her boss, nor the girls in the typing pool were much more dedicated.

Once the Education Committee had decided to reopen the Schools of Art and Science in the evenings, they were expected to play their part in the technical training required by an industrialised workforce but, crammed into shared ac-commodation in the Central Schools, they were completely unable to meet the demand. On 21 November 1941 the committee, under government direction, arranged for the School to offer an accelerated Higher National Certificate in engineering, covering the normal two-year course in six months. That year there were 20 places, in 1942 10 places, and in 1943 16 successful students. To increase the staff, two women tutors were appointed with degrees in mathe-matics. Other courses foundered, only three women coming forward in 1942

68 *A woman operating a press for Ransomes Sims & Jefferies. She is wearing suitable headgear and protective gloves.*

69 *Group portrait of women passing through the training school for workers set up by Ransomes Sims & Jefferies in October 1940.*

to train as supervisors in engineering, so the course could not be held, although that it should have been considered at all marked a revolution.

Training had to be in large part the responsibility of the relevant industries, and factories found themselves drawn more and more into preparing their own workforce. Ransomes, Sims & Jefferies, in particular, developed a school and ways of working that enabled them to use large numbers of outworkers. In October 1940 the company opened a training school in the Old Lawn Mower Works, where production had ceased because of the war. By the end of the conflict it had trained 500 adult men and women to use machine tools like capstan lathes, drills and grinders. Ransomes & Rapier did not open their works college until just after the war but it incorporated the lessons learnt in the previous years.

Even before the war had begun it was creating a lot of additional work and bringing potentially highly profitable military contracts to the region. The first of these were connected to the expansion of existing airfields (such as Martlesham, which specialised in testing new models) and the building of new airfields from 1937 onwards. Radio Direction Finding posts, very 'hush-hush', were set up at Orford Ness and Bawdsey. Based in the countryside, these are a little outside our story, yet they had an impact, bringing advanced technology to rural Suffolk. Number 9 Bomber Squadron Stradishall was adopted by Ipswich Borough Council.

Cranes in Nacton was perhaps the largest armaments firm in the town. It spread over 16 acres, employed 1,200 people at its peak, and added an additional factory building to its site. Besides its normal output of radiators it had soon converted

70 *Gun limbers for 25-pdrs ready for dispatch from the former Ransomes Sims & Jefferies lawnmower works. The view is up Bishops Hill to the trees of Holywells Park.*

to war work, producing mortar and other bombs, machine guns, tanks and army trucks.

In April 1939 Richard Stokes, the Chairman of Ransomes & Rapier, offered to manufacture shells on a no-profit no-loss basis but his offer was rejected, ostensibly because Ipswich was felt to be too exposed to attack for ammunitions work. However, once war had actually begun and other firms had successfully won armament contracts, Ransomes & Rapier still got next to nothing. They continued to win civilian projects linked to the war effort, however, like dockside and harbour installations, cranes and tunnels, including gates to the Blackwall and Rotherhithe tunnels. The Ministry of Supply also placed orders for mobile cranes, excavators, concrete mixers and 20 vibrating concrete finishing machines (Ransomes & Rapier Minute Book Vol. 8). They also managed to secure a contract for the carriages for 25 pounder cannon.

Ransomes Sims & Jefferies' peace-time production had focused on agricultural machinery, goods handling trucks and lawnmowers. Production of all lawnmowers ceased, except for those designed to cut the grass on airfields, but the wartime modernisation of agriculture led to an expansion in all their agricultural

71 *The small engineering firm of Cocksedges was employed in making Bofors guns to be mounted on the converted trawlers operating out of HMS Bunting on Cliff Quay.*

lines. They found that a small crawler tractor designed for use in market gardens, orchards and small holdings with uneven terrain was greatly in demand owing to the need for increased food production.

The shortage of labour and the need for faster operations at ports and in the handling of goods generally meant that machines took over from men. Ransomes Sims & Jefferies developed their range of electrical trucks and had several types of fork lift ready to go into production at the end of the war. They also gained some specifically military contracts: 345 carriages and 400 limbers were produced for 17-pounder cannon; in addition bomb parts, mine sinkers, components for 25-pounder cannon and hundreds of thousands of parts for tanks were made. Women polished gears for the Rolls-Royce engine timing-gear. The firm was, in fact, typical of the way the government spread the components of a single product between many factories. No single air raid could knock out the supply of cannon if production were spread over several. The workers often did not know what any particular component was for, which was better for security.

72 Bofors gun assembly line.

73 Tank turrets stacked in Cocksedges yard.

The smaller Ipswich firm of Cocksedges produced some of the most dramatic munitions and the greatest variety. They received a large order for cast-steel turrets weighing about 3½ tons each, and thousands of smaller inserts, sprockets and so on. Their work with tanks probably had an effect on Ransomes Sims & Jefferies getting orders for specialised adaptations of tank used in the D-day landings. These included engineer tanks, tanks carrying folding bridges and bobbin cable-laying tanks. They also supplied the steel girders for the marine forts like Roughs Tower offshore from Felixstowe (later to become Radio Caroline and then Sealand). Less dramatic but more profitable were the varied uses to which their steel girders were put: steel-framed air-raid shelters, anti-tank and coastal defences, emergency and bailey bridges, replacement girders for bombed-out factories, and girders for RAF hangars.

Hardly any firm, including the smallest, was without some kind of wartime work. The local printing firm of Cowells found itself producing propaganda in German

74 *Arabic booklet printed by Cowells for use in Egypt and North Africa. Far-fetched though it seems, a British plane did actually destroy an Italian plane with propeller alone during an air raid on Suffolk, the incident being recorded in the Martlesham logbook.*

TERROR !

TERROR war Hitlers Waffe als er das deutsche Volk und Reich seiner Partei dienstbar machte.

TERROR war Hitlers Waffe gegen Österreich, die Tschecho- slowakei, Polen, Norwegen, Terror gegen Wehr- lose, Mord an Waffenlosen, Brandstiftung an unverteidigten Städten.

TERROR hemmungsloser, vorbedachter Terror zwang Holland, Belgien und das uneinige Frankreich auf die Kniee.

TERROR solite auch Englands Kampfeswillen brechen. Aber

Ihr habt Euch verrechnet!

Gegen die sprichwörtliche Gleichmütigkeit, gegen die eisernen Nerven, gegen den sturen Willen der Briten vermögen Görings Bomben nichts. Tag für Tag wird Euch diese Lehre deutlicher beigebracht.

BOMBEN WIDER BOMBEN !

Das ist unsere Antwort an Hitler: Bomben und immer mehr Bomben.

BOMBEN auf die Kasernen, auf die Kriegshäfen, auf die Flugplätze.

BOMBEN auf die Kruppwerke, auf Spandau, auf Augs- burg, auf Magdeburg.

BOMBEN auf alle Benzinfabriken, auf Leuna, Misburg, Pöhlitz.

BOMBEN auf die deutsche Kriegsmaschine. Bomben immer tiefer nach Osten hinein.

WIR SCHLAGEN ZURÜCK !

438

75 *'This is our answer to Hitler. Bombs and more bombs.'*

76 *'Thirty War Principles for the German People.' The local printing firm of Cowells was involved in producing propaganda to be dropped on Germany and elsewhere. Carefully designed to look like official Nazi Party publications, with the names of German publishers and authors, this was highly secret 'black propaganda'.*

77 *The result of a 250kg. HE bomb falling on Key Street on 27 February 1941. The canvas sheeting covers some 500 tons of barley from Messrs R. & W. Paul's Malting and Barley Store which ran out of the building and completely filled the street at one point. Salvage of the grain carried on during the night and was successful.*

78 *Damage caused by the first of 13 HE bombs on the night of 9/10 April 1941 included 12 private cars on the premises of Messrs Yandells.*

79 *The second bomb of the night destroyed the fire float and auxiliary fire float, and the yacht used as the parent ship by the NFS. An officer was killed by a wooden splinter. One of the fire floats is being winched to the surface.*

80 *Incendiaries were dropped around Cliff Quay, as well as high explosive, causing extensive fires. This shows the gates of Messrs Jepsons in Cliff Road, with the gasometer behind.*

81 *This heavily camouflaged grain elevator stood on Cliff Quay near HMS* Bunting *and an armed trawler can be seen on the left. This is the only picture of the shore base to come to light so far.*

and Arabic, and had a priority task in printing all the tombola tickets used by the Royal Navy in the Mediterranean. Clothing manufacturers like Philips and Piper turned out army overcoats and britches, or uniforms for the National Fire Service. Larger garages got maintenance contracts for Army lorries, smaller ones fitted local government vehicles with blackout headlights.

Builders merchants making concrete forms, like Saunders, found they suddenly had an enormous demand. At first they supplied sections which could be used as private bomb shelters, the 'Sleep Safe', then they rode high on a concrete shortage caused by the demand for defences. The Ministry of Agriculture next started pressurising reluctant farmers to use silage, silage meant silos and silos meant concrete sections. Finally, the construction of airfields with hangars and barracks right across East Anglia meant huts, and huts meant concrete girders. The other part of Saunders' business was as monumental masons and war meant memorials.

Factories were key targets. Ransomes & Rapier was the first to experience bombing and the only factory to lose several of its men in the butterfly bomb raid already described, although this was not the result of a specific attack on the factory, for which incendiaries or high explosive would have been used.

German intelligence was aware of the importance of Cranes. Luftwaffe records captured at the end of the war identify Cranes as an armaments factory and single it out for attack. It was bombed five times, on 24 March 1941, 4 May 1941, 11–12 May 1941, 2 June 1942 and 28 September 1943. As a result the neighbouring firm of Wrinch's was hit also. Only the Docks and Cranes are identified as specific targets.

82 Not until 3 November 1943 did the Germans make a concerted attempt to disrupt the railway lines around Ipswich. A total of 24 HE bombs, two firepot (Sprengbrand) bombs and 15 incendiary containers were dropped, and the lines are stated to have been out of commission for 22 hours.

83 The highly specialised firm of furniture makers, Titchmarsh and Goodwins, was converted to war work. It stood in a yard off Turret Lane at the back of St Peters Street. The crowded conditions were typical of old-fashioned workshops.

84 The wartime canteen at Titchmarsh and Goodwins.

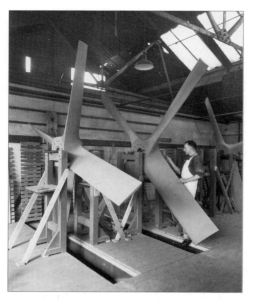

85 *Wartime ingenuity! Floors have been cut away to allow propellers to be rotated while shaping.*

Because Cranes was then on the borders of Ipswich and split between the areas of responsibility of the Ipswich and East Suffolk police authorities there are two sets of reports concerning these raids.

The one on 4 May was serious. The reports differ slightly in the number and order of falling bombs, the one by East Suffolk being most complete:

> The same day at approximately 22.40 hrs another plane following the same course bombed Crane Ltd Works, Nacton Road.
>
> Two H.E. bombs of about 250 kg. were dropped, both making definite craters about 20 feet wide and 8–10 feet deep.
>
> 1st exploded in the yard close to the base of the galvanising shop. This was so damaged that it can no longer

86 *Older skilled men making wooden propellers.*

87 *Women putting the finishing touches to propellers. One has to stand on blocks to reach her work.*

88 & 89   *The reality of life as a Land Army girl. Two workers bundled up on a Fordson tractor; and the fantasy of life as a Land Army girl, a photograph clearly devised to encourage people to help with the harvest on their summer holiday.*

be used. This bomb also caused damage to the core shop and foundry, mainly to glass and outer covering; debris and splinter caused lesser damage over a wider area of the works. The 2nd bomb fell and exploded on the edge of the playing field nearest the works. This demolished a hut used by the Home Guard, and also caused slight damage to the main offices and other departments nearby.

According to the Ipswich report,

> A second ricocheted from ground adjacent to Nacton Road and ex-ploded in the polishing shop of Messrs Wrinch Ltd, destroying a concrete unit shelter. A medium fire was caused at the polishing shop. The two premises adjoin, and the other two bombs dropped one on each side of the combined premises, making craters in fairly open land, and causing slight damage.

It also ignited Wrinch's paint store and the vivid description of the attempts to put out the blaze is a good example of the courage shown by ordinary people with no particular incentive other than a sense of duty. It survives only accidentally, and is best given in the words of the police constable who reported it:

> I beg to report that, following the dropping of bombs, a fierce fire quickly developed in the paint shop of the above works. Two men, Senior Warden Overall and Frederick Perkins of 531 Nacton Road (a street firewatcher), both of Priory Heath, Nacton, at once went to the scene.
>
> They saw that barrels containing turpentine, methylated spirit, as well as numerous other containers of paint, etc. were either burning or were in immediate danger of becoming involved.
>
> Enemy bombers were still in the vicinity and shattered glass and girders made entry to the building perilous, yet these men without thought of their own safety immediately commenced rolling out barrels through the debris so that they were clear of the fire. Some of the barrels were then burning on the outside. The men continued to do this work until the arrival of the fire brigade.

The raid caused a halt in production of about five days until the area was declared safe. A few days later it was the turn of Fisons to receive a direct hit. Cranes was damaged again on 12 May and these raids seem to have been part of a deliberate attempt to destroy the firm. Two bombs, the 15th and 16th to fall in the raid, affected the factory:

(15) and (16) were 250 kg. H.E.s. One ricocheted in soft earth near the entrance gate to Messrs Cranes, Nacton Road, and, clearing a high fence, exploded near the surface of Nacton Road at the main entrance to Ipswich Airport, making a small crater in the roadway. Blast and splinter damage was occasioned to several houses on the Nacton Road between that road and the airport buildings. The other penetrated the end of Messrs Cranes Sports Club Canteen, ricocheted in a tarmac path in front of the canteen, across Nacton Road, partly demolishing a brick-built incinerator building of the Ipswich Airport, and came to rest, unexploded, a few yards away on the surface of the ground.

Fortunately, the Luftwaffe were not able to keep up this sort of pressure for long and Ipswich was not to have its factories bombed out of existence. The last bomb damage to a major factory, on 2 June 1943, was quite accidental. The bomb had not even been released but was attached to the bottom of a stricken Focke-Wulf that crashed into the lock gates, according to the police report:

Full production, following first-aid repairs, was in progress on Monday 7 June at Ransomes & Rapier. Cocksedges lost half a day's production throughout the works, one day in respect of the moulding shop, and full production is expected to be restored in a matter of two to three weeks.

The factory was the major employer of women but they could also volunteer for the services and for the Women's Land Army. Farming and agriculture generally are outside the limits of this book, save in so far as Ipswich supplied the farmer with

90 *Land Army girls demonstrate the manufacture of silage using a Saunders concrete silo, possibly at Thorrington Hall.*

91 *The Women's Land Army Rally in the Council Chamber of the Town Hall in Ipswich in 1942. It was addressed by Lady Cranworth, who complained of the reluctance of farmers to employ them, but noted the good response of the women, 500 coming forward in Suffolk by June.*

labour. Land Army girls lived in hostels in Ipswich and were bussed out to wherever the County Agricultural Committee felt there was a need for them. The wish to grow rather than import as much as possible of the nation's food meant the farmer found the government eager to help in ways they would never have considered in the case of another industry. Women alone were not enough for the farmer's needs; schoolchildren were also used. For many years rural schools had allowed farmers to take boys out of lessons at harvest, even though the practice was viewed with suspicion not only by the Trades Council but also by the Education Committee. That they had good reason to be suspicious is made clear by a minute of 3 April 1944 prohibiting the use of children in 'sugar beet lifting or other work involving heavy strain' and by gang masters, the minute implying that they were being used in this way. Now headmasters, who would have raised a storm at the idea of pupils doing shift work for nothing in the most essential wartime factory, encouraged pupils to help with agriculture. On 31 May 1943 the committee had been informed that the peak harvest period would fall from 7 August to 14 September. It agreed that suitable boys could be released.

Northgate was especially active. On 27 September 1943 it reported that it had arranged a forestry camp and given help to farmers. On 15 May 1944 it was decided that Vth- and VIth-form boys could help on farms for the last two or three weeks of summer term, others helping for a few days at the beginning of autumn. It also ran the forestry camp again.

Sixteen

Schools

As the war progressed schools gradually found ways of making the best of the situation and began to get on top of the chaos of the first two years. The Ilford children had left, the schools were now open and provided with some sort of shelters, and the first and largest wave of evacuation from Ipswich had taken place. There were now considerably fewer children to teach, something that must have made the Ipswich teacher's job considerably easier than that of his or her colleagues in the reception areas.

The terrible state of the school shelters was one of the first bits of unfinished business to be put right. From decisions made by the Education Committee on 22 November 1940, December 1940 and 24 February 1941 it seems that a total of £12,600 was spent on providing electric lighting, waterproofing, ventilation and, finally, heating for the trenches. Progress was painfully slow and piecemeal but the Trades Council refused to take the pressure off the Education Committee. The first point in their deputation to the committee on 9 June 1941 was a demand for speeding up the heating and lighting of trenches. But come October it was reported that there were 'problems in obtaining convector heaters, transformers and cables'. Finally, by 7 September 1942 the committee could congratulate itself that 'heating lighting and ventilation was installed in all schools save St Mary's Albion Hill and Smart Street where the current was DC'. In other words, four years late.

The next stage came in 1943 when, on 8 February, it was decided to line one timber trench with concrete units. As the shelters improved, so the need to resolve the question of public use of school shelters outside school hours became more pressing, particularly as most raids took place at night. The public was granted access to school shelters out of hours by a decision of 6 January 1941, but it warned that 'the ARP must make sure they are returned in good order'.

The committee agreed to heat the trenches on 24 November 1941, but there was no way its electricity would be used to warm the general public. Prudently, therefore, they decided to place the master switches for turning the heating and lighting on in the headmaster's office, which would be locked and inaccessible at night, rather than in the main road where the ARP could reach it. Inter-committee fighting about the shelters continued until 1 June 1942, when the headmaster at Nacton Road reported the school shelters damaged by the public and the Education Committee told the Emergency Committee they were locking the Nacton Road shelter and it was up to the Emergency Committee to arrange to unlock and lock it.

It is perhaps unsurprising that the general public only regularly used three school shelters, the two best and deepest, St Helens Junior Mixed and Clifford Road Junior Mixed, and one in an area without alternatives, St Mary's Albion Hill RC. The Emergency Committee appointed supervisors for these three shelters.

The Education Committee now found it had to face a new problem. It was not just the shelters which attracted keen interest. Schools and their playing fields also represented under-used community resources at a time when it was difficult to fend off outside demands. At first it was for strictly military use, and from time to time different schools would find searchlights, barrage balloons and AA batteries in their playing fields, many of which were covered with barbed wire and obstacles to prevent their use as landing strips by the enemy. Faced with a request to vacate Chantry by the military, the Council was prepared to sacrifice St John's Children's Home instead, placing the children first of all in an empty wing of Heathfields and later acquiring Polstead Hall.

The warden service badly needed group centres in each of its divisions. Chief Warden Woods recounts his frustrated search for centres over the period May to October 1940 and the restlessness the delay was causing to his men. Finally, the wardens were given rooms to use in all but three of their areas (B, D and S). They represented 10 of the 34 schools in the town, three senior and seven junior schools. As well as permanent use of a classroom as a group centre the service often used school halls in the evenings for public lectures on protection against gas, blast and splinters and incendiaries and on first aid. Part of Western Senior was set aside but never, thankfully, used as a gas cleansing centre.

The Home Guard was soon chasing the use of school premises too. London Road School was taken over by them. Full details of Home Guard use have only survived for the eastern sector of the town covered by the 9th Battalion. Seven schools, later reduced to four, were used as posts: A Company used Sidegate Lane but then joined B Company at Britannia Road; D company used Priory Heath; E Company used Nacton Road but moved to Greenwich when Nacton Road was bombed; Clifford Road was used by F Company; and G Company originally used Northgate for a short period as a post. Three school playgrounds were used for parade grounds: Copleston, Greenwich and Clifford Road. The Eastern Girls Senior School was used right at the end of the war in 1944.

Warden Service Group Centres were needed full-time and manned during every alert. Home Guard posts were used every evening and parade grounds every Sunday. Northgate was used for lectures two nights a week. It appears that the Education Committee received rent for the use of their premises.

The committee was not always co-operative about seeing the schools used in this way. For example, on 7 October 1940, when the Home Guard requested the use of a room at Gainsborough Junior Mixed for a post at which men on duty could sleep, they were offered a slit trench shelter. On 4 September the Home Guard asked via the Home Office for use of the hall and six classrooms at Springfield Junior Mixed School for four evenings and Sunday mornings in winter. At first objections were made that if the open fires were used until 9p.m. this would not leave enough time for them to be cleared and relit in time for school the following morning. But after some discussion it was eventually agreed to allow the school to be used with the fires unlit, the Home Guard being allowed to use their own gas heaters at their own cost.

Next came the needs of the newly formed 'pre-service training units', especially the ATC. On 30 December 1940, at the end of the autumn term, the Air Defence Cadet Force was given rooms at Ipswich Boys School. As they developed they sought space at other schools. Turned down at first, they later got use of Western Senior Boys Gym in February 1944. Incidentally, they acquired the musical instruments for their band from those that had belonged to St John's Home. The Sea Cadets used a boat in the Docks and seem to have made no demands on school premises. They were, however, the first group to ask for exclusive use of St Matthew's Baths one night a week at a reduced admission and got Thursdays; the ATC had to be content with Fore Street Baths, re-opened after bomb damage, on Monday nights. Finally the Army Cadet Force were using Whitton, Stoke and Greenwich Schools.

Three schools lost space to British Restaurants. The bottom half of Ranelagh Road was taken for a British Restaurant used largely by the workers at Reavells, and part of the Central Boys School for the Tower Ramparts British Restaurant. Whitton Junior was also used. The Central Boys School building was also shared with the School of Engineering, and on 26 June 1943 was earmarked as a shadow administrative building in the event of a heavy air attack. Thirteen schools were also earmarked as rest centres, opened as needed to take people evacuated from their houses by bomb damage or unexploded bombs.

Every senior school had to open in the evenings as a youth club. Many schools were used by the Ipswich Co-operative Society to run classes in music, mostly choral singing and bands, drama, dancing and rehearsals for Co-op pantomimes and theatre productions which became and remain today a major social feature of the town. The Co-op tended to use the girls' schools while the Cadet Corps used the boys'. The first use was of the Central Girls School for a Co-op Youth Group educational weekend, permission being given on 8 July 1943. By 9 February 1945 the committee was agreeing to let the Co-op use Nacton Junior Mixed School, Clifford Road Junior Mixed School and Springfield Infants for educational classes, Sidegate Lane for dancing and dramatic work at the weekends, and Eastern Senior and Priory Heath for dance and drama in the evenings. Rosehill and Whitton were used on Saturdays for Co-op Junior Clubs. The Co-op Juniors also used the Central School fortnightly for rehearsals. A whole range of adult and youth education was taken over and run by the Ipswich Co-op Members Educational Committee.

Some schools were even being used for Sunday schools and church services. Arising out of these educationally relevant wartime uses were other requests for essentially social functions, evening events and dances. The basic policy was to allow wardens and Home Guard as well as any school-based youth club to use the school for social events but not other bodies, like businesses, nor could tickets be sold openly to anyone.

So for the first, and indeed the last, time the resources of the schools were being used to something like their full capacity, in some cases five evenings a week and weekends. Such intensive use caused its own problems, principally an enormous amount of extra work for the caretakers. Smoking was banned on school premises, not for health reasons but because of the extra work it gave the staff. In 1942 the ATC banned smoking and asked the youth clubs to follow suit, but in those days, when heavy smoking was an almost universal male habit, it was extremely difficult to get members of youth clubs and the Home Guard to comply. Instead, a request for Home Guard officers to use their discretion was introduced. Caretakers, hitherto almost invisible to members of the committee, began to be mentioned at most meetings, and finally the Chairman found himself sitting down with the school caretakers to negotiate on their grievances. It was reported that,

> 18 November 1943 Chairman had had an interesting and useful talk with the caretakers of the schools most used. Caretakers want time and a half Saturday, double time Sunday. Difficulty of making schools thoroughly clean for start of terms when outside bodies continue to use buildings.
> Use of lavatories by the Home Guard.
> Periodical overhaul and tidying up of ARP and emergency hospital equipment.

Sensibly, what the Chairman decided to do was charge the users: 'Caretakers to be paid 3s. for use of a school on Saturday with 1s. 6d. per classroom and per hour, and 5s. for Sunday opening and 2s. 6d. per room and per hour; PAYABLE BY THE HIRER.'

Teaching was not a reserved occupation and soon began to experience the loss of all males of military age in the successive waves of conscription. By June 1940, 41 male teachers under 30 had been called up. On 7 February 1941 it was reported that 52 per cent of staff were eligible. At one point the shortage of male teachers became so great that the committee tried to institute a pool system of male teachers who could be sent wherever help was needed. The headmasters managed jointly to prevent that plan coming into operation. On 18 March 1941 the committee heard of the first death in action of a conscripted Ipswich teacher: Mr J. Carswell BA (Lond.), assistant teacher at Eastern Senior Mixed School and a corporal in the Auxiliary Military Pioneer Corps, had been killed in a London air raid on 26 February.

Older teachers were allowed to stay on past retirement and well into their sixties. In 1945 three heads and eight teachers were past retirement age, but the solution to the shortage was the creation of pupil-teachers, novices who continued their training on the job. These teachers were deployed on a pool system. Class sizes expanded rapidly, however, and for the first time clear statistics were collected for the committee. Several junior schools had many classes with over 50 pupils.

Free school milk and school dinners were other wartime innovations. As more and more parents made use of school dinners, provided free to poorer children, it became less necessary for the Education Department to provide special doses of malt extract for the malnourished. During the transitional period, while schools were still getting their kitchens, it was common for children from one to be marched across town to eat their dinners at another. Then a school meal container delivery service was set up, partly at Clifford Road, to deliver meals to those schools without space to install their own kitchens.

With the coming of the school meal service came a problem that still bedevils schools, supervising the dinner hour. Essentially, the teachers had lost a two-hour break in the middle of each day. They had been part of the mass meeting of 23 April 1941 which demanded that midday meals be provided, and united with the Ipswich Trades Council and Labour Party and the Ipswich Committee against Malnutrition in pressing the Educational Committee to 'explore all possible ways of increasing the number of school children for whom hot midday meals are provided by the authority'. Now the teachers agreed, unwillingly, only to supervise the children during the period they were actually eating, and not for the whole break. By 1945 the Secretary of the Ipswich Branch of the NUT was recording the opinion of a large minority of his members that, 'School meals as envisaged under the new act will detract from parental responsibility and consequently as a long-term policy will prove detrimental to the character of the British nation.'

The jewel in the education authority's crown was the fee-paying grammar school, Northgate, with new buildings and playing fields on the edge of town. Most of the parents, 70 to 80 per cent, received scholarship grants to pay the fees, entering into bonds to repay them if they withdrew the children from the school or if the children did not complete their studies. At the beginning of the war Northgate was the only school with its own canteen and dinner service, and the only school whose pupils got subsidised transport. It was one of the first to get its trenches dug and its pupils back in full-time education (by 21 September). The Education Committee soon managed to get the Auxiliary Fire Station and Home Guard post moved off its premises, and after their departure it was used as a rest centre, especially in connection with the Cemetery Road parachute mine incident, but remained largely resistant to the demands for external use that besieged other schools. It had only to fend off a demand from the British Welcome Club for the use of its showers. It is no surprise that the glamorous Air Training Corps was based at Northgate. It also kept its headmaster.

Yet Northgate's position of privilege was under constant attack. Within the first year or so of war subsidised transport was extended to all secondary schools. A school meals service became universal. Mrs Lewis and Mrs Whitmore continued to demand, among other things, that allowance be made in the scholarship exam for pupils whose education had been disrupted by the 1939 re-opening fiasco. Attempts were made to make the means testing on which the authority's grant was based shift to earnings after tax, and to increase the amount of grant and extend upward the limits so that in fact all children should be supported in this way.

All these disputes were to be swallowed up by the great changes being set in place nationally, ready to be introduced at the end of the war. But, for the time being, children were passing through an impoverished system under intense pressure. Despite evacuation, the loss of so many classrooms to other functions as well as the loss of teachers meant crowded classes. Teachers were more likely to be superannuated or still undergoing training. There were fewer playing fields and fewer sports, particularly for boys. Over a thousand hours was lost to alerts, with large parts of the school day spent in shelters or, if the raid had happened the night before, with children falling asleep at their desks. Some primary schools organised mattresses and regular sleeping sessions for the children. Some schools were damaged in air raids though, thankfully, in Ipswich the raids that affected schools all happened outside school hours.

From 1942 onwards, however, there seems to have been a marked change in attitude towards children right across the board seeing musical, theatrical and, finally, even cinema performances. Ipswich children, rather exceptionally, had access to a wide variety of educational films that were shown at the Museum's High Street art gallery, and the committee was also prepared to pay an outside lecturer to give talks on natural history and birds. A selection from the minutes of such events includes:

> Mid-April 1942 In Ipswich the London Philharmonic Orchestra gave a special performance for local schoolchildren, Ipswich Council having accepted their offer to play for a fee of £150.
>
> 6 September 1943 Heads can decide whether children attend exhibition 'March towards freedom from want' put on by Ipswich Industrial Co-operative Society.
>
> 20 November 1943 Children's Folk Dance Festival held at North Eastern School, about 340 children from Ipswich schools attended it.
>
> 22 March 1944 Lecture recital on music by Mr Sydney Harrison arranged by Cop Ed for senior pupils.
>
> 3 April 1944 Senior pupils of Northgate allowed to attend performance of *The Bachelor* by Turgenev.
>
> 26, 27 April 1944 Very good public attendance at the Youth Club Drama Festival held at Eastern Senior Girls.
>
> On 22 May 1944 it was recorded that in the previous and current years Mr Bird had given illustrated lectures on Suffolk flora and fauna to schools for a fee.
>
> 4 September 1944 Ipswich Industrial Co-op Society to be allowed to show the films *When we Build Again* and *World of Plenty* in those schools whose heads agreed.
>
> 20 November 1944 The Adelphi Players to perform *Twelfth Night* in three schools.
>
> 12 February 1945 Attempts to be made for children to see film *Henry V*.

Seventeen
The Forgotten Campaign

Perhaps one of the least known aspects of wartime Ipswich and the naval war in general is the protection given to the vital East Coast shipping convoys. Ipswich was an important centre for this service. From nearby Wattisham the RAF ran regular convoy protection patrols, picking the ships up at certain map references and escorting them on to the next station's patrol flight. The Royal Navy hired a sizeable part of the Lowestoft trawling fleet, provided them with a few Oerlikon guns and transformed them into 'armed patrol trawlers' often complete with their usual skippers and crew. Twenty of these auxiliary patrol trawlers (at least two of which had been hired for the same purpose in 1914-18) and 11 motor launches were based in Ipswich.

This was without doubt the aspect of the war in which the boundary between civilians and armed services was most indistinct. The Navy were fighting with civilian vessels, enlisted civilian crews alongside armed merchant marines, from bases in the midst of a town. As much of the naval activity was refitting by local firms a lot of what went on was obscured by the wartime need for security.

In July 1940 the part of the port of Ipswich outside the actual Dock, known as Cliff Quay, was magically transformed into a royal naval shore base known as HMS *Bunting*. As an establishment it had a chequered organisational career, being for a time an out-station of the Harwich naval base and, especially, HMS *Badger* at Parkeston Quay, by then becoming a satellite of HMS *Woolverstone*. The Navy parked a superannuated steam yacht (constructed in 1896) alongside a closed-off section of the quayside and took some warehouses and offices over from British Fermentation Products. Just to confuse matters, the original steam yacht *Bunting* was replaced by a twin-screw motor yacht called HMS *Freelance* until it swapped names with the steam yacht and became the new *Bunting*. In 1943 the base was expanded by the expedient of mooring a pleasure paddle-steamer from Weymouth known as the *Empress of India* next to *Bunting* to serve as an accommodation ship.

The base also served as the workshops for the Ipswich firm of Cocksedges. Early in 1940 the company was asked to assist in fitting degaussing gear to a converted trawler, as this was to be the method used to overcome magnetic mines. It was the start of about six years of work on ships including destroyers, MLs, MGBs, MTBs, fleet sweepers, corvettes, all types of landing craft and merchant ships; approximately 1,500 naval and 800 merchant ships were dealt with. Ships were converted to minesweepers and part of the work was the maintenance of approximately 30 of these. About 130 men were engaged seven days a week at Ipswich Dock. Cocksedges also made the mountings for the Oerlikon guns fitted on the converted trawlers.

Reavells had been building air compressors for the Navy since the First World War. These were used in connection with the recoil and clearing of cannon, and especially in the charging of torpedo tubes. In 1928 they introduced a 3,500lb. per square inch compressor. Made in Ipswich, these were sent away to be fitted in Chatham and elsewhere. Some of the contracts Reavells secured in 1942 were for ships not launched until after the war. Another specialist local firm was Bull Motors, who made 'super-silent' electrical motors as auxiliaries on submarines. Mann Egerton had a contract for some of the small specialised craft used at D-day.

All this activity meant that the Docks and Cliff Quay became a restricted area for which all civilians needed a special pass. These were issued to all the employees of the many civilian firms that continued to work there by an Army sergeant from an office in the Old Customs House.

At least five of the small ships based there were sunk in action: HMS *Cape Finisterre*, HMT *Adonis*, HMT *Franc Tireur*, HMT *Red Gauntlet* and HMS *Hayburn Wyke* (also *Heybourn Wyke*). The crews that served on these ships between them gained one CGM, one BEM, four DSCs, five DSMs and 31 mentions in despatches.

Following some engagements almost the entire crew was honoured. For example, on 21 March 1941 the former trawler *Hekla*, hired in May 1940 as an auxiliary patrol vessel and renamed HMS *Liberator*, engaged enemy aircraft off the Nore. A. Halliwell, skipper, Lieutenant James Mugridge, Petty Officer H. Hutchinson, Able-Seaman H. Johnson, Able-Seaman W. Kirby and cook H. Miller were all mentioned in despatches. *Liberator* was then converted for use as minesweeper between January 1942 and May 1946.

Vessels were sunk in the Orwell. The Felixstowe Police Station war diary records as item 410 the destruction of a converted Danish collier:

> Sunday 24 August 1941, 1530 – Danish collier *Skagerak* blew up and sank in river Orwell opposite Trimley St Martin. Crew of 23 – 16 Danes, 1 Mexican, 1 Swede, 2 RA Gunners, 2 RN Gunners, 1 Pilot (Read of Ipswich). Four dead, 14 missing, 5 survivors. Believed destroyed by a parachute mine. On Saturday 30 August two bodies from the *Skagerak* were recovered near the wreck.

The Ipswich coastal trading vessels belonging to R.&W. Paul's fleet continued to operate during the war, and an incident involving them shows what the merchantmen on these coastal convoys had to face:

> The *Oxbird*, master W.R. Lucas, belonging to R.&W. Paul was attacked on the way to Middlesborough at 8.20a.m. on 10 July 1940 – the aircraft approached us at roughly 800 feet and dropped two bombs on the starboard beam, all of which fell about 300 feet from the ship. He then gave us two bursts of machine-gun fire which also fell wide of the mark. We opened fire with our machine gun and fired rockets and succeeded in keeping him from making a further attack. No damage was caused and no one was

injured. The aircraft then proceeded towards the light vessel and dropped two bombs both of which fell wide.

(Roger Finch, *A Cross in the Topsail*)

On the night of 9 and 10 April the Luftwaffe made a determined attempt to put the Ipswich Docks and the shore base out of action. Fifteen fighter bombers dropped 13 high explosive bombs and hundreds, if not thousands, of incendiaries on the Docks and quayside. This was a highly sensitive area in any case, as the ammunition store of HMS *Bunting* was immediately adjacent to the premises of British Fermentation Products, which held up to 3,000 gallons of pure alcohol, and in turn bordered the Anglo-American petrol storage site. The Chief Constable's report describes what happened in the civilian areas of Cliff Quay that surrounded the naval base:

> The incendiary bombs were of the non-explosive type and were released from containers holding approximately 36 bombs. A rod and base plate from a container was found on the other side of the river. The bombs covered the whole of the quay and many dropped in the petrol installations. Hundreds were used and many fell in the river. Auxiliary naval vessels berthed at the quay opened fire at the raiders with Lewis guns.

The naval base and its explosive magazine stood in the midst of this sea of flames and members of the base won awards for their bravery that night. Because, for some reason, the Admiralty questioned whether or not they had deserved mention, a file of correspondence survives (PRO ADM 1/11430) which describes their actions in great detail and certainly convinced the Admiralty:

> These ratings under Leading Seaman Abbott were conspicuous throughout the whole fire for the manner in which they ignored all danger from either enemy action or from fire when entering burning buildings and were undoubtedly responsible for preventing an explosion of the magazine. The actions of Leading Seamen Abbott and Cozens, in entering the magazine with a hose when the heat inside was such that Mills bombs and small arms ammunition was exploding inside it, was worthy of the highest praise.
>
> Seaman Bailey for a considerable period played his fire hose into the burning timber from a position to leeward of the fire and his action undoubtedly largely contributed to fighting the fire away from the magazine.
>
> Leading Seamen Abbott, Cozens and Smith and Seaman Bailey were fighting various outbreaks of fire continually from 23.00 on 9 April until 5.30 on 10 April.
>
> These ratings entered the sick bay and a workshop which were both eventually burnt out, in addition to which they entered the base office and a store shed preventing the spread of the fire to these latter buildings.

Eighteen

Rattling the Can:
Parades, Propaganda and National Campaigns

Drums, flags, parades and the rattle of collecting tins was a constant colourful accompaniment to the progress of the war. They were publicised on posters all over the town and prominent newspaper efforts were made to promote the many government drives. Perhaps the first of these were collections for the Spitfire Fund in autumn of 1940. Old saucepans and anything made of aluminium was gathered. Chief Warden Woods's men, collecting in Christchurch Park, had done well, perhaps too well, for Woods was forced to record in his diary that one warden found raiding the tins had been arrested. He received a prison sentence.

It was not until 1942 that the government really got into its stride, starting with a highly organised salvage campaign. The corporation arranged for people to use two sets of bins, one for food refuse which could be used as pig feed. The bin men received a bonus for collecting and handling this waste equivalent to the profit the council made selling it to pig farmers. The Council claimed that salvage from its waste collection brought in £5,000 a year. Schoolchildren collected glass jars. David Routh remembers that the school then sold them to a dealer in scrap glass, but he and his friends would collect in the name of the school then sell the jars directly to the dealers, so that they, and not the school, got the tiny commission.

Iron railings began to be coveted and statues to disappear. Railings at the hospital went without any fuss. So too, after a decision of 7 September 1942, did the railings from the Eastern Senior Mixed School, Priory Heath Junior School, Priory Heath Infants School and the Central Senior Boys School in Tower Ramparts. Since 1901 a 9 ft high bronze statue of Queen Victoria had stood in the middle of the lawns in front of Christchurch Mansion, a figure of patriotic pride to some but also of gentle mockery to others. It too was sacrificed to the war effort and made the sum of £50 in scrap. Unnoticed and almost unrecorded, the captured German machine guns that had flanked the main entrance of the Mansion since 1919 also went. Scrap became highly valuable and sought after and those who helped themselves from waste containers found themselves before the magistrates, who had to deal with a constant trickle of offenders. One school stood firm against the iron holocaust. Northgate managed to protect its railings until September 1944, when the Education Committee could hold out no longer.

Gordon Kinsey describes what happened to the books of Ipswich in *Aviation: Flight over the Eastern Counties:*

October 1942 The Ministry of Supply announced that it had selected Ipswich to inaugurate a nationwide Book Salvage drive and called for 150 tons of books to be collected in a fortnight. Ipswich was chosen because its residents were said to buy more books than any other town of comparable size. From the outset it was made clear that the books collected would be divided up into those that should be preserved, those that would be suitable reading matter for the forces, and those that could be pulped. It is doubtful whether such fuss had ever before been made about books. A band of the Royal Marines and another of pipes paraded the streets trailed by 400 schoolchildren with Union Jacks. At an evening ball at the Public Hall the Mayor crowned a Book Queen, Miss Kay Sheppard. The organisers set out to collect an average of eight books from each household, and they managed ten − a total of 294,587 volumes.

These salvage schemes remained in place till the end of the war and were given fresh impetus from time to time. For example, on 4 October 1943 the Education Committee agreed to allow films on paper salvage to be shown in schools; it agreed on 24 January 1944 to send subscriptions of old textbooks to the War Organisation of the Red Cross and Order of St John Prisoner of War Department, and on 4 September 1944 that 9-23 September should be set aside as a Book Recovery and Waste Paper Drive. Departments of the Borough began clearing out their own stores of waste paper. On 20 June 1942 St John's Home was able to send 400 books and 30 sacks of waste paper for salvage, a total of two tons (Minutes of the Children's Sub-Committee of the Public Health Committee).

In the interests of economy the police began tearing up and using for notes the backs of old forms reporting the theft of bicycles, which perhaps says something about the degree of optimism they had in clearing these up.

'Dig for Victory' was another campaign that struck home. Allotments and vegetable gardens were planted and ordinary people took to rearing chickens and rabbits and even joining pig clubs. The Council was under pressure to seek out and use any idle plot of land, and even its public parks were eyed up. Large parts of Chantry Park were converted to arable and much of the rest was let to grazing. To everyone's relief, no doubt, but possibly also to many people's surprise, Christchurch Park was discovered to be unsuitable for agriculture. Council house tenants were encouraged to convert their gardens to growing crops, but they were not allowed to take over the gardens of nearby vacant houses and use those as well because of the problems this might cause if they were re-let. Empty gardens caused problems for the enthusiastic smallholder as they harboured weeds, but the Council refused to employ people to weed them. As the Council had been buying blocks of land for various projects, which had then been frozen for the duration of the war, all sorts of waste land was fenced off and converted into allotments. There was a large plot on the corner of Spencer Road and another on Whitton. The Allotment Holders' Association became a powerful voice within the Council. It raised questions over whether the smoke from Fisons factory was poisoning their crops and was able to get the Education Committee to grant them new access routes to allotments over school grounds.

Enthusiastic heads might encourage a school allotment, and as early as 1940 Smart Street Primary School arranged for the land between the school trenches to be cultivated as allotments. Working on the allotment became part of several lessons. At least two schools converted large parts of their playing fields into new allotments, 28 on North Eastern and eight on Sidegate Lane (Education Committee Minutes for 27 April 1942). There were none on the extensive fields of Northgate close by. The heads of North Eastern and of Stoke who had granted access through their schools were outraged by allotment holders pushing their wheelbarrows over the playground or children playing on the fields in the holidays.

Headmasters in 1941–3 were encouraged to get their children collecting acorns and beech mast to supply the County Garden Produce Committee, provided they spent no more than half a day a week on the task. This was considered suitable for the junior schools.

The Borough had for some years run its own small farm at the Heathfields Institution. Now it increased its small dairy herd, stopped producing vegetables and purchased 20 pigs to be fed on hospital waste. Vegetables, fresh eggs, poultry, rabbits and even slightly illegal pigs could all be acquired off the ration and helped to support the nation's diet. Anyone who produced more than they could use themselves or distribute amongst friends and relatives, often as barter, and started selling it, needed to be very careful however. While Reginald Bales was acquitted of selling home-grown apples, the magistrates found him guilty of selling the apples at a high price and failing to display a written price and of a further offence of not displaying the price for his carrots. In total he was faced with £7 2s. in fines. A producer of strawberries was also convicted of selling his goods at too high a price; he faced a fine of £279 plus £5 costs.

Salvage and gardening were successful and important schemes. Despite the some-what grotesque razzmatazz that accompanied the drives, and any slight queasiness that a book lover must have felt about a Book Queen being crowned to preside over the pulping of thousands of books and records, recycling of waste became a significant part of the wartime economy and helped promote an atmosphere in which waste was simply unacceptable.

Not all schemes were so straightforward however. The great National Savings drives started in 1942, with 'Warship Week'. These were skilful marketing campaigns with a great deal of official pressure behind them. The idea was that sufficient money would be raised in a town to pay for the building of a warship. Ipswich was given the target of £1,000,000 to be raised by public subscription. Endorsed by the Council and even promoted from the pulpit, 'Warship Week' was celebrated with parades of Royal Marine bands and each part of the Council was expected to come up with ideas. The Museum commissioned a huge poster of the proposed HMS *Orwell* painted on a roll of lino and displayed in Lloyds Avenue, along with some of its collection of model galleons and a further collection of warship models of truly outstanding amateurishness lent by an enthusiastic Lieutenant Commander. All contributions were received with great pleasure.

In the prevailing climate it took considerable courage to air a dissenting view. But, nevertheless, one voice was raised, and a highly influential one at that. Richard Stokes, the town's MP, said, 'I have taken no part in the Warship Week in Ipswich, because I think it is a swindle. I don't think it makes the slightest difference to the length of the war; not the slightest difference to the number of war weapons you will have; not the slightest difference to anything conceivable, whether you subscribe or not.'

He was, of course, right. It takes a long time to commission and build a warship and HMS *Orwell*, which was launched on 2 April 1942, was certainly not built with the money raised in Ipswich, which amounted to £846,000. Far from being used only to build warships, the money was placed with big financial organisations who would end up the beneficiaries of the three per cent interest on the deposited sums. Unsurprisingly, Stokes' views caused great offence and he was vigorously attacked by those who had taken part in the campaign, all the way up to the Bishop of St Edmundsbury. Stokes was unrepentant. He objected, he said, to the lack of financial knowledge amongst people and the way the true purpose of the week had been disguised. By requesting people's excess money the government was simply taking it out of circulation, depressing financial activity and demand, and reducing inflation. 'If the government wants the money, they should take it. It is a ridiculous waste of time and effort to continue these weeks, which are insulting to the intelligence of the people,' he said.

When the 'Wings for Victory' savings campaign came around the next year Stokes attacked it from the outset, in much the same fashion. He demanded publicly of the organiser, 'Can Mr (A.V.) Bishop truthfully tell the people of Ipswich that a single extra aeroplane will be provided, however much or little they subscribe?' One of the other organisers of the local campaign, a Mr Shurety, manager of Mann Egerton, replied angrily for Mr Bishop, saying that if Stokes were not known for his integrity he would have to accuse him of financial sabotage. He went on to say,

> It is of course true that no fewer bombers or machine guns would be made if War Savings Certificates were relegated to the limbo of forgotten things. The mass of investors in war certificates do not, regrettably, have current accounts in the joint stock banks. Mr Stokes should look with benevolence on propaganda directed to two ends – to restrict senseless spending and to discourage 'the stocking under the bed'.

It was claimed that Ipswich had exceeded its target that year, but not too much should be made of that. Nationally, the Savings Campaigns had decided that it was far better to set a low target which would be triumphantly exceeded than, as in 1942, set a high target unlikely to be met, which would then be seen as a failure.

War savings weeks became part of the year's ceremonial round, along with the parading Boy Scouts, the rumble of processional tractors driven by the Women's Land Army, the marching feet of Special Constables, the pipes and drums of the Black Watch, or groups of wardens lining up on the Town Hall steps for ceremonial group photos. In May 1943 over one thousand Guides and 300 Brownies camped at Alderman Road. Schoolchildren were roped in to make the numbers up, two from every school, with two male teachers and any members of the Education Committee who had nothing else to do.

'Salute the Soldier' week in 1944 raised more than £1,000,000 in Ipswich and was combined with Youth Athletic Sports Days. Ceremonial plaques were presented to the mayor by Lord Belstead, the Chairman of the War Savings Committee, and Colonel Rice was also present.

War savings drives were not the only call on the purse of local people. The rattle of the collecting tin for flag days was also common in the town centre. Those licensed by the Watch Committee in the years 1943-5 included Remembrance Day, the Earl Haig Fund, Warrior's Day, the Lord Lieutenant of Suffolk's Fund, the British Red Cross Society, the French Red Cross, the Duke of Gloucester's Red Cross, St John Ambulance, the YMCA, the NSPCC, the Waifs and Strays, the Salvation Army's Self Denial Appeal, the Catholic Women's League, Huts and Canteens Committee, United Aid to China, The British Empire Cancer Fund, King George's Fund for Sailors, the British Sailors' Fund, Soldiers, Sailors and Airmen's Families Association, or the National Air Raid Distress Fund.

92 H. Samuel's jewellers in Tavern Street converted for the promotion of National Savings

One can't help feeling that so many charities, many in the same field, must have been tripping over each other to some extent, or that the enormous resources behind some made it impossible for those charities having to carry a great deal of the social burden of the war to compete. In the three years or so of its existence the Mayor's Prisoner of War Fund, a charity with a very direct connection to Ipswich, under the direction of the manager of Mann Egerton, only raised about £20,000.

By 1944 the relentless series of drives was beginning to provoke resistance. Circular No. 1649 of the Board of Education brought to the attention of the Ipswich Education Committee the more that needed to be done to turn 'Make Do and Mend' into a real public success. The committee recorded 'the steps which had been taken in the past without any appreciable results to interest housewives in the matter,' and noted, with a collective sigh that can still be heard emerging from the Minute Book, 'But still, after discussions with HM Inspectors, the Principal of the Women's Evening College and the supervisor of school canteens are going to arrange demonstrations.' These were held on 2 May at the advice centre in the Buttermarket. By 22 May 1944 the 'Make Do and Mend' demonstrations had been discontinued. The Principal of the Women's Evening College also gave help to Messrs Footman, Pretty and Co. in the organisation of a 'Mend and Make Do' exhibition in Waterloo House on the Cornhill. Garments were lent from the school classes, but 'It was disappointing to note the lack of response from the public.' Finally, they had to admit, 'Girls are more interested in dressmaking than make do and mend.'

93 *A Dornier DO17 bomber on display in Christchurch Park. The plane was forced down at Wickhambrook and taken on tour to various places around the county.*

Empire Day in 1942, as described by R. Douglas Brown, was a major celebration of patriotism and solidarity:

> In Ipswich, for example, the Mayor Alderman R.F. Jackson took the salute outside the Town Hall as units of the Home Guard, the Army Cadets, Sea Cadets, Air Training Corps, the Scouts, the Guides, the Boys' and Girls' Brigades, the St John Ambulance cadets, the NFS and the ARP Messengers marched past. Later Ipswich saw its largest ever parade of the ATC.

Two years later, on 14 April 1944, the Education Committee outlined its plans for Empire Day that year. Mr Job was going to train a Youth Choir and the Salvation Army Band would accompany the hymns. The Army Cadets would be in charge of orders for the day and there would be two processions, one for pre-service training units and one for voluntary organisations. The Bishop's Advisory Council for Youth Work suggested that the official form of service be used. The great and the good were

94 *The High Street Exhibition Gallery of the Museum was used intensively during the war years for educational film shows and all kinds of exhibitions, including the 'Wings for Victory' savings scheme in 1943.*

invited, the Bishop, the Rural Dean and the President of the Free Church Council, and it looked like the propaganda triumph of 1942 would be repeated. But by 5 May neither the Lord Bishop or Quentin Hogg could take part in Empire Youth Day and it was decided to cancel, although supervisors could arrange something in their individual centres. Then they had to plan for the following year.

For 1945 it was decided to make the celebration voluntary. Each centre could make its own arrangements but a prominent public celebration would not be held. It was agreed to move the popular and separate Youth Week so that it culminated in Empire Day; the suggested Youth Thanksgiving for the End of the War service would not be held after all, but also combined with Empire Youth Day, and no collection would be made at the church service. It looks as though the organisers were concerned that if they were not careful then a lack of real support for Empire Day would become too evident.

Nineteen

Errant Girls

It still comes as something of a shock when talking about the war to a group of older people when a highly respectable, white-haired old lady speaks of the occasion she was offered ten shillings for a good time by an American serviceman. Yet there is no doubt that this was an important element of life in wartime Ipswich. The dispassionate reports of the Medical Officer for Health make it quite clear that the war led to profound changes in the area of sexuality. Dry as these reports are, they are irrefutable evidence of the massive changes that took place. The Medical Officer did his best not to spell matters out, but the figures he gives tell a clear story. Ten thousand people in Ipswich were away from home, most of them men, including married men, in the Army. Logically, therefore, the number of births should be lower than in peacetime. But the birth-rate was increasing as each year went by:

> A total of 1,786 live births were registered in Ipswich in 1945 as compared with 1,774 the previous year. This represents a birth rate per thousand of the estimated civil population of 20.1. This rate compared with the pre-war rate of 15.4 in the year preceding the war is obviously weighted to the advantage of the birth rate owing to the absence of some 10,000 of our normal population which would form the denominator of the ratio [i.e fertility levels appear to have increased]. However, on comparing the actual number of live births we find there were 1,459 in 1938 as against 1,786 in the year under consideration, thus showing an actual rise. The number of illegitimate births in 1938 was 59 compared with 251 this year.

He did not attempt to calculate those births to married women whose husbands were away from home (some authorities did) but there is only one conclusion to be drawn from these figures.

Unmarried girls were also having more children. In the report for 1946 the crucial figures from the table of births by sex and legitimacy are as follows:

Illegitimate births

1936	56	1942	106
1937	71	1943	95
1938	59	1944	189
1939	74	1945	251
1940	77	1946	204
1941	79		

It is no coincidence that the major alteration at the beginning of 1944 was the arrival of so many American troops in the previous year. Mrs Gray suggests that at a certain point morals seemed to go out of the window. She says that her own woman doctor helped very many girls who had got pregnant, even though it was illegal, and she also says that in every area there was a women who knew what to do if you hadn't left it too late.

The calendar of cases brought before the magistrates in 1943-4 underlines the same story: a woman warned for soliciting; two women charged with committing indecent acts in an air-raid shelter, although this case was not served and dismissed; a man charged with procuring a 13½-year-old girl for immoral purposes; five women charged for being in protected areas or 'premises appropriated for use by allied powers', one of whom was fined £10 or two months in prison if she didn't pay while the other four got fines from £1 to £2. Failure to produce an ID card, being in a regulated area and improper use of an air-raid shelter jointly brought one woman one month. There were also a number of cases involving indecent assault on boys under sixteen, one male was charged with soliciting and another with being in a prohibited area.

The creation of so many public shelters, some provided with beds and open at all hours, provided opportunities for sex and caused the Council problems:

November 1943 Emergency Committee
Mr Sisam reported the use being made of the public shelter for immoral purposes. The Chief Constable reported that the Magistrates Clerk would advise the Council that these shelters were public places and cases could therefore be taken before the Magistrates. It was agreed that it was undesirable to close the shelters to the public and the only course was to take these cases before the Magistrates.

It was not just the shelters that proved so convenient. The public parks, especially Christchurch, were popular in the blackout. On 11 February 1944 the Watch Committee received a letter from the Education Committee dated 26 January asking it to consider 'the question of the moral danger in the streets of Ipswich at night-time. After discussion it was suggested that a system of voluntary women patrols might be considered. The Home Office was to be asked if any other town had such a scheme.'

On 19 May 1944 the Education Committee requested 'Some form of supervision in the public parks. Agreed to represent to the Watch Committee deep concern at the standard of behaviour in the parks and the need for immediate action in the way of patrols either through more women police, special constables or women patrols.' The Watch Committee recorded further representations on 2 June 1944 passed on by the Secretary of the Education Committee from the Youth Advisory Committees 'on behaviour in public parks and mainly Christchurch park'.

There was not much practically that could be done. It was reported back to the Education Committee on 21 July 1944 that, 'The Chief Constable had promised that officers on duty in the vicinity would include the park in their patrol where possible. Inspector Harrington very kindly undertook to enlist the help of the American police.'

Attempts were made, not very energetically or successfully by the sound of it, to establish a night shelter for girls stuck in Ipswich:

> 26 August 1944. A letter dated 22 inst. had been submitted from the Secretary of the Women's Section, St Clement's Ward Labour Party expressing concern that there was no shelter for girls in need of protection at night-time. The Secretary to be told provision at Heathfields [the old Work House] was available.

> 22 September 1944. St Clement's Women's Section Labour Party repeat request for night shelter.

Official notices inevitably have a tendency to emphasise the starker aspects of the situation. However, they make it clear that the pronouncements of various 'concerned bodies' quoted in the press were not just examples of puritanical outrage at young people having a good time for once. A selection of them has been put together by R. Douglas Brown:

> The probation officer for Ipswich, Miss W.E. Grant, stated in her report for 1944 that more girls were beyond control and had come before the courts. She referred to girls going out with Americans to the country for dancing; not all girls who went out by transport returned the same night. The West Suffolk County Medical Officer of Health told a Sudbury audience:
> 'Unbelievable things are happening in some of our villages and people say they can do nothing about it. There are not enough strong people in them to say not only that these things are wrong, but that they must not be.'
> At another meeting – in Newmarket – the Recorder for Ipswich, Mr Grafton D. Pryor, said: 'I am not going to condemn the youth of the country wholesale, but I do say there is a very lax moral note prevailing among some of our young people.'

The memories and comments of local people also create a picture of increased sexual activity. One man, a schoolboy at the time, remembered The Dales (an area of scrub behind the open-air swimming pool) was also used by Americans and their girlfriends. The whole area would be littered with packets of French letters, the first time he had come across them. The boys were convinced the Americans were deliberately sending over extra large sizes as a form of boasting. They used to measure themselves against them in private.

Before the war he was not aware of commercial sex in the town and expects there was simply too little money. Of course, they were aware of which married women had soldiers going in and out when their husbands were away. Some turned a blind eye but in a few cases neighbours would write to the husband. During the war there was a lot of money floating around and prostitution was very obvious. A couple of more middle-class women set up brothels in houses. A lot worked out of the small streets running from Princes Street down to the station. Our schoolboy and his friends could see the women pick up clients, disappear and return in about half an hour. He estimated that some would have 30 to 40 in a day. They were often quite well-known figures in the town. One of them, Olive, went to London after the war and committed suicide soon after; others were girls they had grown up with.

The girls were, of course, playing with fire and it was inevitably the youngest and least experienced that got badly hurt. Dorothy Gray remembers one such tragedy from her time working at Stowmarket:

> One young girl should have been on the bus every day but she got very friendly with the Americans. I am not going to say the name because it is all over and done with, but when I was in reception I could see anybody who was coming, had to mark them in more or less. Well, this particular day the father of this girl turned up, couldn't understand why his daughter hadn't been home all night, did anybody know, so of course one or two people said she'd been friendly with these Americans but it turned out she was a country girl. When they went along this particular lane which was between Needham and Stowmarket and across a field they found an American bivouac that they'd put up with loads of tinned stuff and god knows what in it, but the girl was in there. Unconscious, and she'd got all the money pinned on her – whether or not she survived I do not know, but she'd been very badly used. That was one of the sad things. You had the sad as well as the funny and I never did hear what happened to her because they had to take her to hospital, and as I say that's what her father found. Nowadays there'd be a hell of a police hue and cry.

Some places got a bad reputation that remained for years after the war. A woman and her young girls from the north of England moved unknowingly into one such, Priory Court, where the Unitarian Chapel stands. They found themselves subject to knocks on the door at night, teasing at school and even pointed references from the blue-nosed comedians introducing the strippers at the Hippodrome. It drove them out and the court was renamed.

This was not conventional prostitution. The town had seen nothing like it before or since. Ipswich was full of airmen facing death on every raid and was filling up with troops aware that they were about to be hurled into D-Day. Husbands and boyfriends had vanished to who knew where and might never be seen again. When someone remembers the couples embracing through the wires that surrounded the bases it is the desperation, sadness and loneliness of both boys and the girls that is recalled. It was certainly true that girls were officially encouraged to attend dances at the local bases. Military transport was arranged from pick-up points like the *Cricketers* in Ipswich and formed part of the official duties of some officers, British as well as American. Careful parents kept their daughters away.

The strict rules which governed ordinary courtships could not be maintained either. Father was probably not there to demand his daughters were back exactly on time, and even if he were his daughters now had iron-clad excuses. As Dorothy Gray says,

> If you were in the pictures the siren went and they'd put on the screen that the sirens had gone, and you'd either have community singing in the pictures or they'd continue with the pictures according to how near the problems were. And when the picture had finished or when the singing had finished you'd go in the foyer and kip down there. Any excuse to be out late.

The demands of various wartime duties and jobs also provided greater opportunity for men and women to meet, and there were so many more men for the girls to choose from:

You had so many different tribes, you might well say. There was the Australians, the New Zealanders, Canadians, Yanks when they finally came, there was the Black Watch round here, and my sister used to have the time of her life, she played the field, she enjoyed her war.

War certainly could face people with quite new and unexpected moral problems. One person has told me of how 'early in the war' his mother had married a Canadian airman, who soon afterwards was posted missing, believed killed in action. After two years she met and married a Polish man, but at the end of war the first husband returned. He never told me quite how they resolved matters. These pressures were the background against which other changes in the attitudes of society, that would otherwise have taken decades to occur, took place.

Sex education started in the war. When Ipswich Association of Youth put its proposals for youth clubs to the Education Committee on 11 July 1940 they suggested 'the services of a doctor might be asked for with a view to giving at each Centre frank talks on sex education.' Nothing was done until 3 September 1943, when Mr Cyril Bibby and Miss Violet Swaisland of the Central Council for Health Education delivered three lectures on the practical problems of sex hygiene, not to club members but to adult leaders, closing the centres to do so. '19 November 1943. Sex education lectures to be provided to the teachers desirous of lectures on sex education under the auspices of the Central Council of Health Education.' The Board of Education pamphlet, 'Sex education in Schools and Youth Organisations', was to be used. The committee also discussed talks to parents. Specialist lecturers were to address parents at Western Senior Schools as a trial. Should parents from other schools attend? Should audiences be mixed? By 5 June 1944 they could record with relief that the parents' meeting at Western Senior had been a success despite a relatively small attendance.

Finally the talks, discussed first in 1940, could go ahead:

> 10 January 1945. Sir Drummond Shiels MC, MB to give three lectures illustrated by films to young men on 3 and 17 February and 3 March in the Central Senior Girls School. Arrangements for young women would be made when the success of Sir Drummond's course was known. Sir Drummond is to lecture to parents at Eastern Senior Girls School in March.

The Public Health Committee was responsible for passing on information to the adult community. On 2 September 1943 it was told that the Minister of Health had vetoed both the compulsory registration of V.D. and instruction in the use of prophylactics, but government policy was forced to change under pressure from the military who did not wish to lose large numbers of soldiers to the disease as the figures rose. By the end of the war the Medical Officer of Health for Ipswich could report that many more men and women were seeking medical help in the early stages of syphilis rather than waiting until the disease was in its untreatable stages. What gave the Medical Officer considerable pleasure was the great increase in the numbers of men and women attending clinics and finding they were not infected after all: 'It is encouraging to note that while only 15 female non-venereal cases attended the Centre in 1940, there were 129 patients in this category in 1945.'

The figures for returning servicemen were even more striking. Around 400 had themselves checked on returning to civilian life and 251 were free from any infection. These figures show that the old culture of ignorance, fear and shame concerning sex was disappearing. As the Medical Officer reported, 'This indicates the increasing willingness of persons to seek advice and reassurance and reflects the nationwide publicity campaign against the venereal diseases.' It also shows a greater climate of responsibility and lack of hypocrisy amongst the returning men. The number of births to married women listed at the beginning of this section means that many men, working out when they had last been home on leave, would have had questions on their minds. Yet many, perhaps most, kept these questions firmly to themselves.

Twenty

Bad Boys

If there were errant and wayward girls there were also bad boys. A clear gradient from simple high spirits and a little wildness ran all the way through to vandalism and more serious misbehaviour. Often it is uncertain how this behaviour was to be judged. Wartime certainly provided boys with the opportunity for dangerous behaviour not open to them in peace. David Routh described some of the pranks of his friends:

> The area of The Dales was a special place for him and his friends, who formed the Broomhill Gang. There was no railing around the park and so many ways in and out that the police could not get them for starting fires. In the middle were some disused huts and if necessary you could sleep there overnight. One of their games was to get hold of signal flares and set them off. At first they had to hold the flare at arms length and pull the cord but once some of the boys started getting onto the American bases they got given Verey pistols and by the end most of them had these and fired off the flares. The police couldn't catch them. No one went short of cigarettes from the bases either.

The collecting of shrapnel and other aeroplane relics also provided the opportunity for dangerous games. Russell Bridges recalls:

> On one occasion we were out on our bikes, which had been fitted with trailers behind to carry things in, and we had been collecting leaves near Grundisburgh to use as compost. A plane crashed near Grundisburgh and we rushed over to get to the site just after it had crashed. It was burning and ammunition belts had been thrown clear. These we picked up and hid in the trailers of our bikes under the leaves. As we set off for home we were passed by a policeman on his bike, blowing his whistle and ordering everyone away from the wreck.
>
> In my father's garage we worked the heads free from the cartridges and used to pour the ammunition onto little scraps of paper where it burnt beautifully. Having got rather blasé about them we put one round in my fathers vice and set it off. It burst the casing of the shell and the bullet shot through the garage, through the closed doors, and through the walls of our neighbour's garage. He was a wholesale dealer in sweets and the bullet went through his stock. It was discovered at the end of the war in a crate of sherbet lemons.

Russell Cook was part of a group of six boys fanatically keen on collecting ammunition and bits of planes. His father, who was in the AFS, encouraged him and brought back ammunition from wrecks for his collection. Usually this involved riding at top speed to reach crashes and incidents before they had been properly sealed off. It seems that it took longer for USAAF incidents to be brought under control. Once there they would fill their pockets with whatever they could get hold of and cycle away pursued by the cries of authority. One of the boys had a policeman father and seemed to be very well informed as to what was happening. It led to their raiding the dump on the heath into which all the cleared incendiary bombs had been thrown one dark evening. They also got under the perimeter wire at Woodbridge air base and ransacked planes there. They would come away with whole belts of machine-gun and cannon ammunition. This they would disassemble, extracting the explosive and burning it or sticking shell cases into the ground without the heads and using them as fireworks, besides setting off tracer rounds and other examples of pyrotechnic ingenuity and danger. One favourite game was to arrange bullets on a tray placed over a gas burner and covered over with a dustbin lid and wait for them to ignite. On one occasion the boys were ransacking a crashed Liberator in a wood. One boy was hiding ammunition belts up a tree for later removal when he found a pilot's glove. He picked it up for a souvenir then found the hand was still inside.

Technically, a lot of this was highly illegal: entering prohibited areas, stealing vital munitions, wasting police and fire brigade time as they responded to the shooting flares. It was also very dangerous but, strangely, was viewed as high spirits in a way that taking and selling cigarettes from a shop would not have been.

The most common types of bike in Ipswich during the war were 'ASP's, as they were called – All Spare Parts. With petrol severely rationed and public transport restricted, and people needing to make journeys to isolated posts at all hours of the day and night, the bike became *the* method of transport. They were in short supply and bicycle theft an uncontrollable epidemic. Case after case came before the magistrates, whose records also include a number of cases of boys charged with stealing quantities of sweets from their employers, probably newspaper boys pinching from the local sweet shop.

The peculiar conditions meant it was very easy for boys to miss school. As David Routh said,

> The rule was that if the siren went on the way to school, then if you were more than half the way there you were supposed to go onto school, under half way you were supposed to go home. As far as I was concerned half way to school meant at the school gates.

A number of boys evacuated to Leicester simply stopped going to school altogether. Enver Chaudhri described his time there:

> Our education was supposed to continue while we were at Leicester and our books were sent there, but although I was there for about four months, not one day's teaching did I get. We were supposed to take lessons at Leicester Technical School, and one day we were all requested to attend the college to receive our books, which had arrived. We were assembled in a natural history laboratory, which had a skeleton of an animal on the master's desk. As the books were brought in to be put onto this desk, all the boys made a dash to pick out

the best copies, with the result that the pile fell on top of the skeleton and flattened it. We straightened it up as best we could, but one or two parts wagged that had not wagged before. That was the one and only time we went to the Technical College, and we had no further education at all. Perhaps we were no longer welcome there!

He and his best friend Stephen then spent their time hanging around Leicester learning to smoke from dog-ends presented them by grown-ups, trying to get either sweets or coins out of self-service machines, and similar amusements. When he returned to Ipswich his friend managed to burn down a field of wheat when the two got bored during a sports match.

None of this ranks as major crime but, while Enver and his friends never went any further, it is clear that some boys were at risk of drifting into more anti-social behaviour. A sharp increase in convictions for juvenile delinquency attended the disruption to the schools. The number of young people under 17 found guilty of breaking the law in England and Wales rose by over one third between 1939 and 1941; the figures for malicious damage and petty stealing rose by 70 and 200 per cent respectively. Six times as many small boys were birched on the magistrates orders in 1941 as in peacetime. That year a 17-year-old was sent to prison for looting a bomb-damaged home and two Ipswich boys, aged 12 and 9, got four strokes of the birch for theft on probation. The birching was done at the Town Hall police station. The Watch Committee found there was a growing call on the Remand Home and that for the first time boys were beginning to abscond from it. There was an investigation into setting up a Girls Remand Home, too, but in the meantime Ipswich girls were placed with the Norfolk Remand Home in Bramerton.

As early as 12 February 1943 the Ipswich Trades Council and Labour Party had passed a resolution that 'in view of the increase in juvenile delinquency the Borough Education Committee be asked to consider the setting up of a Child Guidance Clinic at the earliest possible moment.' In 1944 the Education Committee received complaints of serious vandalism by schoolchildren. The local paper carried an advert reading:

> Behaviour of children on trolley-buses complained of. THE ASSISTANCE OF THE PUBLIC IS URGENTLY REQUESTED in securing the prosecution of the persons guilty of DELIBERATE DESTRUCTION OF TROLLEY-BUS FITTINGS AND UPHOLSTERY, which has during the past few months reached serious proportions. Will any passengers witnessing any suspicious action kindly report same immediately to the 'Bus Conductor, a Policeman, or notify me at Russell House.

Two cases in the magistrates records may refer to acts of this sort. Albert Lanton was committed to trial at the assize for sabotage (an act likely to interfere with persons engaged in essential services), and William Studd was convicted of sabotage but only bound over in the sum of £2. (Sabotage here is clearly not the politically motivated act of terrorism.)

> 26 June 1944. North Eastern playing field damage to pavilion windows through stone throwing by two boys. Stoke playing field pavilion had been damaged. Priory Heath Junior Mixed about 40 windows damaged by catapults, damage to shelter trenches.

This last led the Education Committee to ask the Watch Committee on 28 June 1944 whether there was any way to stop the sale of catapults, to which the answer was no.

> 4 September 1944. South Eastern playing field damaged. Greenwich Junior Mixed School theft of wood from shelter trenches and malicious damage to windows, four children responsible.

> 28 May 1945. Further damage had occurred to the shelters on the Priory Heath site and repairs to the gates and fencing had proved to be of no avail in keeping out local youths and children. The Corporation Electric Supply Department to remove electrical fittings and wiring from all trenches.

There was trouble at the youth clubs as well. On 14 October 1943 deliberate damage to the blackout had taken place at the Western Youth Centre and obscene remarks had been written up; a temporary assistant caretaker was partly responsible. There had been trouble with certain members from the Whitton Estate leading to assault on a supervisor.

The Sessions Book for the Eastern Division 1943-9 lists 21 cases tried at Ipswich of minor theft, involving 31 soldiers between 18 and 22. They were often stealing in groups of two to three and most cases included strings of multiple offences. Most were straightforward 'magpie' offences and many offenders were simply bound over, presumably because they were in the forces anyway. A number received borstal sentences.

Robert Beattie, aged 18, received a three-year borstal sentence for breaking into the dwelling house of Diana Ewen at Reydon, and stealing some clothes, and then into the Pier Pavilion at Southwold and stealing £1 0s. 11d. worth of cash and cigarettes. The clothes stolen amounted to a single gentleman's civilian dress, making it look as though Beattie were trying to go Absent With Out Leave for some reason. Convicted in 1943, he was of course released in 1946 having spent the rest of his war safe inside. That may even have been the intention of the judge because it is hard otherwise to reconcile the fate of Beattie with that of Sydney Formston, aged 18, who was clearly part of a group convicted of seven counts of theft but only bound over. Nine cases of servicemen caught AWOL came before the Ipswich magistrates in 1943-4, almost invariably with other petty thefts in addition, such as the one who had stolen three maps to aid his flight.

As the war progressed there was a growing problem of boys and girls getting a little out of control. V.E. night was to provide notable instances. For reasons of morale the wartime approach was to put a brave face on problems, but according to most modern ideas about children's behaviour, the Second World War provided almost optimum conditions for encouraging deviance in children. Absent fathers, one-parent families, disruption, moving home several times, fostering (which is what evacuation amounted to), little or disturbed schooling, perhaps a succession of different men in the house, underlying fear and occasional exposure to violent death and destruction. Even granted that society has changed, it is interesting to think about why the problem was not as bad as it might have been.

Twenty-One
Aliens and Americans

The early years of the war was not a very good time to be a European in England. Even long-term residents with dual nationalities would find themselves investigated closely if they tried to join the forces. Cresswell had instructions from MI5 to report on 'Edward Austin Zantboer, Dutch father, living 15 Parkingtons Dwellings, Bramford, Ipswich; Peter van der Heijden, Dutch father, American mother, wants to join air force.' As early as 12 September 1938 the Chief Constable was sent a list of Germans living in Ipswich to be arrested in the event of an emergency. This list is no longer in the file.

Ipswich was covered by the Aliens Act, which meant that no foreigner could reside in the area without special permission from the Chief Constable, nor were they permitted to own cameras, binoculars or radio equipment without licence. Looking back from the safety of 1945, the unit historian of the 9th Battalion Home Guard laughed at their persistent spying on an elderly German farm labourer near the airport; it was unlikely to have been so funny for the man at the time, when those in his position were taken to the internment camps in Devon or the Isle of Man.

Many of the refugees from Central Europe were German-speaking Jews and often highly educated professionals. There was no point in a German-Jewish doctor applying for a post with the Ipswich Borough medical institutions, however. In 1942 Dr Freitze, late of Prague, applied for the post of Assistant Medical Officer vacated by Dr Meikle. It was suggested that he could be put on a month's contract to see if he would suit. He was not appointed. A year later the post again became vacant:

> Ed. Comm. Minutes April 1942
> The committee then interviewed Dr Ferdinand Frank, at present living in Bradford on Avon Wilts, and Dr Konrad Hirsch living in London. It recommended the appointment of Dr Hirsch for three months in order that it might be ascertained whether he could carry out the duties satisfactorily. Dr Hirsch undertook to commence duty on 11 May as temporary Assistant Medical Officer of Health and School Medical Officer.

Hirsch had fled to Britain in 1936 from the continent, where he had been persecuted because he had Jewish blood. His medical education included three years at Edinburgh University. The story as told by R. Douglas Brown is a minor triumph for toleration, but the truth is rather different. Hirsch was successfully appointed on a three-month contract on 16 May 1942. Forty days later, on 25 June, the Public Health Committee decided not to keep him on beyond the trial period. The Education Committee had no real option but to follow suit (as School Medical Officer he was technically employed separately by them) and on 8 September 1942

> It was decided on the motion of Alderman J.R. Staddon seconded by Mr G.A. Mallet that Dr Hirsch did not fill the requirements of the Council and that when his three months probationary period ended he be informed that his services will be no longer required. Mrs Lewis voted against this decision.

As the war progressed so the refugees were swelled by the numbers of men belonging to the various Free European forces who had made their way to England to continue the fight. These were often rather strange and insular units about which it is difficult to get details. In East Anglia there was a Czech RAF squadron (311), two Belgian squadrons (349, 350), eight Free French squadrons and Danish and Norwegian ones too. Before D-Day Free French paratroopers trained at Nacton. They were actually a Breton unit with Breton officers earmarked for the liberation of Brittany.

But before the Americans the largest single grouping was undoubtedly the Poles. With their distinctive caps and shoulder capes they struck local people as sad, exotic and romantic. All three branches of their armed forces were present in the Ipswich area. The Polish Army had a unit at Westerfield whose job it was to run armoured trains throughout East Anglia. There were 10 officers and 30 men. Since the days of the Russian Civil War Poles had supposedly been experts in armoured trains. At various times there were Polish squadrons and Polish flyers based at Ipswich airport. One of these was a prince, Prince Obolensky, and he is buried in Ipswich cemetery.

In 1940 Julian Kowolski of the 302 (Polish) Squadron based at Duxford shot down a Junkers 88 near Ipswich and was forced to land damaged at Ipswich airport. On 30 July 1940 Sgt Chlistowski, based at Ipswich, was killed in an air accident at St Osyth in Henley (Ipswich Airport log book). Poles were back at the airport in November 1943 and Lt. Karpinski appointed Polish Liaison Officer. The three Polish destroyers stationed in the mouth of the Orwell were mentioned in Chapter Ten. Martlesham also hosted a Polish squadron, who brought a complete V1 rocket there that had landed without exploding. It was captured by members of the Polish Home Army, at extreme risk to themselves, and retained for scientific analysis by Polish fliers.

In September 1941 the *Ipswich Journal* reported the large numbers of Polish officers attending the performances of the London Philharmonic at the Public Hall. In 1942 the Anglo-Polish ballet performed for a week at the Ipswich Hippodrome. In 1943 the Earl of Stradbroke became the president of an Anglo-Polish Friendship Society, organising different events in Ipswich and elsewhere, and a Polish Army Choir toured the region. Christchurch Mansion hosted an art exhibition of sketches of Polish troops in their camps around the country.

Then there were the Irish, quite possibly a bigger group but one which has gone largely unnoticed. Technically citizens of a neutral power, not an ally, and containing a section within their community that considered itself to be at war with the United Kingdom, Irish labourers nevertheless dominated building sites, the lifting of sugar-beet and several other essential aspects of daily life. Some had joined the British Army, yet just before D-Day Richard Brown commented on the group in terms that show his own prejudices but also reveal the true complexity of the situation:

> Wonder how much has already been said to Jerry agents about our aerodrome positions and planes by the Irish labourers over here? There are crowds over here, a wild lot too by reports, and they regularly go home each seven weeks for a short stay in order to avoid paying income tax over here on their earnings. Den said the traffic at Stranraer was very heavy at weekends. Glad we are taking care of such an obvious leakage and wonder what the next steps will be?

Future research may well expand our knowledge of these various groups, add to the list and demonstrate that they played a greater part than has really been appreciated. It was inevitable, however, that their contributions, as well as those of the Commonwealth forces (Canadians were based at Ipswich Airport for a time and the South African government organised large-scale food aid in the form of donations of dried fruit to the elderly), would be overshadowed by the final arrival of the Americans. Even before the American government had entered the war some units of the LDV had been equipped with obsolete American rifles, Ipswich men had been sent to train as flyers with the American Air Force in Florida, Ransomes & Rapier had been receiving supplies under Lend-Lease, the inhabitants of Ipswich, New England had equipped and dispatched a mobile canteen, and the Eagle Squadron, which consisted of Americans who had volunteered to join the RAF, had been stationed at Martlesham.

When the troops arrived they brought with them a sense of glamour, of overwhelming might, and of an inevitable, if distant, final victory. Ipswich had no American bases as such but it was the major centre in the whole of Suffolk for Americans on leave, and their bases at Martlesham and Debach were only a cycle ride away. David Routh remembers as a schoolboy seeing the men on leave at Broomhill Baths. They would go there with picnics of food from the bases and set gramophones on the grass surround to the pool. It was there that he first saw men using powder and deodorant; it was carbolic soap for him. They introduced circuit training to sports and the butterfly stroke. When first seen this led to an appeal to the president of the Ipswich Swimming Club about whether it was alright. Temporary extensions were put on the boards for exhibitions of specialist diving.

To the boys of Ipswich the Americans were not only heroes, but also the source of sweets. Dorothy Gray thought them full of themselves, 'God's gift to women'. It is clear, however, that many girls and women agreed with this self-assessment. Getting an invitation to visit an American base became something of a major goal for many locals. Just looking at the gates of an American base became something of an outing, as Richard Brown describes:

> It's been hot with not a sign of a cloud and we've cycled out to find Debach aerodrome. Undoubtedly it is an American Liberator station. We were stopped at a road halt by an American in green khaki with peaked field cap, green sunglasses and a large half-smoked cigar, who inspected our identity cards very courteously. Quite a lot of similar chaps were about with the short American rifle and several jeeps, trucks, cars and a concrete mixer passed us manned by Negroes, also adorned with white rimmed green sunglasses. Several planes were about the dispersal points, all Liberators, and mostly the new aluminium colour. The runways were huge.

British civilians were encouraged to fraternise with the Americans and Welcome Clubs were organised. The one in Ipswich had premises in Tower Street. It was meant as a place where people could socialise away from the pubs. So, gradually, an American Ipswich grew up, with the Welcome Club, an American PX nearby, between the club and Lloyds Avenue, lorry service to the bases, a centre for black troops in St Peters Street, a post for American military police in the railway station, apparently, and favourite pubs like the *Mitre*. David Routh described the social club:

> There was an American service club at the top of Lloyds Avenue. They had a jukebox, perhaps the first in Ipswich, that played all the swing records, some from bands you had never heard of, on the old 78s. A friend of mine had a mother who worked there and she would bring home all the records after they came out of the box.

American troops poured into Ipswich on packed lorries from seven o'clock in the evening at the weekends and were picked up in Princes Street at eleven. English girls were taken to dances on the bases from the *Cricketers*. Those girls and Americans who had passes to go to Felixstowe might travel back on the last train, known as the 'passion wagon'. It was quite usual for hands to remove all the light bulbs from the coaches.

The Americans worked hard to ensure a smooth reception from their war-battered hosts. There had already been a delicate amount of food-aid, and a whole range of other goodwill events were staged:

> 10 January 1944. During the holiday season American troops in the district had entertained between 600 and 700 schoolchildren and in return the teachers in collaboration with the WVS were arranging for scholars to entertain a number of American soldiers. Talks in schools on American life and history were being arranged through a special service officer of the USAAC.

> 20 November 1944. About 25 pupils from St Helens Junior Mixed school had been invited to a party at an American air station on a Sunday when the children would perform one of their school plays for the men.

There was clearly a black market in American military stores, which were sold in some numbers in Ipswich. It was against the law simply to have such items in one's possession, 'buying, detaining or receiving', so it was easy enough to get a conviction, even if the Americans selling from the base or the street traders in Ipswich were never convicted. The Magistrates Court Register lists four people convicted

95 *A black USAAF serviceman at a game in Portman Road. He seems to have created almost as much interest as the game itself.*

of having American Army boots each valued 18s. 6d., two for having an American military torch value 6s. 9d, two for having army clothing value 16s. 9d., someone with £7 17s. worth of army clothing, four for having army blankets worth 25s., followed by three cases, all dismissed, of possessing American Army overalls. These cases were only the tip of a very large iceberg.

The Americans brought with them a problem all their own: their attitude to race. As the air bases had first to be built, large numbers of the first Americans to arrive were black, the first sizeable group of black people seen in Ipswich for many years. A woman told me of her aunt who, quite late one night, during the blackout when the light in the hallway had been dimmed, went to answer a knock at the front door. When she opened it, she said, she saw nothing but a set of teeth in the air. An American had been billeted on her. After the initial surprise the two seemed to get along. There were, no doubt, English racists but most English people had no ideas about how they were expected to respond. These were allies, they had been told to welcome American forces, and, today anyway, some people say the black Americans were more popular, being in general more polite, quieter and respectful than the pushier white troops. One woman explained that not only had they been carefully groomed to be on their best behaviour but they found themselves better treated than they had ever been before and were suitably grateful. American Army negro choirs sung to packed audiences. Black musicians were popular for dances and pubs.

Black Americans, especially those from the South, lived under the oppression of legal segregation and in fear of lynching. So in Ipswich a Women's Voluntary Service member quoted by R. Douglas Brown, who helped in the local YMCA, found she had to persuade the American blacks that 'they were allowed to walk on the pavement when white people were there, too, that they could use the trolley buses, go into restaurants, shops, etc'. (*East Anglia 1943*) This also came as a shock to white Southern soldiers, especially when they saw local girls with black servicemen. A white ex-serviceman with whom I spoke 'explained' that the blacks who had come over first were able to convince the local girls they were not black but were Native American chiefs; Southern whites could not tolerate this wicked deception of the naive English and so fights started. The truth or otherwise of this is beside the point.

Tensions between black and white American servicemen were undoubtedly high but it is difficult to get evidence in this sensitive area. What lay behind the shooting by black private David Cobb of white Lieutenant Cobney, reported on 1 January 1943 in the *East Anglian Daily Times*? It was said to have arisen out of a dispute over Cobb's being kept on sentry duty. But after Cobb had shot the officer in a struggle he turned, apparently, to the surrounding men to ask for their approval. He was hanged.

Local people remember the fights between black and white servicemen in Ipswich pubs. They noticed the violent way American Military Police beat black servicemen. It quite clearly shocked many of them at the time. Ipswich was the first town from which American officer Colonel (later Brigadier-General) Oliver Haines, of the Inspector General's Department of the US Army, reported after he was sent to look into relations between black and white. He is quoted by R. Douglas Brown.
Dated Ipswich, 21 November, he wrote:

> Blacks were stationed at Eye, at Debach near Ipswich, and in Haughley Park near Stowmarket, where they were particularly popular with the locals because of their swing bands and dances. The white troops were in different towns – Martlesham, Wattisham and Horham. For both races the night life was in Ipswich, with its 150 public houses. There being more white than black troops, their commanders decided that the whites should have access to the majority of places of entertainment, and so just eight pubs, a Co-op dance hall and a Red Cross club were 'reserved' for blacks alone.

This in effect created a segregated Ipswich. Essentially, the black pubs were on the outskirts, the *Mitre*, *Dove* and the *Ivy Leaf* in St Helens, the *Tankard* in Tacket Street and the *Blue Coat Boy* in the Old Cattle Market, for example, while the town centre pubs were white. The famous *Daily Express* cartoonist, 'Giles', lived just outside Ipswich in the village of Tuddenham at the time. At first his local pub served black American, many of whom he befriended and took home. Photographs have been published of him playing the pub piano with black Americans and of them in his garden. The pub was later designated 'white', however, and the management took down all the photographs, much to Giles' lasting disgust. I have heard that the fish shops were segregated. Cinemas were divided into halves for white and black troops, because of the fights that broke out, especially if an English girl were seen with a black American.

The effect of all this on the local population was, in part, confusion. Paul Taylor, who lived in St Peters Street, remembers the Christmas party which the black troops

96 *Outside the Margaret Catchpole in Cliff Lane the vicar is flanked by a black USAAF serviceman and a Chinese engineer sent by the Nationalist Government to study at Ransomes & Rapier.*

who used the Drill Hall as a club put on for local children. He remembers being puzzled as to why all the American Christmas parties were publicised save for this one. Those who were already on the left (like Giles), or at least liberal in their political sympathies, were genuinely shocked at the strength of American racism, while many more either adopted it themselves or found their own existing prejudices strengthened. Women have told me that 'of course, we thought that women who would go with black soldiers were the lowest of the low. It is how we felt then.' Some clearly didn't feel this way because mixed race babies were born. A sad little story was told me of a married woman in the Wherstead Road area of Stoke who was known by her watchful neighbours to be pregnant by a black serviceman. When she gave birth the gossips thought she had got away with it because the new-born baby was light skinned, but when the baby naturally turned darker the gossip mill got going again. Another woman, who was just a small child at the time, told me how it was the custom to put all babies outside in their front gardens in the afternoon and how she liked to come down the street looking in each pram. She was especially fascinated by what is obviously the same black baby, as she had never seen another one. One day it had vanished. She didn't know why at the time but later realised that, although the mother could have passed off a white baby and the father accepted it, a black one would be too obvious and would hurt his pride too much.

One lady said that black Americans were followed by the Mexican Americans, who kept pretty much to themselves but could use the 'white' pubs. She had known three and fallen in love with one, Frank, who spoke both English and Spanish. She became pregnant and they wanted to marry. Her father gave his permission but her mother was uncertain. American officials pointed out the difficulties they would face, the family being illegal immigrants who lived along the Rio Grande and worked in cotton fields. Apparently, they offered to help Frank move to a different part of the States but his family needed him. In the end his officers posted him away, but she kept in contact with his family and does so to this day.

97 *The painting of St Francis at Kesgrave Pond was done by Italian-American airmen from Martlesham.*

With so many fit young men around, trained to be highly aggressive and far from home, Ipswich pubs could be pretty violent places. Some were definitely naval, and woe betide the innocent soldier who crossed their threshold. There was also considerable tension between English servicemen and American ones, who were considered 'overpaid, over-sexed, and over here'. When talking to the Ipswich Stroke Club, I was quite taken aback when one elderly gentleman started to say how much he hated Americans. He had, he said, been in a unit in Normandy that had lost men because the American unit that was supposed to be protecting their flank was actually in a brothel. On his return to Ipswich, he had taken his rifle with him down town on leave in the evening but was stopped by a military policeman who asked him what he was doing with it. Apparently, he told him he was going to shoot as many Yanks as he could. The M.P. explained to him exactly how much time he would spend inside and talked him round. He still felt the same, however, and the anger was still visible in him. The other men present gave the impression of finding his views comprehensible but extreme.

But, despite these undercurrents, the overwhelming reality was that the Americans were on our side. Every dawn the people of Ipswich could hear the young American men fly planes over their heads and every evening see them return, sometimes knocked about and out of formation, and realise what had happened to those they saw about the town. One of the best pieces in Richard Brown's diary describes the experience:

> Later some race over westwards, we see if they are still in fours, and they have an 'in-a-hurry' look as they dash for home. Then out of the cloud, sometimes so misty that they use their searchlights or wing lights, come low-flying Forts in groups or wings of twelve – if there are no losses and if some haven't peeled off at other 'dromes on the way. Stragglers follow, and these sometimes have a stationary prop or the bomb door may be stuck open. Some circle Debach and land and then silence shows another op has been accomplished but we don't know what it was.

Battered and damaged American planes often force-landed or crashed in and around Ipswich. There are differing accounts of what is essentially the same story: '(718) Friday 5 November 1943, 1515 – Crew of 10 from American Flying Fortress baled out, landing safely at Newbourn. Plane flew on, out of Felixstowe Police Section.' (Felixstowe Police Station War Diary)

> On 5 November, a Fortress returning from an attack on Gelsenkirchen, in Germany, crossed the coast with only one engine still operating. At 3,000 feet the 23-year-old

pilot ordered his crew to bail out, then set the plane on auto pilot on a course which would take it back out to sea. As he prepared to jump himself, he realised that the plane was in a downward glide that would take it to the centre of Ipswich so, placing his life at risk, he returned to the controls, pulled the Fortress out of its dive at 200 feet, turned it away from the town, cut the engine and crash-landed it on its belly in a field on the outskirts of the town.

(R. Douglas Brown, *East Anglia 1943*)

Other incidents show clearly not only the sacrifices of the Americans but also how dangerous it was to have so many friendly bombers flying overhead. In one particularly tragic case three British soldiers were killed and one injured by parts of a Flying Fortress that exploded over Felixstowe.

(940) Tuesday 7 November 1944, about 1455 – American Flying Fortress bomber, No.D …561, Home Station, Thorpe Abbots, Norfolk broke up in the air and parts fell in Langer Road area, Felixstowe, the main parts on Coastguard Cottages, near Royal Observer Corps post at Martello Tower, Langer Road. Some of crew baled out between Ipswich and Felixstowe. One found dead at Wherstead. Two bodies fell in Langer Road. Coastguard Cottages used as H.Q. of No. 3 Anti Aircraft Practice Camp (RAF Regiment) set on fire and three members of the Regt – 1022686, Cpl D. Postlethwaite (Armourer), 1281687, LAC L.P. Arrom (General Duties), 1304119, LAC A.C. Coward (Clerk, General Duties) – were killed. F/Lt. Duckworth King, second in command of the unit, was burned and taken to hospital.

(Felixstowe Police Station War Diary)

3 January 1945. Mustang WAF 44-14212 from 434 Squadron USAAF aircraft overshot after continuous cutting of engine and eventually came to rest after pushing through the boundary of the [Ipswich] airfield.

(PRO AIR 28/405 Ipswich)

Forced landings and crashes of American planes were treated as a security matter and were usually taken over very quickly by the Americans themselves, as this report from a local ARP warden makes clear:

DATE OF RAID 26 March 1945
BRIEF HISTORY OF RAID
At 1640 hrs plane heard diving to earth: located and reported by S/W Gooden. On instruction of Police Inspector Green, Head Warden Richardson not permitted to approach incident, information re. description obtained from American Officer. Control ultimately taken over by American AA ambulance and NFS arrived and standing by. Crashed aircraft American P51 (Mustang).

The story of the Americans in Suffolk continued for perhaps another fifty years after the end of the war. It had a deep and abiding effect on the region and will remain part of what gives East Anglia its special nature.

PARTING SHOTS

Twenty-Two
The Birth of the Teenager:
Controlling Youth

The war saw the first formal provision made for all school leavers in the town. The teenage years became a distinct stage in life, a special sector around which a whole series of professionalisms and bureaucracies were built up, bristling with problems, concerns and issues. How were the different services to be organised and controlled, and who was to resource them? The issues were addressed through the minutiae of the various changes being made, but these were often deliberately fudged. ARP and Home Guard, rationing and the blackout may all have vanished by the time of writing, but 'youth culture', really appearing in wartime for the first time, remains with us.

There had, of course, been various clubs and recreational things for young adults to do before the war, commercial and otherwise: the Police Lads Club in Arcade Street, various other groups connected with churches, and the Co-op. In 1942 the Education Committee made grants to a number of independent groups, providing a rough list of those which were in existence before the war: Ipswich Co-operative Youth Club, Ipswich Boy Scouts local organisation, St Bartholomew's Social Club, 1st Coy Ipswich Boys Brigade, 1 and 2 Coys Girls Training Corps (a recent wartime creation), St Joseph's Youth Centre, Alan Road Youth Service and 9th Suffolk Cadets. However, there had been no real attempt by either local or national government to get involved.

When the Ipswich Association of Youth was first established in the early summer of 1940, largely through the initiative of Mr Whitmore, it was not officially linked to the Education Committee and was run more or less directly by the supervisors of each centre working directly with the young people. They were given the use of school playing fields and rooms and at first provided with a straightforward series of activities likely to appeal to their users. On 11 July 1940 the Education Committee acknowledged the creation of the Ipswich Association and allowed its facilities to be used as an HQ in the Youth Office, 19 Tower Street. At first the scheme did not make much use of educational premises. The main playing fields to be used for inter-centre events were those at the Bourne End Police Lads Club, swimming was at St Matthew's and Fore Street, the gym at the Police Lads Club in Arcade Street was used, and ten rooms were set aside in Holywell for the Gainsborough estate area, as well as Whitton Old School and church hall. But these venues were not seen by the committee as suitable for the younger teenagers, there being some concern

98 *Northgate High School encouraged its senior pupils to help with the harvest every year. This photograph was taken in 1943. The headmistress complained of the prejudice of farmers and their unwillingness to employ the girls.*

about school leavers mixing with those who had already been at work for some years. Older teenagers had already formed habits, such as drinking and smoking and the other pleasures of working-class men and women, that were viewed as undesirable.

It was better to provide youth clubs within secondary schools which catered primarily for leavers from that school. This probably reconciled the teachers to seeing 'their' facilities used outside hours but was to have unforeseen consequences. Inevitably it associated the culture of school with the culture of youth clubs, so that organisers saw themselves and were seen as somehow 'teacher-like'. For the disaffected, those that youth club organisers have argued ever since they most wanted to reach, it was a turn-off. Moreover, as youth clubs were only allowed to organise dances for their members, and not sell or advertise tickets, each club became firmly associated with a geographical division of town, and mixing between areas and getting out of the neighbourhood difficult. Going to a youth club in another part of town invariably ran the risk of friction and fights, and the insularity of the council estates was perpetuated.

Each youth club was to be provided with hobby, craft and art equipment. Camping, hiking and rambling were to be organised and a paid warden and wardenness found for each centre. The proposals included one that 'the services of a doctor might be asked for with a view to giving at each Centre frank talks on sex,' which was not implemented, but was not to go away.

In January 1941 the Education Committee saw the results of the first year of the scheme. At Arcade Street Youth Centre around 100-110 boys turned up on the opening night, but soon there were 153 boys, with 80 waiting. Girls joined later. The group activities included physical training, ju-jitsu, boxing and Keep Fit. Activities for the girls including country dancing, rejected unanimously in favour of ballroom dancing, and home nursing, which 'didn't seem to go well'. A discussion group was growing, a dramatics group was to be tried, and an association football tournament had been set up. At Western 127 boys and 25 girls had turned up and at Eastern 140 boys. Each group was developing slightly different approaches; for example, the ponderous slogans of the Eastern club – 'Live Pure, Speak True, Right Wrong, Honour the King' – had no equivalents at the others.

99 *For the Youth Day celebrations, which coincided with the August Holidays at Home scheme, the Borough boarded over the Round Pond in Christchurch Park for the inter-youth club boxing championships.*

A part-time supervisor and four paid helpers had been appointed at each club. Arcade Street had a full-time warden plus four helpers. They were then organised into a separate Youth Committee that reported officially to the Education Committee. By the summer of 1941 the Trades Council had begun to badger the Youth Committee to extend youth club provision to every part of the town. In 1941 the government required all 16- to 21-year-olds, male and female, to register and to be given advice as to what youth organisations and forms of youth service were available, and in one way or another pressure was put on young people to join youth clubs and other organisations. This was really the first time the government had sought to mobilise school leavers, both directly, as members of feeder bodies to the services and voluntary and civil defence units, and also in terms of 'hearts and minds'. So, in 1942, the rather *ad hoc* Ipswich arrangement was identified as unusual by the Board of Education and in 1943 the Youth Committee was taken over by the Education Committee. The Education Committee set up a Youth Advisory Committee to which the Youth Council reported.

This became a very large body with every single interested party demanding representation. Control of youth work was taken away from the teachers and others running the youth clubs by a body on which religious interests and those of the pre-service groups predominated. The list is so extensive that a full committee meeting of 24 people probably involved more people than the attendance at some of the events they ran: District Boys Brigade, Boy Scouts Association, National Association of Boys Clubs, Girl Guides, Girls Friendly Society, Girls Life Brigade Battalions, Girls Training Corps, Ipswich Working Girls Club, National Association of Girls Clubs, principals of Technical Institutes, supervisors of Youth Centres, Inspector Harrington for the police, Sea Cadets, ATC and Army Cadets, Ipswich Industrial Co-operative Society Education Committee, Roman Catholic organisations, the Church of England, the Diocesan Youth Adviser, Ipswich and District Free Church Council and the Salvation Army. The organisations had direct links to the General

Educational Committee and were actively lobbying at the national level with the Board of Education.

In May 1944 the government was demanding information, which club supervisors were to collect, on how many members attended technical evening schools, pre-service units, St John Ambulance, NFS Messengers or any other form of national service. That year also saw the holding of an elected Ipswich Youth Parliament to discuss post-war developments. A hundred Youth MPs attended the first session held at the library lecture room on 1 March to discuss the Housing and Local Plan. This was one of many ways in which ordinary people were encouraged to take part in debates to decide the nature of post-war Britain. From the BBC Brains Trust to educational discussion groups in the services, debate around the Beveridge Report and its proposals was almost universal.

The second session of the Youth Parliament took place in the Art Gallery of the Museum on 16 May 1944 to discuss secondary education. The original proposal, drafted before the meeting, had been intended to endorse the three-tier system that was actually adopted nationally but was already highly controversial. The Parliament refused to endorse this and voted for what was in fact a comprehensive system under a different name: 'to avoid too high a degree of specialisation the three types of school should be included in one building and the pupils share the facilities for general education; schools of arts and crafts and commerce should be included within the junior technical schools'.

This did not go down too well with an establishment already unhappy that its youth registration scheme was not working: 271 of the school leavers in 1944 had said they were going to join a youth organisation but only 42 had done so. The scheme's continuing existence was in question, although in the end it went ahead. Youth club organisers were being canvassed for their views on the future developments of the clubs. Their suggestions for the coming year were practical and linked to the 'Make Do and Mend' campaign. Courses in household maintenance, re-washering taps, fitting fuses and dyeing materials should continue, as should a personal appearance course, and boys (including 'some of the toughest') were taking cookery courses. Supervisors were also still proposing without success sex education courses for members.

They wanted full-time education extended to 16, part-time to 18 to avoid the need for evening schools, and were strongly in favour of restricting hours of employment, objecting to part-time employment of children on paper rounds. Finally, they felt that films were not useful in youth work because cinema films were better. Their remarks still convey a patronising manner, however:

100 *Doris Friend stands next to Flying Officer Lawson Brown on a St John Ambulance trip to RAF Sutton Heath.*

> It was thought that if young people were taught to appreciate good books at school and if youth centres were provided with suitable libraries then the reading of many modern unwholesome novels might be remedied.
>
> Efforts to interest at least a substantial portion of the older members in music other than jazz are proving successful.
>
> Girls are more interested in dressmaking than make do and mend.

Youth club participation in Empire Day had proved a bit of a damp squib and on 21 July 1944 application was made by the Ipswich Club of the Young Communist League of Great Britain to be represented on the Youth Council. It had simultaneously suggested that 1945 should be declared 'Salute the Child' year to follow 'Salute the Soldier', and was seeking to extend its influence on the Council. The proceeds of a dance at Western Schools had been donated to a children's home run by *Pravda*. Reasonable proposals that it should be represented if it had the same number of members as other groups were blocked when the number of members an organisation had to have before it was entitled to representation was raised from

50 to 100. The Young Communists were turned down and they were also denied permission to hire the Central School for their meetings as before. Instead a church youth council was to be added. The actual users of facilities for young people were now in a marginalised minority.

After lengthy discussion the Youth Council was unanimous that any attempt to introduce religious observance or denominational teaching of any kind would be unwelcome. The Education Committee was not pleased with this or with the proposals from the Youth Club leaders and formally entered their complaint on 21 July 1944, regretting the 'absence from the proposals of any reference to service to the Community or spiritual aims'.

Some centres had had reasonably successful discussion groups on religious matters. One reported a 'Brains Trust' composed of four clergymen, two Church of England, one nonconformist and one Roman Catholic, at which the questions were of a surprisingly high level. The organisers remarked the interest of members in religious topics, 'although this interest may not often be obvious'.

What the *ex officio* representatives really objected to was the fact that discussions were not going their way. On 18 September 1944 it was agreed that the Arcade Street Youth Centre should be open to all members on Sunday evenings to enable them to hear the BBC's series of youth services followed by an epilogue, which in turn would be followed by discussion groups and brains trusts. The Youth Organiser who was to arrange all this presented the report on the operation to the committee on 11 May 1945: '25 attended the first broadcast. As the order of service had not been known all attending could take only a very passive part. The young people left looking bored and weary but they did suggest the next be followed with a discussion.' The results of the discussion were not quite what the Youth Advisory Committee or the BBC would have hoped. One feels, too, that the Youth Organiser was beginning to have some sympathy with the views of the young people who attended:

> Discussions after the second and third services were extremely interesting, the theme of service was ignored and they at once turned their attention to religious matters. The points of view expressed included, 'I don't go to church because it's too dull,' 'If God is all-powerful why doesn't he stop the war?' 'I don't believe in Christianity, look where it's taken us,' 'Some people say we must believe the Old Testament and others argue that it's all a myth; which is correct?'
>
> The reporter felt that the fact the services were organised by the Youth Organiser and not at the request or suggestion of the members contributed considerably towards their failure, and that the uninspiring nature of the bare room, none too clean and containing incendiary bomb cases and Spotters Club identification charts, made it unsuitable.

The supporters of official religion still had not learnt their lesson. On 11 May 1945 the Suffolk Standing Conference of National Voluntary Youth Organisations had suggested they 'help' the Youth Council organise a conference on Christianity and the Young Person. The terseness of the reply can still be felt today: 'The Youth Organiser had been to such a conference in London and felt that while parts of the conference were helpful, most of the lectures were of no practical value to those present.'

Twenty-Three

Last Bombs and the Return of the Evacuees

What had been new and untried in 1940 had become the daily routine by 1943-4. People could not see quite how long the war might last but with Britain, Russia and the USA now lined up against Germany, and the collapse of Italy, the ultimate outcome was pretty clear. Nevertheless the German authorities had not exhausted their efforts to kill and maim civilians. There were five raids in 1943, on 14 May, 2 June, 28 September, 7 October and 3 November. Only one was anything more than a tip and run. The last conventional raid, designed for a target of obvious military importance, the Docks and surrounding industries, took place on 2 June

101 *The local Hippodrome re-opened for live performances in 1941 after ten years as a cinema and served up a regular diet of radio spin-offs, glamour and the occasional play or pantomime. Crowds are queuing outside the Hippodrome in August 1944 for the revue* Fig Leaves and Apple Sauce.

102 *A political sketch from* Fig Leaves and Apple Sauce.

103 *A comedy sketch showing National Service conscripts.*

1943. It was both bloody and dramatic, leading to 11 deaths, a spectacular ricochet by a bomb, a German plane crashing into the docks and the gasometer being set on fire.

The low-level dawn raid was a new German tactic, and the height at which the bombs were dropped caused them to bounce on landing. The improved system of Observer Corps alarms was in operation, as was the MAGNA or 'mutual aid good neighbour' scheme; tea vans were present, and arrangements were in place for the salvage of furniture; the report itself uses grid reference numbers: all very much more 'professional' than earlier raids.

Three 500 kg. HE S.C. bombs were dropped on the town with occasional cannon fire. The bombs and damage were as follows:

> No. 1 passed through the roof of 12 Pretyman Road, then through Nos 33 and 35 Hamilton Road, exploding in a bungalow, No. 29 Hamilton Road. The bungalow was entirely demolished, and two women therein were killed. Nos 33 and 35, through which the bomb had passed, were practically demolished, and Nos 25 and 27 on the

104 *Bomb damage in Myrtle Road. Mr and Mrs Martin and Mrs Sheppard died in No. 42, Mr and Mrs Smith in No. 44, Mr Clews, from No. 40, died later in hospital, and Mrs Mabel Brown in No. 46.*

other side were considerably damaged. No. 27 was, in fact, almost demolished. A man and a woman were killed in No. 27. Another man and a woman were injured and detained in Hospital.

No. 2 hit the centre of the metalled surface of Felixstowe Road a few yards east of the junction of Alan Road, making a small impression in the road. The fin came off and struck a shop at the corner of Alston Road and Felixstowe Road. The bomb then ricocheted through the trees in Holywells Park, breaking the top of a fir tree, and then breaking two other trees each approximately twelve inches in diameter, making a ricochet mark 19 feet long behind the cottages at the Bishop's Hill entrance to the Park. The bomb then passed through 37 Myrtle Road, into No. 42 on the opposite side, where it exploded. Thus it ricocheted a total distance of approximately 600 yards. Houses on either side of No. 42 were demolished and serious damage was caused to houses on the opposite side which had been weakened by the bomb passing through them. A man and two women were killed in 42, their bodies being blown completely from the building and found on land nearby. A man and woman in 44 were also killed, and their bodies were found, with that of a woman from 46, blown out of their own premises with the debris onto the site next door. One man from 40 Myrtle Road died soon after admission to Hospital. Three others, one woman and two children from No. 40, were injured and detained in Hospital. Five other injured cases resulted from the houses on the odd-numbered side of the road, through which the bomb had passed. Initial difficulty was experienced inasmuch as the first message of damage and casualties had to be conveyed part of the way by messenger, telephones in the district being temporarily out of action.

Police and a few other people on the spot commenced the rescue of the family from No. 40. A Rescue Squad arrived before this was completed. The Rescue Leader first on the scene speaks highly of the help given by Policemen. It was several hours later that a systematic search of the debris found the last of those killed. During the later stages a squad of American Military Police stationed to the town came along and offered their services. They were put to work helping to move debris, under the guidance of the Rescue Squad. The houses had been reduced to a mass of rubble. The First Aid Post of Ransomes, Sims & Jefferies was only about 100 yards away and casualties quickly received first-aid treatment there.

No. 3 came from a plane which crashed on the eastern side of the lock gates at the entrance to the docks. It is believed that this plane, slightly behind the others, was caught by the blast of the bomb which exploded in Myrtle Road, for in passing over the gasometers at the side of the dock, it dived steeply, hitting the ground on the east side of the lock gates. The bomb is believed to have been still attached to the plane, for in the middle of the marks made by the crashed aircraft there was a deeper groove. The bomb ricocheted from that point, over the river, and passing through the end of an assembly shop, exploded in

105 *Firemen from two units play their hoses on the gasometer to cool it down after the raid on Myrtle Road.*

a pattern store of Ransomes & Rapier, adjacent to the moulding shop of Cocksedge & Co., at the bottom of Rapier Street.

The plane, an F.W. 190, bounced from the east side of the dock, and pieces were strewed from the west side of the lock across the river to Ransomes & Rapier. The body of the airman and the majority of the engine fell on the west side of the river, part of the engine hitting the jib of a crane belonging to Christopherson Ltd, Griffin Wharf, and part hitting the roof of Christopherson's building and entering Ransomes & Rapier's long shop at the corner of Harland Street and Griffin Wharf. Air Force Intelligence soon took over the area covered by parts of the plane.

Four points in the path of the planes were subjected to aircraft cannon fire: the first on the Felixstowe and Bucklesham Roads 650609, the second in roads near Derby Road Station 633619, the third at the Gas Works 622618, and the fourth at 610618. Slight damage was occasioned to dwelling houses in the first, second and fourth cases, and in the third case some dozen holes were made in a one million cubic feet water-sealed gasholder of the Ipswich Gas Light Company, and the issuing gas ignited. Ransomes, Sims & Jefferies' Fire Brigade were soon on the spot, followed quickly by the National Fire Service...

... No outstanding point arose in the operation of Services.

First-aid repairs to property, salvage of furniture, and all other immediate post-raid necessities were put into effect within a few hours after the raid.

Despite the personal tragedies they represented, the raids had become just another wartime routine, relatively easily handled by the civil defence services. They were at the level of a serious traffic accident, not something which could threaten the fabric of society or do more than create a hiccup in the running of the town.

By 1944, however, the Germans were ready to try another kind of weapon. On 26 June the Education Committee discussed the possibility of attack by pilotless planes. The children were to go to shelters on alert or if gunfire were heard, and, if no warning, to take shelter in schools, which is, of course, exactly what they had already been doing. When manned bombing raids were replaced by the V1 flying bombs it barely made a difference, despite the revolutionary implications of the new design. In fact, the bombs could only be aimed in the general direction of the town and many landed relatively harmlessly. I have found records of the following incidents in which V1s missed the town:

> 17 June 1944, V1 passes over Ipswich lands at Woolverstone.
> 18 July 1944 morning, V1 passed over town and crashed in open country.
> (919) Wednesday 18 October 1944, 23.16, Flying bombs began to pass S. of Felixstowe flying S.W.
>
> (Felixstowe Police Station War Diary)

Sometimes they were successfully shot down by coastal defences:

> (931) Wednesday 25 October 1944, 19.26, flying bomb exploded in A.A. barrage S.S.E. of Felixstowe. Three others passed N. and S. of Felixstowe flying S.W.
> 19.30, flying bomb fell and exploded on Brightwell Heath. Damage to two cottages.
> (956a) Wednesday 22 November 1944, from 00.52 to 01.10, flying bombs exploded in A.A. barrage E. or S.E. of Felixstowe.
> (956b) Friday 24 November 1944, from 05.40 to 06.09, seven flying bombs passed N. and S. of Felixstowe or exploded in A.A. barrage E. and S. of Felixstowe.

But when they landed they had the power to destroy. One fell on Maryon Road next to the airfield on 1 September 1944, killing an RAF sergeant and seriously injuring two men and three women. An RAF chaplain had to break the news of the man's death to a relative lying terminally ill in hospital. On 18 October 1944 a flying bomb fell and exploded at Halton Crescent, Priory Heath, Ipswich. There were four fatal and 28 other casualties. To some people these were worse than the conventional bombs, not just because of their scale but because of the uncertainty created in the interval between the engines cutting out and the inevitable explosion. Moreover, there was a general feeling that victory was inevitable and it would be particularly pointless to die so close to the end.

However, the greatest impact of the new weapons was, bizarrely, to end officially the evacuation of Ipswich people to the Midlands. The V1s and V2s were targeted primarily at London, where they had the greatest impact and where, therefore, there was the greatest need to evacuate. Many thousands of Londoners had to be found billets once more and one of the towns selected for their reception was Ipswich. It was not possible for central government to tell Ipswich to take evacuees while at the same time saying that Ipswich should be evacuated, and so the Regional Commissioner had to visit Ipswich, a rare if not unique event, and agree to allow the return of evacuees.

> 17 August 1944
> As to billeting refuges in Ipswich, the Regional Commissioner attended and explained the necessity for billeting refugees in Ipswich. He had in Hertfordshire more London

refugees than could be dealt with and it was necessary to get these placed out as quickly as possible in case the position in London became worse, and there was no alternative but to send a certain number to Ipswich. He agreed that, so far as the special evacuation scheme was concerned, the whole organisation could go into 'cold storage' and that no objections would be raised if a resident who evacuated in 1940 now desired to return.

Much less is known about the personal problems and difficulties associated with this final phase of evacuation, which seems to have been almost entirely forgotten. There was inevitably hardship amongst these people who had been bombed out, but it seems that their 'home' authorities had to deal with any welfare issues: 'August 1944 The Framlingham Egg Depot in Burrell Road could house a Depot to which the LCC could send packages to East and West Suffolk areas for refugees.'

Ipswich had about 300 children billeted on it in the summer but by 16 October 1944 there were only 163 evacuated children in Ipswich. On 7 November 1944 the Education Committee was notified that,

> As 100 of the 300 children who had come to Ipswich from the South of England during the summer holidays were from the area of the London County Council that authority had been approached and sent two teachers. The number of LCC children had now fallen to about forty and one of the teachers had returned to London.

Despite his earlier words, it was only in February 1945 that the Regional Commissioner finally put an end to evacuation from Ipswich, by asking the corporation if they agreed with a government initiative to bring to an end a scheme against which they had been agitating for four years! He hoped in this way to save face by not admitting just what a waste of time the whole thing had been. On 15 February 1945 he addressed a personal letter to the town clerks of the evacuation towns in East Anglia, asking if they favoured the voluntary return, with assistance from the government, of those persons who had been helped to evacuate the towns in 1940. Ipswich Council was in favour of the proposal. The final step was to pay those remaining evacuees some of the expenses of returning home at last. A maximum of £20 each was allowed and evidence that accommodation was waiting for them. Grants were made from 24 May onwards, by which time only 11 men, 23 women and 2 children were left in the Midlands.

Twenty-Four
Ducking and Diving

Over the course of the war people had learned the ropes, and examples of fiddling which would have been thought treacherous or unpatriotic before now seemed like enlightened self-interest. The manager of Ridley's, faced with losing his secretary and his window display designer to Directed Labour in the one case and the Army Catering Corps in the other (the designer had a disability that kept him out of the services but the Catering Corps came up with a scheme that allowed him to volunteer), arranged for the girl to join ARP and persuaded the boy to withdraw his application on the grounds that it would be very silly of him to volunteer to peel potatoes for the last months of the war. Fire guard duty was universally unpopular, and teachers took every legal step to avoid having to do it.

Right from the introduction of rationing, particularly petrol rationing, a black market grew up. A police constable was suspended from duty for siphoning petrol from police vehicles, and a taxi driver was caught stealing and receiving 20 gallons of petrol. Enver Chaudhri relates how a friend of his with a small motor bicycle had to use all his ingenuity to find petrol:

> He discovered that the wrecked cars which scrap metal dealers collected frequently had petrol left in the tanks. He made a habit of visiting these yards under cover of darkness, when one could drain the tanks into a can, as in those days most tanks had drain cocks or plugs. One night he paid a visit to one particular yard, and evidently since his last call they had decided to employ a night watchman, quite unknown to him. There he was, lying beneath a lorry, draining petrol into his can, when he heard a noise. To his horror he saw a pair of feet alongside him. The night watchman had heard the noise of the running petrol but could not understand what it was and was endeavouring to locate the source. The feet moved slowly all round the lorry, while my friend sweated beneath it, not daring to move. Eventually the watchman satisfied himself that all was well and moved on.

In those days, of course, if a policeman pulled a car over it was not to breathalyse the driver but to suck up petrol from the tank and make sure it was the correct colour; dyes had been put in the petrol supplied to the services and to farmers.

Magistrates records are full of people infringing rationing regulations in some form or another. The range of offences includes small cases involving consumers: two cases of altering entries in ration books, two cases of unlawfully accepting the transfer of ration documents, illegally obtaining ¼lb. of lard, illegally obtaining

106 & 107 *No civilian could escape war duty altogether. The most common and possibly the least popular was fire watching. These photographs show the staff of Boots and of the County Council visiting the normally hidden world of the rooftop, bringing with them the blankets and chairs that made bearable the long hours of night-time duty.*

1½ lb. of sugar, illegally obtaining 4 cwt of coal. One case involving furnishing false information under a Consumer Rationing Order and transferring ration documents was treated more seriously, the individual receiving two months in prison. Small shops were convicted of acquiring an excess quantity of sugar and fish for the use of a catering establishment, unlawful possession of meat for human consumption, and selling fish paste at a price above the maximum set. Larger concerns were involved, too, Dewhurst the butchers selling meat they had obtained illegally at above the maximum price (the supplier, shop staff and customers all facing charges). George Hunt's bakeries and dairies were fined for obtaining and selling milk, and Zagni's prosecuted for false weights. I have been told of how at weekends some men would come into the *Inkerman* pub with meat under their coats, then give some away to customers to buy their silence and sell the rest. I was told by another man that his father drove a lorry with hidden boxes of food into the town. He, a small boy, had strict instructions to shout out, 'Dad, this man's fiddling with my trousers,' if the policeman got too close to the hidden compartment. Selling stolen British and American Army stores obviously went on, although to what extent in Ipswich it is impossible to say. But that there were a growing number of people sailing close to the wind over war regulations seems certain.

Twenty-Five
Future Plans, Future Dreams

Exvasion was the strange official term for the projected invasion of Europe. All around them people were noticing the build up to D-Day. Richard Brown first begins speculating about it in his diary on 4 January 1944. There was increased work in factories turning out specialised tanks (Cocksedges, Ransomes, Sims & Jefferies, Ransomes & Rapier) and pontoon bridges, mine-clearing flails, landing boats or even plough attachments (Mann Egertons). On 10 February the Royal Artillery moved out of Nacton and the Free French Paratroop Regiment under Major Puech moved in. The Eighth Army were in numbers around Whitton. Woolverstone on the river was an assembly point for tank landing craft. Everything pointed one way.

Huge daily raids on Germany could be seen taking off and returning, with the inevitable losses and damaged planes. When the invasion finally came a handwritten message was pinned to the front door of the Museum and it still survives. Special services were held in many churches and a hundred people attended a service of intercession at a Youth Club.

As the Allied victories mounted so did the number of German and Italian prisoners-of-war in Suffolk, many based in the nearby camp of Debach. Their distinctive jackets could be seen in many fields as they provided farmers with yet more free labour. They were subject to teasing by local lads. One remembers stealing their packed rations from the hedgerows and learning a lot of unconventional Italian phrases. He and his friends tried them out so much at school that there was an official ban on speaking any Italian. David Routh remembers that the prisoners were bussed into Ipswich once a week to use the baths and showers at St Matthew's Pools.

Feelings could run very high, especially towards the Germans. R. Gordon Brown tells the following story:

A few weeks after the National Day of Prayer a south London vicar appealed in his parish magazine for comforts for German prisoners who were in hospital in his parish. An Ipswich clergymen, the Reverend H.G. Green, vicar of St Nicholas, sent him a tin of rat poison with a note reading, 'Having seen your tender-hearted request for comforts for the blasphemers of God and butchers of men, I herewith send a small comfort which I am sure they will enjoy. I am sorry the tin is not full, but a small dose will do the trick.' The south London vicar to whom the poison was sent passed the note to the Bishop of St Edmundsbury and Ipswich, Dr Richard Brook, who observed in a statement to the press, 'Mr Green must not be taken seriously. He was trying to be funny. In any view, it was a poor joke, cheap and vulgar. He is entitled to his own views, though they are very different from mine. There is nothing I can do beyond telling him that, in my judgement, his action has been most reprehensible, and has brought discredit to the church.'

Pictures on lino presented by German POWs to a young girl whose house was within Debach camp still survive, and I have been told of a German POW who saved a young boy from drowning in a static water tank in Felixstowe. I have also been told that one of the members of the Ipswich Co-Operative Society made a point after the war of helping German POWS get letters to their families. David Routh was set to guard them as a part of his National Service:

> I was stationed in a railway siding near Dunmow in Essex, and amongst my tasks was guarding German POWs. I do not know when the last went home. They were driven in winter to my base by a Polish soldier who hated Germans. He would never put up the cover of the lorry so they arrived all hunched up against the cold like little snowmen. My job was to search them, a task I found embarrassing, as a young lad searching elderly men, and their possessions were so poor, tins full of used dog ends. One of the other soldiers would take them round the corner for a bashing. Most of them were just tired but one was probably still a Nazi, full of himself. He complained to me about the beatings and I reported it. It was discovered the soldier responsible had lost his brother in the war and he was posted elsewhere.

Throughout the whole country and wherever British troops were based abroad discussions were being organised on the future of the country and the implementation of the Beveridge Report and what was to become the welfare state. We have already seen the Youth Parliament in action. Beveridge himself visited a huge public meeting in Ipswich.

Ipswich Council had proposed an ambitious Five Year Plan in 1939. It was now time to dust off these proposals and see what could still be done. The Civic College made a start in two temporary classrooms in Tower Street, teaching carpentry, joinery and plumbing to meet the needs of the building trades. The power station opened soon after the war, and the new Art School at the top of High Street. The Council had decided on the Rope Walk site for the main college and acquired the land in the middle of the war, even though the College was not opened until the sixties.

13,099 houses had been significantly damaged in Ipswich. In line with national policy, the resultant shortage would be tackled by giving council house building priority over private housing, the target for Ipswich being 5,000 new council houses in the ten post-war years. In the planners' and public's minds these estates were to be almost self-contained communities, with a full range of services in each. Officials went to study the Goldsmith's Community Centre in Greenwich and on 3 April 1944 submitted suggestions for an Education Centre for Maidenhall to include secondary, primary and nursery schools, and a community centre and young people's college. There should be separate entrances, 'as middle-aged people did not like the noise and bustle normally associated with youth'.

The first step was to build 112 houses on those sites where work had been frozen in 1939 that already had sewers and services in place; these were largely in

Whitton and Whitehouse. Seven hundred houses were to be built in the next two years and 250 'factory made houses', pre-fabs, were ordered on land near Northgate School. Houses that had been requisitioned to billet troops (78 in Whitton alone, others round the airport) and for other wartime purposes (including many large properties in Fonnereau Road) were soon to be released, and as early as January 1944 one Ipswich estate agent was advertising 'requisitioned properties for investment and future occupation'.

Just before Christmas the Export Group of Agricultural Machinery and Implement Manufacturers invited a party of potential overseas customers to visit two Ipswich engineering plants. A Chinese government engineer came to study engineering techniques at Ransomes & Rapier and can be seen in photographs of the V.E. Day party outside the *Margaret Catchpole* (see p.150). The Works College was to open soon after the end of the war.

Not all the wartime plans ever made it through to fruition. The most obvious case is that of the nursery schools. As early as 4 November 1943 it had been decided that separate nursery schools were to be provided where circumstances permitted, as an immediate wartime measure. In December it was felt that this should mean children from the ages of two to five, not three to five, and it was expected that around 50 per cent of all children would attend. With 40 in each nursery, this would mean that 44 nurseries would be needed to cover the town. The Education Commitee had worked out how this was to be done and identified buildings and sites: ten in existing schools, two using school buildings, 29 on sites selected by the Borough Surveyor in certain areas, and three in the existing wartime nurseries of South Eastern, Stoke and Rose Hill. But by 10 July 1944 nothing had been done. The St Clement's Ward Labour Club urged 'the importance of nursery schools. The Club was told that the Committee had put forward a request for sites.'

But nothing happened even on the 15 sites the Education Committee already controlled. So on 10 April 1945 it was decided that nursery classes would be provided in the existing infants school for the under-5s and that it would actually take over the three wartime nurseries as agreed two years earlier. But it was never to happen, and provides a good example of how the apparently enthusiastic endorsement of a radical scheme can be sabotaged by prevarication.

Discussions with parents had been planned in April 1944. By 16 October 1944 the committee was discussing reports of the meetings which had, unfortunately, coincided with the peak of the V1 raids:

> Attendance had far exceeded expectations. The largest number was at Whitton meeting which was held on a Wednesday afternoon as, with so many of the fathers in the forces, the mothers could not leave their children after darkness in order to attend. Unfortunately, between the preliminary meetings and the first meetings of the discussion groups, there have been frequent alerts and these have undoubtedly affected attendance.
>
> At Eastern Senior Mixed School those present were most keen and when there was an alert followed by an imminent danger warning the group moved to one of the shelter trenches and continued their discussion there.

Twenty-Six
Winding Down the War

The war had created a new kind of British society, highly centralised, markedly egalitarian and focused on one goal. It had taken years to build shelters and train the ARP and the Home Guard but the Home Front had become a way of life. This did not simply come to an abrupt end. It went away bit by bit, cautiously, even reluctantly. The process gradually gathered speed but was so slow to begin with it left people impatient, wondering exactly when it would finish, and when the end came it was something of an anti-climax. The Ipswich Home Guard assembled on 10 September 1944 at the Odeon and voted on whether to stand down or continue training. It voted to continue. Mr Brown was clearly moved by this and his diary entry is one of those where his powers of description are exercised:

> The table on the stage with the Union Jack (unfortunately upside down) draped on it, the four officers in the usual peculiar shadows of the footlights, those lights vaguely round the screen space, the back curtain design of dark-blue and yellow flowers, and the general orange-red-colour background and the heavy dark-green side curtains, the subdued lights in the body of the hall, the overshadow of the circle upstairs and the rows of stiffly-at-attention part-time soldiers: it seemed as though we were really standing down then.

When he entered his memories of the actual Stand Down, after a brief description of the parade he merely wrote, 'I suppose we did do a job of work.'

I have tried to construct a calendar showing the steps along the way for Ipswich and Felixstowe, from spring 1944 to summer 1945, using Emergency and Education Committee Minutes, Mr Brown's Diary, and the Felixstowe Police Station Diary, quotations from which are prefaced by bracketed numbers:

7 May 1944 One of the Ipswich teachers in Northampton to teach Ipswich evacuees is to return after summer holidays, but the teachers at Leicester and Loughborough will probably stay there.

September Request to remove emergency hospital stores at North Eastern (Copleston) School.

September Request to remove barbed wire and obstacles on Eastern playing field.

17 September Dim-out replaces blackout in Ipswich.

(889) Thursday 28 September The Bye-law Controlled Areas beside the Rivers Orwell and Deben were freed. Had been controlled since April 1944.

(918) Wednesday 18 October 166 Platoon of 10 B.D. Coy, R.E. (Lieut. Skinner),

stationed in Felixstowe (came from Wales). Engaged on beach mine clearance, which began shortly after.

22 October The Home Guard parades for unit group photographs.

29 October Original date for disbandment Home Guard.

(937) From November 1944 to February 1945 Land mines on beaches in defence belts exploded by 166 Pln, 10 B.D. Coy., R.E., Felixstowe in connection with demolition of beach defences. Damage unavoidably done to certain houses, cafes, hotel, etc., on or near sea front.

(964) About Tuesday 5 December Detachment of Pioneer Corps personnel to work with 166 Platoon of 10 B.D. Company, R.E. on beach clearance stationed in Felixstowe.

(967) 7 December (about) Coastal strip in which full blackout regulations applied reduced so that a coastal belt from the shore to about five miles inland remained fully restricted. The remainder covered by 'dim-out' restrictions.

13 December Fire-watching teachers to fire watch only once a fortnight, not once a week.

20 December Reduction in the duties of part-time Civil Defence personnel, but only from 48 to 24 hours in each four-week period.

(979) From Sunday 24 December Motor cars permitted to be driven with unmasked head-lamps, the first time since a few days before outbreak of war.

Fire watching discontinued from noon Wednesday 14 February.

(989) Friday 19 January 1945 (about) The use of whistles and handbells by general public permitted after total prohibition since outbreak of war.

23 February Ipswich Corporation workmen replaced the electrical light bulbs in town street lamps.

4 March Last bomb on Ipswich.

(1013) On or about Tuesday 13 March Two sites on fields, one at Shottisham and one beside Levington Lane, Bucklesham, manned by the RAF and set up about four years before for use as decoy fires in the event of air raids on Ipswich or Martlesham Aerodrome, were abandoned. The Bucklesham site had been lit twice when Ipswich was attacked.

29 March Ipswich sirens sounded last time at 12.45 hours.

20 April R. Brown removes the cellophane protection from his windows.

23 April Dim-out ended in Ipswich.

26 April Tower Ramparts Secondary Modern to be used for a War against Japan exhibition.

April Alien Pioneer Corps unit of Spaniards, Italians, etc., stationed in Felixstowe and engaged on beach clearance.

2 May Sirens shut off in Ipswich, factory sirens etc. no longer banned. ARP no longer have to sign on duty nights.

8 May V.E. Day. Weather reports again on radio.

Thursday 10 May, 10.50 Chief Constable says blackout is not officially relaxed but impossible to re-impose.

(1055) Friday 11 May, 15.24 Blackout cancelled all over the country.

17 May Part-time personnel of the National Fire Service in Suffolk stood down at parade in Christchurch Park.

23 May Ex-members of the Home Guard military band wanted to stay together and keep playing. The Education Committee of the Ipswich Co-op asked on their behalf if they could be allowed to practise in the Co-op Youth Centre part of Clifford Road school but were refused.

28 May Shelter Trenches the Board of Education. No general demolition of air-raid shelters possible except where they were a physical danger. The committee told all dangerous trenches had been demolished or made safe.

10 June Empire Youth Sunday held in Ipswich preceded by Youth Week. Special service held at St Mary Tower church.

(1066) Monday 11 June Air-raid warning sirens disconnected.

14 June Wartime allotments on Copleston School playing fields to stop.

27 June Works Holiday Pay. It was decided to recognise the victory in Europe by paying an additional 23 hours on day rate to all weekly wage earners. (Ransomes & Rapier Minute Book No.8)

(1069) Saturday 30 June, 03.30 C.D. (Final) 'Stand Down' Parade, all Services, for East Suffolk, at Little Glemham Park.

7 July The teachers who had been looking after evacuated Ipswich children, Miss Goose and Miss Fairweather, would be returning from Leicester and Loughborough respectively and probably Miss Middleton from Northampton at the same time.

14 July Streetlights back on.

(1071) Sunday 15 July, 21.55 Street lighting resumed in Felixstowe and Ipswich. Trial period on Saturday 14th.

(1075) Wednesday 15 August 'V.J.' Day, national holiday.

108 *Despite the joy of the occasion, the faces in James Street, one of the smaller thoroughfares demolished to make way for the Greyfriars precinct in the 1960s, reveal both the strain of war and the mixture of people already living in the town.*

109 *End of the bogeyman. An effigy of Hitler takes pride of place at a party in Brunswick Road.*

110 *One lad in Phoenix Road is about to tuck into a plate of buns, but for the women glamour has been one of the wartime casualties.*

(1076) Thursday 16 August 'V.J. Day plus 1', national holiday.

(1077) Saturday 18 August Further stretch of beach (260 yards) opened to public, from Cobbold's Point to opposite to Beach Rd E. Other stretches to be opened as cleared. [Clearance will not be completed until autumn 1945.]

3 September Permission for 50 children to be absent afternoon Thursday 26 September for a Victory Tea was NOT granted.

The Emergency Committee had agreed well in advance that the flags of the Allies, Britain, the Soviet Union, the Americans and the Nationalist Chinese, should decorate the streets. They had authorised a dancing platform on Tower Ramparts. But very little of an organised nature had been planned to mark what must be one of the most important turning points of the century. The staggered stand downs of the various services meant that they were not available to add drama to the occasion. Instead, in each neighbourhood an energetic man or woman took it upon themselves to organise the neighbours into finding a bit of land or roping off a street, getting tables set up and putting on some sort of party for the children. Inevitably there would be a snap of the seated children and, surrounding them, women trying to look happy for once, although the strain and the wartime dowdiness is always just under the surface.

After that the younger ones would inevitably gravitate to the town centre and try and find some way of giving expression to their relief and excitement. What happened is vividly described by some of those present. Jack Haste was courting Betty, who was to become his wife, at the time:

We decided to go into town, and although we thought the war had ended everything was exactly the same, of course. The pubs were running out of beer but the town centre was packed solid. It was great, there were chaps with saxophones and drums and bands, military chaps, all ad-libbing, nothing organised, free for all and anywhere you got together. Beer was brilliant, but I don't know that there was much. I know there were lots of sailors in the town, all the Americans came in, American soldiers came in, the airmen and the army, so lots of men in uniform, and then I was about 18-20 years old. So we were walking through town, it was a riot really, it was good really, but it got out of hand. The Cornhill was solid, they were all cheering and shouting and doing things but, naughtily, there were some boys breaking windows, and Ridleys had their windows broken, new windows. They might have put their hands in and pinched a tie or something, this was about 8 o'clock in the evening, so being involved with the company we popped up to see the governor's house where he lived and he let us have the keys and we came back again, cleared the glass away from that window, emptied that window and just shut up again. All the while this was going on, this party, but I thought we done our bit, so that was that. But by ten o'clock we were going to wander round and we got on the Cornhill. A policeman or policemen had tried to arrest some boys for throwing stones, no, men, they were men to me then, chaps, fellows, not children. They could have been drunks, no, men, sailors. And then there was a bit of a thing going on with the Americans and the sailors taking the mickey out of each other, you know, 'Go back to America.' I know it was noisy, raucous, and you know the police station, you know where it was, down the side of the Town Hall, they were throwing stones at it, at the police station, yes, and it was crowded and Betty and myself got in Barclay's Bank doorway, which was there just the same. I remember standing there like this, 'Look at this, this is fun,' and this dreadful noise, and then they locked the police house doors, and then they chanted, 'Let them out, let them out, they've got

111 *The VE Day crowds on Tower Ramparts. There is a dancing rink on the left.*

to be let free.' The policemen locked their station up; they'd got their prisoners, taken chaps in who had been naughty. The whole crowd was saying, 'Let them out, let them out, don't be stupid, the war's....' Everybody's for them. The police were being a bit ... so, well, anyway. Someone phoned the Military Police up to clear this mob, for it was a mob, and the Military Police, this blooming great army truck I reckon, came up from Princes Street and blocked the end of that road just where we were, Arcade Street, Barclay's Bank, and out jumped all these Military Police and they'd got their truncheons out and their helmets on and they said, 'Come on, Come on,' and they were blowing whistles and giving orders out and making people turn around, 'No, you go that way.' So we slipped quietly round the corner very quickly and nipped down the Thoroughfare. I could see things were going wrong, you could get hit by a brick or something, or nobbled, or something could have gone wrong. I think Betty thought the same, time to get away a bit.

David Routh was on a different part of the Cornhill with his friends and had a different perspective on events:

On V.E. day there were tremendous celebrations in the town. A friend of mine tried to climb up one of the tram poles but found there were already people at the top. So he broke away from the other lads who suddenly noticed him again perched on the top of the sign giving the banks name on the outside of Lloyds Buildings on the Cornhill. He was taking down the flags and throwing them to the admiring crowd. The police in the Town Hall basement station did not like this and, led by a one-eyed Inspector, began to push through the crowd to arrest the lad. The crowd did not like this and pushed me and my friends one way and the police the other, not letting them through. There

were some scuffles and the police took prisoners. The lads all scattered and met back on
The Dales. Meanwhile rumours went out that there was to be more serious trouble in
retaliation on the police the next night. American servicemen and sailors from Shotley
and Harwich and so on were planning to come into town. That evening the Americans
were confined to the bases and the town swamped with American Military Police in
their white helmets with a few British redcaps. Everything was very quiet.

The American Military Police were the hardest men I had ever seen. They would
use their truncheons to smash the collarbone. I had seen them in action when some
pubs had to be cleared.

Enver Chaudhri would not have gone to the Cornhill at all had it not been for
his grandmother who woke him up about 10.30. He went down with a friend.

Together we went to the town centre. The Cornhill was solid with people, singing and
cheering, dancing up and down the streets, arm in arm, eight or so abreast. We all joined
in, despite the fact that they were mainly strangers. At one time the police arrested a
sailor who had inflated a condom and was endeavouring to tie it to the top of a lamp
standard. The Police Station was alongside the Town Hall, on the Cornhill, in those
days, and the bad lad was taken inside. The crowd took umbrage at this and the Police
were barricaded in their own headquarters for quite some time. Gradually we met up
with various friends and it was about 5a.m. when we eventually returned home.

None of this mayhem gets a mention in the Watch Committee Minutes save in a
very roundabout way. The Chief Constable made a point of assuring the committee
of the arrangements for V.J. day and of reporting after V.J. night that there had been
no loss of control. Enver, who drove around on a motorbike with a dust bin lid
tied behind it, remarks,

The Police remembered their previous experiences of V.E. Day and were rather apt to
use their truncheons on anyone who overstepped the mark. One of my friends told me
that he was chased along Tavern Street by a policeman for no reason whatsoever.

So hostilities ended with the various elements of wartime society giving them
their own special send off: from the official choreographed presentations and marches
for middle-aged civilian men, through makeshift neighbourhood attempts to give
children a party, to the Dionysian spectacle of young men and servicemen still
trapped in the forces fighting, drinking and having a go at the police.

Even then, of course, the war had not been wound up. It was to take years before
the last Ipswich serviceman was demobbed or the last POW returned. It was to take
about two or three years before the last German or Italian POW returned home
too. The plight of displaced European persons was not to be fully resolved until
the collapse of the Berlin Wall. Rationing continued along with National Service
for another decade and there is still an estate of wartime pre-fabs in Ipswich. The
names of dead servicemen have still to be added to the war memorial, although it
may happen at any moment. The American bases are still here.

The shooting stopped in May 1945 but much of the structure of wartime
British society survived well into the fifties. Some people will carry their wounds,
physical and emotional, to their deaths. In ways large and small the debates of
wartime continue.

Endword

Cracking the Shell

Any notion that I would be able to cover every aspect of the war and follow up every detail of every story vanished so long ago that I can hardly remember if I ever believed it might really be possible. There are whole areas of wartime life, entertainment, the arts, religion, transport, food, housing, that have not been covered. There are many loose ends, people to whom I have not spoken, stories not followed up. I have made no comparisons with other towns. Still, one has to start and stop somewhere.

I have tried to separate the information from my personal opinion and analysis and allow, as far as is possible, all the different sources to tell their own tales. Some conclusions became more and more obvious as the study progressed. Was there a myth of the Home Front, of cheerful civilians all pulling together, volunteering, helping each other out and not locking their back doors? The romantic image certainly conceals a more complex reality, one in which civilians certainly did volunteer and work selflessly for very long hours but could also lose all sense of proportion and quarrel with those around them, where wardens stole Spitfire Fund collecting tins and policemen siphoned petrol. People were still people during the war. That said, there is much truth in the traditional picture of wartime Britain: by and large the most divisive aspects of British society were ameliorated and people were often convinced that social issues would be resolved once the war was over; ordinary people did do extraordinary things, and were encouraged to queue for trolley buses and show kindness to their neighbours. The various civil defence and Home Guard services developed a range of darts matches, social dances and sausage suppers that created a new set of activities to bind a neighbourhood together. There were wonderfully glamorous dances on American bases. Everyone had to do their bit, and because everyone had a bit to do they could feel they had a value and a stake in things; the terrible feeling of being on the scrap heap that blighted so many lives both before and since was lifted.

The picture is not so much inaccurate as incomplete. It has to be set against a backdrop of disrupted families and childhoods, prostitution, of pervasive fiddling and evasion of unpopular duties and of bureaucratic inefficiency and meanness. The fact that people had a better diet during the war is, perhaps, less a compliment to British wartime society than a criticism of pre-war inequality. Wartime was one of extreme contrasts, crowded pubs and dances followed by hosing down the machinery at Ransomes & Rapier into which pieces of your friends and workmates had been blown, parades and exercises married to prolonged exhaustion and boring diet.

It is a commonplace that the war profoundly altered the position of women. Certainly the material from Ipswich bears that out, but it also hints that perhaps that alteration was a bit more complex than is sometimes presented. Professional women found more senior posts open to them, and moved towards equal pay. They were no longer faced by their employers with the requirement to resign on marriage. By and large they kept their jobs in the post-war world. But working-class women were in part compelled through direction to join the labour force at the bottom end. They tended to lose their positions in the semi-skilled jobs they had filled when the men returned and were thrown back into unskilled part-time work. The effect of the Women's Land Army was to subsidise farmers so they didn't have to compete with the wages available in industry.

Post-war English society is clearly structured by age group as well as both class and gender. Fashions, speech patterns, recreational behaviours and attitudes are far less distinctively regional or even class-based than they were. Both conscription and directed labour took people on the basis of their age and put them in close contact with others of the same age but from different areas and backgrounds. These groups shared experiences that others did not. The Second World War saw not the creation but a rapid growth in the idea of youth and the teenager. This was intensified as the army lessened the regional basis of its units and extended to women too. Youth clubs and pre-service training also took people more out of multi-aged family units, or church or political party clubs, and into new specifically 'youth' groups.

Years before *Windrush* Ipswich began to become a multi-racial community and had to do so with only American segregation as a model.

One final case from a minute book sums up themes that I find running through all the material. If, in most of our minds, the 'typical' victim of the First World War is a young man blown to pieces in a trench, the typical victim of the second war would have to be a civilian child. What is most obscene about total warfare and, especially, area bombing is the way the weakest and most vulnerable are made to suffer. This was not only a result of enemy action but also of the archaic Poor Law attitudes, inefficiency and, on occasion, the almost unbelievable meanness of officialdom.

The war gave rise to a generation of children whose sufferings have never been properly acknowledged. On 4 January 1942 the Welfare Committee had to deal with the case of Daphne Walters, aged six and injured in an air raid in May the previous year when her mother and brother were killed and two other sisters were injured. The child had been in hospital for some time and then gone into lodgings with one of her sisters who had been maintaining her. This sister was shortly getting married and was unable to look after Daphne any more.

Relief in kind had been granted to the case, but in the meantime a communication addressed to the Ministry of Pensions asked them to deal with it as the child had been orphaned as a result of enemy action. A reply was received to the effect that as she was illegitimate Daphne did not come within the definition of 'child'

112 Chief Constable Cresswell receives his medal from the Lord Lieutenant of Suffolk in 1945.

for the purposes of the Personal Injuries (Civilians) Scheme and, further, that she was not entitled to War Injury Allowance as she was under the age of 15 years. It was further reported that the child had to attend at the St Albans Hospital for further treatment.

So the system devised to protect six-year-old Daphne, orphaned, injured, turned away by her sister and needing a further period in hospital, found a reason not to pay her. This was typical.

In the case of Ipswich alone people were moved in elaborate operations that were enormously disruptive and damaging to places as dangerous or even more dangerous than those from which they had come. School trenches were not dug in time for schools to re-open to accommodate evacuees, giving rise to conditions which led to most evacuees making their own way home in spite of the government. Despite regarding evacuation as a vital part of national policy, the government allowed it to be done voluntarily in Ipswich, so that no clear arrangements were made. (Children from other towns travelled as organised school parties.) Once again, most gave up on the scheme and came home.

There was no civilian shelter policy to ensure decent protection for all. In Ipswich not all those who wanted Anderson shelters ever actually got them. Barrage balloons went up locally in 1942, only after the bulk of conventional bombing had ceased. We have seen how public shelters could not be unlocked after the parks closed at dusk. The co-ordination that would have allowed one adequate shelter to be built for both schoolchildren and neighbouring streets was missing so that school shelters stood empty and unused at nights, weekends and holidays, and were built to lower specifications; children were expected to spend long hours in winter in what were effectively holes in the ground without heating, lighting or drainage. Some members of the public were able to rest night after night in deep communal shelters provided with a canteen, first aid and ticketed bunks, while others tried to sleep in damp, unlit, unheated holes with a bit of tin over their heads.

Wardens were appointed to deal with bombing but not given proper posts or telephones with which to report incidents. Middle-aged and indeed elderly men were encouraged to volunteer for duty one night in four in order to save lives in a raid but begrudged a kettle. Wardens were sacked in Christmas 1939 and Easter 1940 and more recruits and volunteers called for that same summer. Local government and employers quarrelled over who paid wardens for the loss of income during a raid in working time but no one worked out a system allowing them time off after night duties. The public were allowed to form a militia but it was then given a suicide mission and never properly armed.

The wardens were expected to work in the blackout at what could be a dirty job in which clothes got soiled or torn or soaked. Throughout his diary of 1939-40 C.J. Woods is trying to get overalls for his men, indeed is promised them, only for them never to arrive. Why not? Was the need for overalls completely unforeseen? Wartime shortages is hardly a convincing answer. So early in the war peacetime stocks had not yet been run down. Moreover, if it were impossible before Dunkirk, why was it possible in 1941, when materials were in even shorter supply, to issue first overalls and in the fullness of time a battle-dress style of uniform and good thick warm overcoats?

Clearly, those that ran the town, and possibly many of those who administered the country, did not really have their hearts in prosecuting the war to final victory but were instead digging their feet in about spending. No one can now be clear about their motive: it may simply have been an instinct that a deal would be struck anyway; at the worst, they may have been more influenced by the climate of opinion represented by Mosley's drive for a British peace than they would ever have allowed themselves to say. After all, their children were not going to those ill-provided schools, but to the fee-paying Northgate at the very least; for the most part they were not sending their wives and children on government evacuation schemes but were moving privately to elderly relatives with large houses, to farms on which they had spent holidays before the war, or to West Country hotels. The heads of major departments of the Borough and most of the senior committee members were not ARP wardens or special constables or ordinary volunteers in the LDV.

113 *Wartime prefabs near Northgate School.*

114 *Ipswich war memorial. When this photograph was taken the names of local servicemen killed in the Second World War had still not been added to the monument. Civilian and civil defence dead are not recorded.*

Returning to the example of the little girl, Daphne, after pressure was applied by Richard Stokes the Ministry of Pensions finally caved in and she got some help. Continual pressure from dissident members of the committee, the heads, the Teachers' Joint Committee, the Trades Council, trade unions and the Ipswich Labour Party and ward Labour parties eventually forced the education authorities to get their act together. Major social programmes could be got through as well as those directly related to the war. In 1939-40 it was impossible to get overalls for essential service; by 1942-3 dinners were provided in every school. Despite lack of plans, shortage of materials and all kinds of other wartime difficulties, civil defence and Home Guard were by 1945 well equipped, properly trained and completely ready to meet the challenges of 1940.

In every aspect of life the same kind of change was under way: the Chief Warden was not allowed to fire Warden Wilkinson despite his bluster; the Chairman of the Education Committee found himself having 'very useful' chats with school caretakers; firms started providing tea to staff; fees for Northgate became a thing of the past, and subsidised transport was extended to all schools. It is impossible to imagine local government in 1930 or '39 agreeing to the idea of a Youth Parliament, or attempts being made to involve parents in education policy, or Communists being allowed to hire schools, or the existence of sex and health education, never mind greatly improved knowledge of contraception and sexually transmitted diseases.

The war was the greatest test English local government had faced since the 1660s and the first years of the war found it failing. One can point to the enormity of the task, one can say that few European states did any better, one can raise the inevitable objection that everything is so much easier with hindsight. These things do not alter the facts; if one asks whether English society was ready in 1940 to face the reality of aerial attack and a potential invasion the answer has to be no. It survived because Hitler failed to push his attack home and declared war on Russia and, finally, through an alliance with Japan, found himself confronting the Americans as well.

Genuine grassroots change tends to be reflected in tiny details, and not in statues pulled over or streets renamed. Essentially, the old hierarchy and local elite cracked during the war under the pressure of its own obvious failure to manage the conflict and challenges from below. It had only cracked, however, and not broken. The Youth Service was hijacked by the Church, even if the Church didn't know what to do once it had got it. Ipswich School was somehow, no one knows how, not made a Direct Grant school. Procrastination prevented nurseries being set up and the government was able to let them drop. Works Councils were forgotten.

It had been the BUF that loudly denounced the old parties and pronounced itself the future. It was not their kind of brutal modernism that triumphed. But the old guard in Ipswich was not replaced by the revolutionary left either. The Ipswich variety had deep roots in Edwardian socialism, in radical dissent, and looked to the Rochdale Pioneers rather than to Engels. Even the Youth Parliament had been foreshadowed by a Socialist Ipswich Parliament, or elected debating society, held for a few years in the town before the first war. Mrs Lewis was certainly influenced by Marxism but was always far more a Quaker than a revolutionary. It was the Co-op rather than the C.P. that became a force in the social life of the town. The Labour Party in Ipswich remained dominated by the figure of Stokes, whose politics were based on a kind of benevolent managerialism.

Some of the changes in Ipswich can be summed up neatly by the life of Mrs Lewis. She started her political career as the wife of a left-wing Unitarian minister investigated for MI5 by Schreiber, the Chief Constable before Cresswell. He deserted her. She was a committed Quaker and helped organise Peace Pledge Union meetings before the war. Throughout her time on the Education Committee and elsewhere, she was continually urging the Council to move in a humane direction, whether on a small scale by organising Christmas treats at the cinema for the Ilford children, or, more significantly, by campaigning to get welfare payments paid directly to mothers. Together with Mrs Whitmore she put in a lifetime of committee work, and the two women ended up as first and second mayoresses of the town: from wife of suspect revolutionary to mayoress, from the margin to the centre.

Index

compiled by Peter B. Gunn

Page numbers in **bold** refer to illustrations